ADMINISTERING EARLY CHILDHOOD SETTINGS

The Canadian Perspective

Fourth Edition

Marilyn Yeates

Donna McKenna

Carolyn Warberg

Centennial College

Karen Chandler

George Brown College

Prentice
Hall

Toronto

Canadian Cataloguing in Publication Data

Administering early childhood settings : the Canadian perspective

4th ed.
Includes bibliographical references and index.
ISBN 0-13-082201-9

1. Day care centres — Canada. 2. Early childhood education — Canada. I. Yeates, Marilyn.

HQ778.7.C3A35 2001   362.71'2   C99-933041-1

ISBN 0-13-082201-9

Vice President, Editorial Director: Michael Young
Executive Editor: David Stover
Senior Marketing Manager: Sophia Fortier
Associate Editor: Susan Ratkaj
Production Editor: Joe Zingrone
Copy Editor: Diana Thistle-Tremblay
Production Coordinator: Peggy Brown
Page Layout: Janette Thompson (Jansom)
Permissions Research: Susan Wallace-Cox
Art Director: Mary Opper
Interior Design: Dave McKay
Cover Design: Sarah Battersby
Cover Image: Superstock/Lisette Le Bon

1 2 3 4 5   05 04 03 02 01

Printed and bound in Canada.

Contents

Chapter 10: Families and Early Childhood Programs —A Vital Partnership   191

Chapter 11: Community, Resources, and Advocacy 204

Preface

This is the fourth edition of *Administering Early Childhood Settings: The Canadian Perspective*. Each of the authors has been involved in teaching Early Childhood Education students at the college level and kept the needs of students in mind when completing the fourth edition. The main emphasis of most early childhood programs is to provide a solid foundation in child development, in understanding, creating, and implementing high quality programs, and in the other fundamental knowledge necessary to be a responsible, ethical, enthusiastic, and professional early childhood educator. This book provides an introduction to the administrative practices, standards of professionalism, and advocacy.

Features included in this edition:

- an emphasis on safety issues when working with groups of children
- updated government and societal influences on child care
- the importance of anti-bias attitudes, respect for divers ethnocultural and family beliefs throughout the child care and administrative practices

The appendices include sample forms and checklists, Internet Web sites, and pertinent addresses that reviewers suggested remain as a resource to beginning educators.

The organization and chapter titles have not changed because they seem to reflect how the administrative material is introduced to students for the first time in most educational settings. The need for high quality Early Childhood Education programs forms the fundamental basis for success of child care centres and therefore is introduced in Chapter 1. While it seems impossible to keep up with the trends, direction, and role of the government, Chapter 2 attempts to help students glean a better understanding of government's effect on programs, families, and funding.

Chapter 3 provides students with what is probably their first yet very important understanding of how a philosophy is formulated as the underlying principle for curriculum development. Curriculum development is covered in Chapter 4.

Students have studied and seen a variety of physical environments, particularly as experienced in their practicums. However, the essential elements for planning and the areas and equipment to include are examined in detail in Chapter 5. The key to quality will always be the characteristics and professionalism of staff, which is re-emphasized in Chapter 6. Chapter 7 is a separate chapter on leadership styles and challenges. This area remains critical for students to explore because of the importance of understanding how a centre comes together. Often this is not a priority for students to consider as they grapple with the many other aspects of child care. However, it takes little time for new educators to realize how leadership styles can be used to effect the overall smooth operation of a centre. Thus the inclusion of this important chapter.

Chapters 8 and 9 may not stir initial interest but once students understand the impact of financial planning, new insights begin to occur. Initial interest with the administrative forms, procedures, and other organizational materials required to operate an efficient centre may take time to develop. Once understood, a new respect for the operation of an overall quality centre emerges.

The last two chapters, Chapters 10 and 11, focus on the need for partnerships with parents, involvement in the community, and the role of advocacy. Positioning these subjects at the end of the book is not meant to diminish their importance. Quite the contrary, as the future of early childhood programs rests on the involvement and commitment from parents, early childhood educators, and other professionals by advocating together for quality, affordable, and accessible programs and settings for young children.

A note on terminology may be useful. In the field, the terms *early childhood educator, E.C.E., teacher, practitioner, caregiver,* and *worker* are applied to those who work with young children. Traditionally, the distinction has been made that a caregiver is someone who works in a child care centre, while a teacher provides a more educational function. This distinction is not a clear one, since the line between education and nurturing in the early years is blurred. Throughout this text, the terms *early childhood educator, provider,* and *caregiver* are used synonymously.

We continue to dedicate this book to you, today's students, as you enter the rewarding and sometimes difficult field of early childhood education. The rewarding part—the children, their families, and your colleagues—far outweigh the difficult aspects of trying to gain the recognition desired by the profession.

We continue to thank, respect, and appreciate our many colleagues for their support and encouragement to update this book. Thank you to those who took time to review the book: Carolyne Willoughby, Durham College; Malcolm Reid, Medicine Hat College; Jane Hewes, Grant MacEwan Community College; Joanne Baxter, Mount Royal College; Martha Friendly, Child Care Research and Resource Unit, University of Toronto. We would also like to thank our colleagues for the feedback that assisted the team in including new thoughts, perceptions, and insights beyond our own.

Our thanks once again to the team at Pearson Education Canada—especially to Susan Ratkaj, who worked very hard to keep us on track and complete the fourth edition.

As college teachers, our job is to share information, encourage thinking, and support new ideas. It is through this process that we have been able to formulate our ideas about the field and focus on what is critical for the beginning teacher to know and understand. Our thanks to the many students throughout the years, especially all the graduates of Conestoga College, who have helped us in this endeavour. Living with our own families has added to our understanding about how we all best learn and grow. You have enriched our thinking and our lives and made our concepts and perceptions about children and families real.

Donna McKenna, Carolyn Warberg, Karen Chandler

HIGH QUALITY EARLY CHILDHOOD— A DEFINITION

A high quality early childhood experience meets a child's needs and interests at each developmental stage. This chapter identifies and discusses some of the issues affecting quality, under these headings:

- *The need for a system*
- *What is quality early childhood education?*
- *Indicators of a quality environment*
- *Indicators of quality: The child's environment*
- *Indicators of quality: Caregiver characteristics*
- *Indicators of quality: Contextual factors*
- *Methods of achieving quality*

Overwhelming evidence points to the importance of early childhood experiences in determining health and social success throughout a person's life. Early childhood programs that nurture, protect, and educate young children affect not only the children themselves, but also their families, communities, and the larger society. The social and economic benefits of quality early childhood settings reach into every segment of Canadian society—parents are able to work or attend school, while children receive the best nurturing and early childhood education possible.

Significant economic and social changes over the past two decades have propelled the early years and care for children to an issue of national importance. Trends include increased global economic competition, a shifting economic base, changing demographics, and an influx of mothers into the workforce. Research shows that early childhood education is crucial to Canada's future economic position. It provides members of the next generation of workers with a solid foundation of skills, competencies, attitudes, and behaviours that will ensure their success in a more technologically based economic environment. This perspective has caught the attention of policy makers.

Equally compelling should be that quality early childhood services promote healthy development of children today. There is substantial evidence that the quality of early childhood experiences has long-term effects on an individual's performance in the education system, their behaviour in adult life, and their risks for chronic disease in adult life (Fraser Mustard 1998). Recent human development research confirms how important the first five years of life can be for children's lifelong abilities, health, and well-being. This is a crucial time for brain development, when the structure of children's brains is strongly influenced by the world around them. The quality of care that children receive affects the way they think and learn. Unhealthy physical, emotional, and social environments can have lifelong consequences. In fact, children who have been well cared for have brains that are physically different from those of children who experienced less favourable conditions in their early years.

Many young children spend more of their waking hours with caregivers than they do with their parents. Roughly two-thirds of Canadian children under age six receive non-parental care while their parents work or attend school. Human Resources Development Canada (1994) estimates that young children receive nine hours a day for 250 days a year in non-parental care. The research has consistently shown that non-parental care is not harmful when it is provided by people who are warm and responsive to the child. There is clear evidence that the first six years of life are crucial for the development of the language, interpersonal, and intellectual skills that will determine adult competence. Society has an obligation to adopt policies that encourage children's development.

THE NEED FOR A SYSTEM

Canadian children live in a world that is often very different from the one their parents were raised in. There are more single-parent families, and most families with two parents need two wage earners. The typical Canadian mother works outside the home, usually at a full-time job. Often she returns to work soon after the birth of a child—the latest census figures indicate that significant numbers of mothers of young children are employed outside the home. Most single parents are women, and women's wages are generally lower than men's. Many single parents raise their families on incomes below the poverty level.

These developments make the provision of a quality early childhood environment a major challenge of the new millennium. The need is shown in the statistics: for 1998, the latest year for which full statistics were available, Human Resources Development Canada reported that there were an estimated three million children with working mothers and only 438 188 regulated child care spaces. These figures argue a great unmet need for quality child care, and show why families, child care advocates, and women's groups have been pressing, over a number of years, for the development of a national child care policy.

As early as 1970, the Royal Commission on the Status of Women identified the child care crisis in its report. The Commission pointed out that parents required supplementary child care to allow them to meet both work and parental responsibilities, and emphasized that society had a role in contributing to the development of these services.

Recognizing the benefits to Canadian families and the larger society, the federal government announced a national child care policy in late 1987. However, it is still not in place today. In 1999, Canada's federal, provincial, and territorial governments announced an agreement on how to implement a National Children's Agenda that has the potential for a coordinated policy framework to address the needs of children. Among the areas of focus in this initiative: supporting parents and strengthening families; enhancing early childhood development; improving economic security for families; and providing early and continuous learning experiences. Chapter 2 discusses in more detail Canadian child care policy and the unmet demand for regulated early childhood services.

Parents who seek child care outside their homes ought to be able to choose from a variety of options, since family needs and preferences can vary greatly. In a formal, regulated system, families should be able to select from options that include licensed home child care, group care, and parent–child resource centres. For young children to develop and learn optimally, the early childhood setting must be prepared to meet their diverse developmental, cultural, linguistic, and educational needs. These services should meet the needs of infants, toddlers, and preschool- and school-age children, providing full- or part-time care on a regular or flexible basis.

Some families choose to look after their children at home and require flexible work schedules to allow for this. For example, one parent may work part-time, or on a night shift, providing care for the child during the daytime hours when the other parent is working. Other families may prefer to make private arrangements, but need access to information and referral services to accomplish this.

In reality, this range of services is not available in most communities across Canada. Families have been left to struggle on their own, balancing work demands with their children's needs. The supply of child care is inadequate, especially for school-age children and infants. Virtually no child care exists in some areas of the country, and where there is adequate supply, quality is uneven. Where a full range of quality child care services exists, many parents are barred by the high cost.

In a 1999 study by the Canadian Policy Networks, three-quarters of Canadians want a new child care system that provides economic supports for children in their first three years of life. Progress is needed to increase the total number of regulated spaces, but there cannot be a large-scale creation of spaces without a general agreement on standards that must be met. Standards must be established that reflect the kind of high quality environment Canadian children need. Program standards identify what needs to be in place in a setting to support provision of quality child care.

To understand the place of such standards, we need to look at the question of what defines quality. What are the components of a high quality setting? How do these elements interact? How can parents assess which situation is right for their child? Answers to these questions will guide the efforts of practitioners and spur action to upgrade the quality of our nation's early childhood services.

WHAT IS QUALITY EARLY CHILDHOOD EDUCATION?

Quality has become a central topic of study among early childhood educators and developmental psychologists, and no single issue related to child care is as complex, controversial, or important. Over the past 25 years, we have moved beyond debates about whether early childhood experiences help or harm development, or which types of early childhood services are best. The question today is, "How can we make them better?" Peter Moss, a European child care expert, cautions us about only looking to child care for working parents. He believes every country should have a comprehensive early-years policy that provides flexible, coherent, and high quality services with equality of access for all children, whether or not their parents are in employment.

Early childhood services can be analyzed through several perspectives:

- its enhancement of children's development
- its services to working parents
- its position within a range of family support services

These are not mutually exclusive—all three should be goals in any early childhood setting. But each provides a different way of analyzing a program's operation, and together they show the diversity of issues related to high quality early childhood education.

The first perspective emphasizes the child's development. The professionals directly involved in providing child care stand most directly behind this view, along with parents, who are also vitally concerned with their child's development. The term "quality" refers to situations that support children's well-being and enhance their social, linguistic, and intellectual development. Good child care meets children's needs and stimulates their interests at each developmental stage. For example, infants need good physical care, a nurturing environment, and affection, and opportunities for interaction, exploration, and sensory stimulation.

From the parent's perspective, the child is entitled to be safe, healthy, adequately fed, active, and happy. The service must be reliable, affordable, consistent with the family's values, and similar to the kind of care the parents themselves would provide. Other factors important to parents include flexible scheduling, a location convenient to home or work, provision of care for more than one child in the family, and care when children are sick.

The third viewpoint acknowledges that quality child care cannot be provided in isolation, but must be part of a broader range of services to children and families. Parents may need services that provide support, counselling, and referrals. For example, families that have a child with special needs benefit from this coordinated service. In a comprehensive family support services approach, staff may be drawn from the fields of health, education, and social work.

Each perspective highlights part of what is involved in substitute care, and needs to be considered by caregivers, parents, advocates, and policy makers. The different emphasis provided by each illustrates how complex the issue of quality is. The *ecological approach* provides a way of thinking about the overall question.

The Ecological Model of Early Childhood Settings

Ecology is the study of how organisms interact with their environment. Researchers in the early childhood field use this broad perspective in assessing child care environments. An ecological approach to understanding these settings looks at the interaction among children, parents, and early childhood educators, and their relationship with the environments in which they work and live.

An ecological look at early childhood considers not only how to structure environments to foster children's growth, but also how these environments interact with influences outside the setting. Often efforts to improve child care have seen each program as a self-contained classroom, and so concentrated on internal factors, doing things like buying new equipment or adjusting curriculum. But experienced practitioners have come to understand that the impact of such changes will be limited, if a setting fails to consider the wider environment within which its programs take place.

Many writers incorporate Bronfenbrenner's (1979) framework for looking at early childhood settings in his ecological model of human development. His model can be adapted to provide a framework for understanding the influence of contextual factors on a child's daily experience. He thinks in terms of four levels, each embedded within the next (see Figure 1–1). Bronfenbrenner's model provides a way of moving beyond the immediate setting, to consider in turn the layers of influence acting on the developing child, along with the impact of child care upon family, community, and society.

At the heart, the *microsystem* (*micro* = small) is centred on the developing child himself or herself within his or her immediate settings—the early childhood environment, a school classroom, a family day care, or the child's own home. It is made up of the physical environment, the resources within it, appropriate curriculum, the interactions between the parent, caregiver, and child, and the interactions among the children.

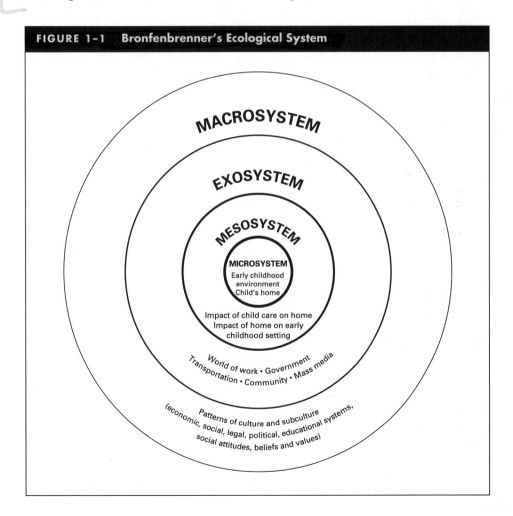

FIGURE 1-1   Bronfenbrenner's Ecological System

The second circle is the *mesosystem* (*meso* = middle), where different microsystems are linked together through relationships, such as teacher–parent interaction, or through employment practices that affect the family, such as maternity-leave benefits. For example, the relationship of the early childhood environment with the home would be considered here. These interactions will be influenced by how different adults perceive the child, and by child-rearing beliefs. A critical factor is the necessity of the environment to be welcoming to all those who use it—the child, the staff, and parents.

Outside this is the *exosystem* (*exo* = outside), which represents the social structures, both formal and informal, that influence the settings the child experiences. In this dimension, one must consider the roles and influences of various government agencies and policies for early childhood settings and the family, the local economy, the mass media, the workplace, and the immediate community. Administrators need to be aware of funding sources and how to access them, and where to refer families for support. It is also essential that they keep current with government philosophies that underlie policies.

All these sets of relationships are located in a *macrosystem* (*macro* = great). It includes patterns of culture, such as the economic, educational, legal, and political systems. These would include attitudes toward the family and the role of motherhood, and community definitions of appropriate environments for young children. The macrosystem defines what is possible: for example, a society that believes children belong to their parents, rather than to society at large, will greatly restrict government involvement in child care. Perhaps the most important macrosystem issue is the public image of early childhood: how the families who use the service are viewed, and whether the workers are valued and respected or patronized and held in disdain.

The quality of early childhood services depends on the interactions of these four dynamic systems.

INDICATORS OF A QUALITY ENVIRONMENT

Quality is best understood as a blend of desirable factors. Adult–child ratio, group size, caregiver education and experience, curriculum, physical environment, quality of adult–child interactions, adult work environment, level of parent involvement—all are aspects of quality.

Research has identified a number of these discrete indicators of quality (the term *indicator* is frequently used in the professional literature to refer to the individual characteristics of a program). Many of these indicators are interrelated, and their mutual impact ultimately affects the child's well-being. Deborah Phillips' *Quality in childcare programs: What does the research tell us?* (1987) provides an overview of significant research into the factors affecting quality. Doherty has written extensively of elements of quality, synthesizing more than a hundred research studies conducted in the past 15 years in Canada, the United States, Europe, and elsewhere, identifying a common core of caregiver behaviours and program characteristics associated with positive outcomes for children in both the short and long term.

The Canadian Child Care Federation (1991) defines quality early childhood environments as those that:

- support and assist the child's physical, emotional, social, and intellectual well-being and development, and

- support the family in its child-rearing role.

Research divides the discussion of early childhood quality into terms of *structural quality* or *process quality*. *Structural quality* generally refers to variables that can be regulated, including adult–child ratio, group size, and the education and training of caregivers. There is increasing evidence for the importance of a centre director's level and type of education. Structural variables are so interconnected that to speak of them separately as unique contributors to overall development is difficult. *Process quality* refers to interactions, the provision of developmentally appropriate activities, caregiver consistency, parent involvement, and warm, nurturing, sensitive caregiving.

Process variables have a direct influence on children, but because they require interpretation on the part of the experts, these variables are more difficult to regulate. For example, most people would agree that a teacher should be sensitive to the children in her or his care. Caregiver consistency encourages the development of trust and provides an environment in which a child feels free to explore. This approach supports learning. But it is difficult to imagine how a supervisor could assure sensitivity during hiring, or through a job performance evaluation.

However, structural quality and process quality are related, and structural quality can be regulated. While it would be difficult to measure a teacher's sensitivity, research suggests that teachers with more years of formal education are, as a group, more sensitive (Whitebrook et al. 1990). Therefore, a requirement of formal education is intended to ensure that teachers are more likely to be sensitive.

Careful and systematic research on child care programs has appeared since 1970. The National Day Care Study (1979) conducted in the United States has had a profound impact on legislation both there and in Canada. This study identified group size and specialized caregiver training as significant elements of child care quality in centre-based programs for preschoolers, with staff–child ratios a further crucial element in infant and toddler care.

While research has helped answer many questions, others remain unanswered. Those interested in the improvement of quality in early childhood services must consider the setting's relationship with the external environment, and the exploration of this relationship helps provide a research agenda for the new millennium.

Licensing and regulatory systems that are well designed and effectively administered can help assure the provision of early childhood programs that will nurture, protect, and educate young children. Regulation by itself does not ensure quality: it is designed to prevent programs from harming children, rather than to promote programs that enhance development. But if regulation does not ensure quality, it is an important factor safeguarding it. The responsibility for regulation rests with each province and territory. Early childhood services are patchwork, provided by a variety of agencies and auspices, with minimum regulation. Chapter 2 expands on the topic of regulation.

Throughout the next sections, the following indicators of quality environments for young children will be examined:

The Child's Environment

- adult–child ratio
- group size
- curriculum
- physical environment
- interactions
- continuity of care
- cultural continuity

Caregiver characteristics:

- education and experience
- stability and staff satisfaction

Contextual Factors

- funding, auspice, licensing standards
- relationships with the external environment
- parent involvement

INDICATORS OF QUALITY: THE CHILD'S ENVIRONMENT

Adult–child Ratio

One of the most important indicators of quality is the ratio of caregivers to children. A program should have sufficient numbers of trained staff to meet the needs of the children and promote their physical, social, emotional, and cognitive development. Each caregiver should engage in a stimulating and sensitive fashion with a limited number of children.

Children in settings with a high adult–child ratio are more likely to receive appropriate caregiving and experience developmentally appropriate activities. An adult who is responsible for too many children, can do little more than attend to their physical needs and safety. The caregiver is also likely to feel stressed in such situations, which increases the probability of harshness and restrictiveness. Fostering child development in young children requires frequent supportive, individualized interaction between adult and child.

Research indicates that optimal ratios vary with the age of the child. Reduced ratios appear to be especially important for infants and toddlers: ratios higher than 1:4 for children under three have been observed to result in increases in child apathy and distress. For older children, the more children per adult, the more time staff have to spend managing and controlling activities, and the less time they have to interact with children.

Group Size

For children older than the toddler stage but under five, adult–child ratios may be less significant than group size (see Table 1–1). The total number of children within each group is clearly linked to program quality. Where groups are smaller, caregivers spend more time interacting with children and less time simply watching them. As well, peer relationships may also be enhanced because moderate-sized groups permit children to have a choice of playmates while protecting them from overstimulation.

The determination of maximum group size needs to reflect the developmental needs of children, along with practical considerations such as the demands on the caregiver's time. In smaller groups, children are more verbal, more involved in activities, and less aggressive, and they make the greatest gains in standardized tests of learning and vocabulary. Group size should be evaluated and defined to facilitate adult–child interaction, individualized attention for children, and constructive activity among them.

Maximum group size should be determined by the distribution of ages within the group, the activity, and the inclusion of children with special needs. The group must be small enough to permit caregivers to manage both individual and group activities effectively.

TABLE 1–1	Staff–child Ratios within Group Size									
	Group Size									
Age of children*	**6**	**8**	**10**	**12**	**14**	**16**	**18**	**20**	**22**	**24**
Infants (birth–12 months)	1:3	1:4								
Toddlers (12–24 months)	1:3	1:4	1:5	1:4						
Two-year-olds (24–36 months)		1:4	1:5	1:6**						
Two- and three-year-olds			1:5	1:6	1:7**					
Three-year-olds					1:7	1:8	1:9	1:10**		
Four-year-olds						1:8	1:9	1:10**		
Four- and five-year-olds						1:8	1:9	1:10**		
Five-year-olds						1:8	1:9	1:10		
Six- to eight-year-olds								1:10	1:11	1:12

*Multi-age grouping is both permissible and desirable. When no infants are included, the staff–child ratio and group size requirements shall be based on the age of the majority of the children in the group. When infants are included, ratios and group sizes for infants must be maintained.

**Smaller group sizes and lower staff–child ratios are optimal. Larger group sizes and higher staff–child ratios are acceptable only in cases where staff are highly qualified.

SOURCE: Canadian Child Care Federation, *Definition of high quality child care* (1991).

This will encourage the appropriate development of independence, self-assertion, problem solving, cooperation, and friendliness.

Health officials also recommend group-limiting strategies—that is, keeping small groups of children consistently together—to reduce the spread of infection in early childhood settings.

Curriculum

Young children learn from all their experiences. In high quality early childhood environments, caregivers with education in child development use their skills of observation and assessment to plan appropriate experiences. Curriculum includes such items as program goals, planned activities, the daily schedule, and the availability of materials and equipment. It should facilitate the development of the whole child.

Children need a wide choice of developmentally appropriate activities and opportunities to explore their own interests. Practitioners who use developmentally appropriate practice as a guiding philosophy recognize this approach: addresses the development of the whole child in all developmental domains, including social, emotional, aesthetic, moral, language, cognitive, and physical; and are individually, age group, and culturally appropriate, incorporating the emerging needs and interests of individual children within the group. Curriculum planning is based on an early childhood educator's observation of each child's special interests and developmental progress. Children need adequate amounts of uninterrupted time to persist in self-chosen tasks and activities.

Cultural relevancy must be an integral and continuous part of the program, just as it is part of Canadian society. In an anti-bias curriculum, the early childhood educator models and conveys respect for differences and encourages children to recognize the many options open to them regardless of gender, age, ability, race, or culture. Children and parents are encouraged to share aspects of their culture and lifestyle.

Different curriculum approaches emphasize different aspects of child development. In general, research shows that highly structured programs emphasizing cognitive and language development are particularly effective with disadvantaged children. In programs structured by adults, children show less independence and initiative, but do better on intelligence and achievement tests. Children in open or child-centred programs are observed to be more independent and persistent. Children in moderately structured programs appear to fare best overall, demonstrating gains in creativity and self-esteem as well as cognition and achievement.

Whatever the approach, a program's success is related to how clearly its philosophy is defined. Curriculum is discussed at length in Chapter 4, "Making Curriculum Work."

Physical Environment

Whether indoors or outdoors, the environment affects the behaviour and development of both adults and children. The setting needs to provide opportunities for exploration and learning. Physical environment affects the level of involvement of children, and the quality of interaction between adults and children. According to the research, children demonstrate higher cognitive skill levels and greater social competence in environments that are safe and orderly, contain a wide variety of stimulating material, and are organized into learning centres.

In examining the impact of the environment, one must consider:

- both indoor and outdoor space
- the overall size, design, and layout of space
- the availability of materials and equipment
- the health and safety needs of children

Child care environments must ensure a minimum number of square metres per child. Studies have found that as the number of children in a space increases, so do aggressiveness, destructiveness, and apathetic behaviour.

Equipment requirements are more difficult to quantify, since many types of equipment contribute to the objective of high quality care. Equipment should be age-appropriate, and designed to develop skills at various age levels. Materials should be available in sufficient quantities to allow choices by children and avoid unnecessary competition.

The environment must be safe and healthy. Staff in quality early childhood programs educate children about safe and healthy practices, and act to prevent illness and accidents. Further considerations around the physical environment are discussed in Chapter 5, "Physical Environments."

Interactions

Although many factors contribute to the quality of an early childhood setting, perhaps the most important factor is the interaction between the adults and the children. Adults who are sensitively responsive excel at reading and understanding each child's verbal and behavioural cues and are able to anticipate children's needs. Optimal development is enhanced by relationships with adults that are positive, supportive, and individualized. Adults support developing independence by helping when needed, while allowing children to do what they are capable of and want to do for themselves.

Young children also develop through peer interaction, and here adult intervention is again crucial. The schedule should provide many opportunities for children to play with and beside other children. Teachers support children's beginning friendships. Interactions between children and staff should provide opportunities for children to develop an understanding of self and others, characterized by respect, affection, freedom from bias, and humour.

From a child's point of view, early childhood experiences are a joint enterprise of parents and caregivers. This fact is recognized in some studies that examine the joint effects of home and early childhood environments on child development. There is some concern about caregiver/parent relations here—Galinsky (1988) revealed that caregivers often harbour negative attitudes about the parents of children in their care. Galinsky further revealed that these attitudes vary with the caregiver's perceptions of the quality of parental childrearing, parents' education and marital status, and whether the parents are using subsidized care. This research points to a key area needing to be studied further, and indicates a need for additional caregiver education on how to meet a variety of parental needs.

Quality of interaction is interrelated with other factors we have discussed: ratio of adults to children, caregiver education, continuity in relationship, group size, and program size. In her summary of research, Doherty-Derkowski (1995) suggests ratio has a direct influence on the child's experience of caregiver responsiveness, or lack of it, and this ultimately affects the child's well-being and development. This aspect of a program can be assessed using instruments such as the *Early childhood environment rating scale* (Harms et al. 1980, 1989, 1990, 1996).

The importance of caregiver characteristics that impact the quality of interactions are discussed in Chapter 6, "Staffing—The Key to Quality."

Continuity of Care

A secure attachment with a primary caregiver provides a child a sense of security necessary to reach out and explore people and things in the environment. Such an attachment is based, in part, on the availability of a consistent caregiver who responds quickly, sensitively and appropriately to the child's needs. It is suggested that the child remain with the same caregiver for the first 36 months of life. In a primary caregiving system, babies still interact with all adults in the environment, but they are assigned to a particular adult who meets most of their caregiving needs and serves as a primary contact for parents. Lally (1995) advocates for the development of policies and practices that endeavour to keep children and caregivers together in familiar environments. This approach aids the child by providing a supportive emotional climate within which to work through the development of identity, rather than having to repeatedly form new relationships while at the same time trying to define self. Poor wages and working conditions are a significant factors in staff turnover.

Cultural Continuity

In addition to facilitating security through the provision of consistent caregivers, a setting must possess cultural content. Culture is a fundamental building block of identity. The early childhood experience should be in harmony with the culture of the home. Different cultures have unique ways of viewing the world, preferred ways of social organization, unique language patterns, learning styles and concepts of acceptable behaviour. Early childhood educators should pay great attention to incorporating home practices into the early childhood environment. Staff should reflect the culture of the families served, and the environment should include pictures and objects from home. There are a number of recent Canadian resources to assist settings in developing culturally appropriate curriculum. Bernhard et al. conducted research into practices, documented in *Paths to equity: Cultural, linguistic and racial diversity in Canadian early childhood education* (1995). Chud and Fahlman, in *Honouring diversity with child care and early education* (1995), have collected materials for curriculum in teacher preparation programs.

INDICATORS OF QUALITY: CAREGIVER CHARACTERISTICS

Education and Experience

The teacher is the most important factor in the quality of child care. Among the important variables that affect a teacher's performance are the amount and kind of formal education, experience in child care, and length of service.

It is important to foster a knowledgeable, confident self-identity.

Research studies consistently report that postsecondary education in early childhood is associated with adults who are more likely to be responsive, to provide children with stimulating activities, to provide activities that are developmentally appropriate, and to support parents through the provision of child development information. The benefits of postsecondary education are found in family day care as well as among centre staff. Research has found that appropriate staff training in child development contributes to positive outcomes for children in areas such as increased social interaction with adults, the development of prosocial behaviours, and improved language and cognitive development. Appropriate training for staff is linked to more social interaction between caregiver and children, more cooperation and task persistence among children, and less apathetic, unengaged behaviour among children.

The amount of teacher preparation, both preservice and in-service, predicts program quality, which in turn is linked with positive child outcomes, especially in terms of language and representational skills—critical areas for later school success. Caregivers with more education have less authoritarian styles and more knowledge about child development.

In contrast, experience alone appears to have little association with positive child outcomes. By itself, caregiver experience is not a predictor of effective caregiving, and in the absence of other factors has been linked to less cognitive and social stimulation among children, and more apathy among infants. To emphasize this point: in early childhood care as in other fields, experience is valuable. But experience alone, without other supporting factors, does not appear to necessarily make an effective caregiver.

Teachers should be trained in the requirements of children with special needs, and given an awareness of the social and political forces affecting early childhood programs. They must possess the knowledge, skill, and competency to interact sensitively and successfully not only with the children they care for, but also with adults. A number of studies (Almy 1975; Feeny 1985) have probed beyond training to examine the significance of personal characteristics of staff, such as motivation, communication skills, and enjoyment of children. One study suggests that important teacher qualifications are rooted in basic personal qualities.

Stability and Staff Satisfaction

The structural variables of experience, level of education, specialized preservice preparation and in-service professional development as well as salary and working conditions are tied to staff turnover and therefore the consistency of care. Increased stability in child care arrangements is linked with positive child outcomes in both the short and long term. Caregiver stability is particularly important for infants and toddlers, because they are in the process of forming attachment relationships. It is an increasingly serious problem, with annual teacher turnover rates in the field of 21.7% (Doherty 1999), and estimated to be even higher in family day care. It is important to note that this national figure masks considerable differences across the provinces, with a high in Alberta of 44.8% and a low in P.E.I. of 15.5%.

Stability is only one of several ways that job satisfaction among caregivers affects child behaviour and development. Studies indicate that salary is the best predictor of job satisfaction: higher salaries are associated with higher job commitment that views child care as a career. Whitebrook et al. (1990) also found that teachers earning salaries at the higher end of the range worked in centres with better quality. In the studies *You bet I care* (1999) and *Caring for a living* (1993), Goelman and Karyo et al. found that the nature of the work, feeling that they, the workers, were making a difference, and relationships with coworkers are the most satisfying aspects of working in child care.

Caregivers who are satisfied with their jobs are more likely to provide encouragement and guidance to children. Caregivers who are dissatisfied tend to be more harsh and restrictive with children, and less likely to provide activities that will support and encourage child development. Chapter 11 discusses the need for concerted efforts of professional and advocacy groups to meet the personal and professional needs of caregivers.

To improve job satisfaction, the field must:

- improve salaries
- raise the status of the early childhood profession
- increase teacher involvement in decision making
- ensure that caregivers receive their breaks and lunch hours
- provide opportunities for continuing education and professional development

INDICATORS OF QUALITY: CONTEXTUAL FACTORS

Funding, Auspice, and Licensing Standards

Quality is affected by many contextual factors, such as funding, auspice, standards, and regulations.

Canadian child care is heavily dependent on parent fees for revenue. Caring for young children is a labour-intensive service, with cost depending on the child/staff ratio and the wages and benefits paid to the staff. Research has repeatedly demonstrated that teacher salary levels influence the way educators behave with a child. As we have seen, quality requires favourable ratio and group sizes, adequate supplies of appropriate equipment and materials, and reasonable compensation. All these require adequate funding. Government funding, other than fee subsidy, assists programs by providing additional operating funds. To date there is no Canadian research looking at the effect of government grants on quality. However, findings do support the value of government funding over and above fee subsidization, such as salary grants, as a means of encouraging quality.

The term *auspice* is used to describe the way in which a program is operated. In Canada, such auspices include municipal, non-profit, and commercial programs, and the availability of each possibility varies widely across the country. In Canada, the for-profit category includes unincorporated owner-operators of one or two programs, centres or homes that are part of a local system with two or more settings. Non-profit programs may be sponsored by a parent group, an organization such as the YMCA/YWCA, a voluntary board of directors, a municipal government or a First Nations band. The operation of for-profit child care has been controversial in Canada for many years.

Friesen (1995) explores the issue of auspice in some detail in his paper *A sociological examination of the child care auspice debate*. Auspice influences quality through its effect on wages, working conditions, and job satisfaction. In fact, the auspice of a centre is often the strongest predictor of quality.

Studies support the conclusion that high quality child care is more likely to be found in non-profit than in commercial auspices (Doherty 1999). Teaching staff in a non-profit centre generally have higher levels of formal education and more specialized training in child development, and the setting usually has better staff–child ratios and teacher consistency. This is not to deny the existence of high quality for-profit programs, or poor quality non-profit programs. However, the issue of auspice is more complex than it has often been portrayed. The differences in sectors suggests that various factors are at work and that quality depends upon more than the auspice label.

The establishment and enforcement of standards is part of the administration of a child care system. In Canada, child care is primarily delivered by voluntary organizations and commercial operators. Provincial/territorial governments regulate child care by establishing standards that must be met in order to obtain a licence to operate. Family child care providers can operate without a licence provided they do not exceed a certain number of children as specified in their province's legislation. The level of regulatory requirements exerts an influence on child care quality. Regulation can encourage quality by setting standards for structural elements. Regulation can only be effective if there is both adequate monitoring for compliance and strict enforcement of the required standards. Licensing requirements are usually minimal and measurable. Programs can move to higher voluntary standards and gain professional recognition.

Relationships with the External Environment

Any effort to improve the quality of early childhood programs needs to direct some attention to developing and maintaining good relationships with external parties. Early childhood programs benefit from cultivating good relationships with community members such as legislators, bankers, doctors, licensing officers, elected officals, and community leaders. Children benefit when they learn about the community as a vital component of their curriculum. Field trips, visits from a police officer, or trips to the market are a few of the ways for children to be involved in their community.

Community interaction should include:

- awareness and appropriate use of community resources
- communication and interaction with elementary schools
- sensitivity to changing community needs
- cooperative projects within the community, such as multi-generational projects and public education endeavours

Early childhood environments are a vital part of any community. Chapter 11, "Community, Resources, and Advocacy," examines this aspect more.

Parent Involvement

With increasing numbers of children spending many hours per day in early childhood settings, caregivers and parents, more than ever before, are partners in many aspects of child rearing and socialization. Studies have shown that children benefit when parents and staff share a common commitment to acting in the best interests of children, communicate openly and have mutual respect. Parent involvement can cover a range of activities, from a simple newsletter for parents to active partnerships between parents and staff.

Parents and staff should communicate about child-rearing practices such as discipline and routines, in order to minimize potential conflicts and confusion for the children and ensure some cultural continuity. Studies suggest that open and regular communication between caregiver and parent has a very significant impact on positive outcomes for children. This is especially so where the parent is observant and informed, and perhaps serves as a mem-

Parent involvement in early childhood settings enables them to feel that they are contributing to their community.

ber of the program's board of directors or advisory group, participating in the evaluation of the program. Chapter 10, "Families and Early Childhood Programs—A Vital Partnership," provides more examples of how to involve parents in early childhood programs.

Quality early childhood is a collaborative endeavour, with children moving back and forth between home and program. Future research needs to examine the combined effects of the child's experience in child care and at home.

Methods of Achieving Quality

The mechanisms that can be used to maintain quality fall into three general categories:

- regulatory methods
- voluntary standards
- other non-regulatory methods

An effective licensing and regulatory system can be the cornerstone of any national effort to assure quality in early childhood programs. Licensing provides the necessary foundation upon which all other efforts are built. Government licensing requirements tend solely to address structural indicators such as staff–child ratios, even though process dimensions may be more important for quality. Nonetheless, regulatory requirements based on the findings of research increase the probability that all children in licensed settings will receive higher quality care.

Quality levels higher than the minimum required for licensing may be established by making such standards a condition of funding, or by requiring that staff meet certain levels. A funding agency can define the level of quality it is prepared to purchase. For example, a municipal government may require a centre in which it is purchasing subsidy spaces to meet higher standards than those set by the provincial government. These additional standards will in effect raise the quality level of care. The Canadian Child Care Federation has a research project, Partners in Quality, which developed occupational standards for home providers, child care centres, administrators, and family resource programs.

Two additional measures focus on enhancing the quality of child care through the development of professional standards of practice. Standards can be applied at both the program and the individual levels. *Accreditation* is a process by which a representative body, recognized by both service providers and the community in general, establishes standards for service that are above the mandatory requirements of government. Programs apply on a voluntary basis for evaluation against these standards and if found to meet or surpass them, are granted accreditation status. Accreditation is usually a voluntary process, although it could be required of a program by funding bodies. This trend is beginning in some states such as Oklahoma, which provides additional funding for those programs operating at higher standards.

The second method takes the form of *certification* of qualified individuals. Specialized training in early childhood education is essential for people to become competent teachers. Certification ensures that individuals have completed specific training programs and demonstrated specific competencies in working with children. Certification of early childhood graduates can provide assurance that the individual is able to translate theory into good practice. Three provinces—Ontario, Alberta, and Nova Scotia—provide voluntary certification for members of professional organizations. Accreditation and certification are elaborated on in Chapter 6.

Staff can improve the quality of a program through public education, membership in unions and professional organizations, and consultation with other professionals. Other important methods for encouraging quality include evaluation of the setting, staff training, parent education, and the provision of various types of support for the caregiver.

Children are not aware that early childhood settings vary in form, function, auspice, or regulatory environment. What makes a difference for them are their relationships with teachers and peers. High quality child care services for Canadian children and their families depend upon the cooperation and support of all segments of the community.

IN CONCLUSION

More and more, policy makers and the general public understand that the achievement of optimal, healthy, and overall development for all children is beneficial not only to our children and their families but also to society as a whole. It should be gratifying to early childhood educators that many of the truths about developmentally appropriate practice are being borne out in the new brain research studies and are being read about and listened to with great interest in the popular press by the general public.

At the heart of providing quality early childhood settings for Canadian children and their families is the need for changes in attitudes. Policy makers will move only within the limits of what they believe public perception to be. As identified in the macrosystem, the public's attitudes toward the roles of women must be altered. There needs to be an increased valuation of women's work in the home; an increase in the wages of women in external employment so that their pay is commensurate with their knowledge and skills; and a change in the common assumption that women (rather than men) are the primary caregivers of their children. These beliefs about motherhood, women's roles, the nature of families, and caregiving need to be revisited, since they impede the process of redistributing the costs of quality early childhood education into the public realm.

ACTIVITIES

1. Identify barriers to providing quality early childhood services.

2. In small groups, identify and discuss indicators of high quality child care from one of the following perspectives: parents, staff, community professionals.

3. Select one dimension of quality and develop the criteria to measure it.

4. Assess the quality of an early childhood setting using one of the following tools:
   - the Early Childhood Environment Rating Scale
   - the Child Care Inventory
   - the Early Childhood Work Environment Survey

5. Choose an aspect of your field placement site where you think quality could be improved. Identify a method and, if possible, implement it.

REVIEW QUESTIONS

1. Identify five components of quality early childhood settings.

2. Name the systems in Bronfenbrenner's ecological model.

3. List four ways to improve quality.

4. Discuss two characteristics required by caregivers to provide responsive caregiving.

5. Briefly identify how quality settings for early childhood benefit Canada economically.

FURTHER READING

Canadian Child Care Federation (1999). Research Connections CANADA: Supporting Children and Families. Ottawa.

National Association for the Education of Young Children (1998). Accreditation criteria and procedures of the national academy of early childhood programs (revised). Washington, DC: NAEYC.

Penn, H. (1999). What can we learn from Europe and elsewhere about child care policy? **www.childcarecanada.org**

CHANGING ROLES OF GOVERNMENT

Early childhood educators should be knowledgeable about the ever-changing roles of government, licensing procedures and other regulations pertaining to the provision of services for young children. This chapter looks at:

- *Child care in Canada—a national issue*
- *Role of the federal government*
- *Role of provincial and territorial governments*
- *Role of local governments*
- *Milestones in legislation*
- *Provincial legislative offices, regulations, and early childhood organizations*

Canada underwent enormous social and economic change, and social policies and programs also changed to meet the challenges and needs of Canadian families. Each level of government plays its own role in child care. Governments express their priorities through funding allocations. The provision and quality of child care in Canada are heavily affected by government funding priorities, whether these priorities are expressed through federal–provincial transfer payments, income tax deductions, direct operating grants, individual subsidies, or budget restrictions. Although they attempt to respond to the needs of society within a constitutionally and legally defined framework, each government acts on its political objectives through the way it collects and spends tax revenue.

The development of health, social, and educational programs in Canada has historically been influenced by the federal government. There has been a steady decline in the federal role in social programs as evidenced by child care policy over the past decade (Friendly 1999). Health, education, social services, and the regulation and funding of child care services are the responsibility of the provincial and territorial governments. Municipal governments enforce local bylaws such as zoning, building and fire codes, public health regulations, and the like. Municipalities may have a role in the allocation of subsidized spaces. Some directly operate child care services and may be involved in the supervision of programs.

CHILD CARE IN CANADA—A NATIONAL ISSUE

Early childhood programs can play a role in meeting a broad range of national policy objectives. These include promoting the optimal development of all children, reducing child poverty by enabling parents to enter the workforce, supporting the effectiveness of the current workforce, and promoting women's economic and social equality.

Canada has historically been divided by regional, language, and cultural issues, and finding consensus on social policies continues to be challenging. Progressive social policy analysts feel the government must recognize the challenges and needs of Canadian families. They believe that government should make quality child care a priority, and that providing quality care for all children will support government objectives of employment creation and reduction of poverty. There is concern that many Canadians are worried about family breakdown, job security, and global competition, and that the impact these issues have for

Child care workers need to join with others and speak out in order to get public support for services for children.

the security of their families and for their children's futures has not been considered seriously enough. Although child care has been on the national agenda for several decades, and despite many discussions and consultations, there is no national legislation or set of standards.

Over the last 25 years, there has been a steady increase in the numbers of families where both parents or the single parent work outside the home or attend school. "In 1994/5, 32.4% of children aged 0–11 (1.5 million) were in some form of non-parental care while their parents worked or studied. Of the children who were not in care, 39.6% (one million) had been in child care at some point in the past" (*Growing up in Canada,* National Longitudinal Survey of Children and Youth 1996). Consequently, government policy with respect to child care has become a matter of increasing public concern. Children require care while their parents work. In general, the rapid changes in Canadian families and the growth in the need for child care have moved far ahead of the will of governments to respond and shift resources.

Canadians want children to have a strong start in life. Unfortunately, too many children are not receiving the full benefits of Canada's success. In Canada, in 1998, over 21% of the population, or 1 498 000 people, lived in families with an income level below the poverty line. The 1998 report card on child poverty in Canada noted that 13.1% (932 500) children lived in families with incomes of less than $20 000 annually. Lack of child care contributes to a perpetual cycle of poverty.

Our economy has seen a shift away from predominantly full-time jobs that lasted an entire working life to frequent job changes, increased demand for retraining, and more contract and part-time work and self-employment. These changes have been difficult for many low-income families. This pattern is reflected in a decline in their full-time employment between 1984 and 1996 (National Child Benefit Progress Report: 1999). Some groups tend to be overrepresented among those who are living on low income, including: lone-parent families, First Peoples families, recent immigrant families, and families led by persons with disabilities.

With enormous changes in family structure and the dramatic increase in the employment of mothers, families and children have a greater need for early childhood care and education programs than ever before. In 1997, 52% of women were employed. Mothers represent a large part of this increase. Between 1976 and 1997, the employment rate for women with children rose from 39% to 66%. Fifty-nine per cent of all women with children under the age of three and sixty-two per cent of women whose youngest child was between three and five years were employed. According to the study *Preschool Children: Promises to Keep* (National Council of Welfare 1999), by the time the youngest child reached six, 71% of all mothers had paid jobs. For women who are single parents—a social group whose numbers have greatly increased over these 25 years—the availability of child care often makes the difference between independence and welfare.

These figures indicate the great need for child care, and the even greater unmet need for licensed spaces. Very little regulated care exists in Canada. The Child Care Resource and Research Unit estimates that there are regulated child care spaces for only 8.4% of children who need them. Most parents rely on often unpredictable unregulated care by family members or neighbours. Exact figures for those in unregulated care are impossible to obtain. Doherty et al. (1995), in *Child care: Canada can't work without it,* track figures from 1983 to 1993 and document that the gap is widening. In 1983, there were 2 135 705 children under the age of 13 with mothers in the paid labour force who were not receiving regulated child care services. This number had increased by 636 513 ten years later. Furthermore, the rate of growth of supply is decreasing. According to Human Resources Development

Canada (1994), growth for regulated spaces from 1971 to the late 1980s ranged from 10% to 16%, but in 1993 it had slowed to 3.5%.

School-age children and infants are particularly underserved by the licensed sector. Child care services are dependent on parent fees to cover their operating costs. However, many parents cannot afford the fees that regulated services must charge in order to survive. Consequently many parents who would prefer to use regulated services are left to make informal, often unreliable, arrangements.

Table 2–1 shows the total number of regulated child care spaces in Canada at the end of 1998 organized by province.

THE ROLE OF THE FEDERAL GOVERNMENT

The main reason Canada does not have a national child care policy is because of challenges in the way Canada works. Because Canada is a federation, the federal government does not have the power to enact a child care program without the agreement of the provinces. The functions of the federal and provincial governments with respect to child care are complex and interrelated. Many issues relating to family policy fall under provincial jurisdiction. While divorce law is federal, marriage laws and the enforcement of child support are under provincial jurisdiction. Child care falls under provincial jurisdiction, but indirectly receives some funds from the federal government. The federal government provides maternity and parental leave, but leave from employment is governed by provincial legislation for most Canadian employees.

With respect to supporting children, the federal government traces its role in child care to the introduction of a tax exemption in 1918 (Government of Canada (1994a). The 1942 Dominion-Provincial War-time agreement initiated a 50–50 federal/provincial cost-sharing

TABLE 2-1 Interprovincial Comparison of Licensed Child Care Spaces 1998	
Province/Territory	
Newfoundland	4 275
P.E.I.	3 717
Nova Scotia	10 994
New Brunswick	9 204
Quebec	82 302
Ontario	167 090
Manitoba	20 490
Saskatchewan	7 124
Alberta	61 562
British Columbia	68 978
Northwest Territories	1 145
Yukon	1 307
National total	438 188

SOURCE: Working Paper; *Child Care in Canada (1999),* The Child Care Research and Resource Unit, University of Toronto. Statistics reprinted by permission of The Child Care Research and Resource Unit.

arrangement. This involvement was expanded after the Second World War with the Family Allowance Program. Subsequently, the influence of the federal government became primarily financial, through cost-sharing payments it made to provincial government budgets for child care and related services.

The federal government made provision to share the cost of child care for low-income families in 1966, under the Canada Assistance Plan (CAP). To receive federal contributions, the provinces had to spend the money first, then apply to the federal government to match eligible expenditures specified in the plan. For a limited number of families in financial need, subsidies were available. Funding was only available to programs that were regulated and not-for-profit. The criticism of this arrangement was that the poorer provinces did not have the matching funds to spend on child care.

Child care services are funded through a patchwork approach comprising parent fees and federal, provincial, territorial, and municipal funding. The 1995 federal budget brought about major changes in the cost-sharing approach that has been in effect since the Second World War.

In 1994, the Liberal government began a process of reforming Canada's system of social security. Child care was seen as part of this agenda. It was viewed as a critical support for employment, because it provides working parents with the assurance of care for their children. The 1996 Throne Speech indicated that the assent of a majority of provinces would be necessary for the federal government to embark on new social programs (this includes child care). If this principle had been in place in 1966, the federal government could not have implemented the Canada Assistance Plan or the Canada Health Act.

Canada Health and Social Transfer (CHST)

In the 1995 federal budget the Minister of Finance, Paul Martin, announced that cost-sharing with the provinces and territories for welfare and social services (including child care) under the Canada Assistance Plan (CAP), and health and postsecondary education expenditures under the Established Programs Financing (EPF), would be rolled into a single block fund starting in April 1996. This fund was called the Canada Health and Social Transfer (CHST). According to Department of Finance Canada (1995), this move continues "the evolution away from cost-sharing in areas of provincial responsibility, which has been a source of entanglement and irritation in federal-provincial relations." As a result, provinces had $23 billion less to pay for education, health, and child care services.

Although the 1966 Canada Assistance Plan had limited conditions on how the funds were spent, the provinces and territories needed to expend funds in order to receive the federal dollars. CHST does not require a matching of funds, nor that the moneys be directed to specified areas. The absence of conditions enables provinces and territories to redirect money previously spent on child care to other areas. Child care advocates want the federal government to establish principles and conditions for the CHST and enforce them as it currently does with the Canada Health Act in funding health services. Many felt the changes of CHST halted improvements to child care.

Federal Income Tax Measures Related to Child Care

The discussion of tax concessions in Canada is complicated. In 1988, Canada converted a number of tax deductions to credits. Although these changes were touted as distributing benefits in a more progressive manner, most families suffered a substantial loss in benefits. Tax deductions or tax credits do not contribute to creating more regulated services that would enable parents to have greater choice of child care arrangements. In 1997, the federal budget announced a new child benefit using the existing tax benefit, the Working Income Supplement, and additional dollars from several sources.

A national child benefit, a cornerstone of European income security and family policies, is not new to Canada. This approach has been around since the mid-1940s with Canada's universal family allowance program, which was eliminated in 1993. The National Child Care Benefit (NCB) is a partnership between Canadian governments. Federal-provincial-territorial ministers responsible for social services designed the NCB as an investment in the well-being of the child. The primary goals are to improve benefits and services available to low-income families with children and to help them move from welfare to work and stay employed. The program enables the provinces and territories to either top up benefit amounts or provide supplementary benefits to working poor families such as dental or drug benefits or child care services. In July 1998, there was an initial investment of $850 million to low-income families as a supplement of the child care tax benefit. In 2000, the federal government is investing $1.7 billion per year.

The objectives were agreed upon by the federal, provincial, and territorial governments:

• to help prevent and reduce the depth of child poverty;

• to promote attachment to the workforce—resulting in fewer families having to rely on social assistance—by ensuring that families will always be better off by working;

• to reduce the overlap and duplication through close harmonization of program objectives, benefits, and simplified administration.

To achieve these objectives, the federal government increased its benefits to low-income families with children, corresponding with a decrease by provinces and territories in social assistance payments. Provinces and territories were to provide complementary programs to improve work incentives and services for low-income families with children.

Concerns about this approach include that low-income mothers are impelled into the labour force in the absence of quality child care options. Due to the absence of coherent plans for early childhood care and development, public funds are spent in fragmented, poorly focused programs (*Child care and the integrated tax benefit*). The 1999 report by the National Council of Welfare, *Promises to Keep,* summarizes that the debate around providing good, affordable, and accessible child care continues in the face of overwhelming evidence that public investment in child care is as good for the country as it is for children and their families.

Although critics feel there are some serious failings to the program, there are also two promising features: the program signals a re-entry of the federal government onto the social policy stage and a potential strengthening of their role in income security for families; this benefit could be an important first step to prevent and reduce child poverty (Freiler and Cerny 1998).

The Future Role of the Federal Government

At a time when Canada is undergoing social and economic upheaval, social policies and programs must respond to the changing needs of Canadian families. A society that is interested in the long-term social and economic security of its citizens and a healthy and prosperous future must be committed to the care and nurturing of children. Canada is one of a few major industrialized nations without a child care policy. In parts of Europe, child care is viewed as a citizenship right, as part of early childhood development, and is seen as important for young children regardless of the employment status of the parents. Because child care is regarded as a societal responsibility, services are publicly funded. Policies that enhance child development contribute to the social and economic security of the country. It is time for the federal government to make a commitment to a broader set of social responsibility goals and recognize the legitimacy and value of caring for children.

THE ROLE OF PROVINCIAL AND TERRITORIAL GOVERNMENTS

Provinces and territories are responsible for:

- the regulation of child care services
- funding arrangements
- jurisdiction over child care standards, policies and procedures, and guidelines

By the late 1980s all the provinces and territories had enacted child care legislation and had systems for monitoring compliance of legislated requirements. Most were providing some form of direct funding to regulated child care services. However, Doherty et al. (1999) found that some provincial and territorial governments were retreating from their responsibilities for child care services. These responsibilities can be divided into financial and regulatory.

Financial Responsibilities

Each province and territory has developed its own system of planning, regulating, and funding child care services. Even under fiscal constraints, total provincial and territorial expenditures for child care services have grown in recent years, increasing from approximately $700 million in 1989–90 to $1.1 billion in 1993–94 (Government of Canada (1994b)). The major means of supporting child care is through subsidies for low-income families. There is considerable variation among provinces and territories regarding which parents are eligible for subsidy and the amount of subsidy.

Many provinces and territories have developed grants that provide assistance for capital costs, equipment, staff salaries, or other program expenditures. These grants provide improvements to program quality without increasing parental fees, thus providing assistance to all families. This source of funding is steadily eroding.

Table 2–2 identifies the percentage of revenue from three primary sources for centres. These resources strongly influence wage levels and the kind and quality of services a setting can offer. Although nationally centres obtained 49.2% of revenue from parent fees, there was heavier reliance in some provinces such as Newfoundland (82.1%) and Nova Scotia (72.7%). Manitoba was the province with the lowest reliance on parent fees. See Table 2–3 for an interprovincial comparison of monthly child care costs. The variation on the extent of reliance on fee subsidy for centre revenue reflects different provincial policies. The fee subsidy program in Newfoundland has been capped since 1993, with the result that once the allocated funds were spent, parents were unable to obtain a subsidy.

There is a wide variation in the cost of child care. While the provinces and territories each provide child care subsidies for eligible low-income families, eligibility criteria and the amount of subsidy vary across the country. For example, the study *You Bet I Care* found substantial fee increases occurring in Alberta for infants (approximately 62%), toddlers (42.7%), and preschoolers (39%) since this province reduced its operating grants each year since 1990. Each province and territory sets its own limit on the maximum subsidy, and these limits vary widely. Some provinces require parents to pay a minimum user fee for child care regardless of their income level, whereas others expect them to pay a substantial difference between the subsidy rate and the real cost of care. The amount a parent pays is determined by either an income test or a needs test, where a parent must declare amounts paid for rent, food, transportation, etc.

Many believe that needs and income tests stigmatize child care and the families that rely on subsidy. A subsidy system does not guarantee low-income Canadian families equity of access or affordability, and has the potential to segregate children based on their parents' economic status.

In recent years, some provinces have implemented improvements to their child care systems. In 1997, Quebec implemented a comprehensive child care policy that gave concrete expression to the educational dimension of early childhood services. Half-day programs for five-year-olds were extended to full day. Four-year-olds had a supplemental half-day program provided at no cost to the parent. By 2001, there are an additional 85 000 spaces to be created for children from birth to age four. The regulations required double the current number of trained staff. British Columbia added infant care spaces and referral to child and family support services. However, most provinces and territories maintain that they cannot provide adequate funding of services, and subsidies have not increased to reflect the cost of

TABLE 2-2	Average Percentage of Revenue from Three Primary Sources by Province 1998			
Province/Territory	**Parent Fees**	**Fee Subsidy**	**Other Gov't Grants**	**Totals**
British Columbia	49.4%	38.5%	8.9%	96.8%
Alberta	53.8%	36.2%	7.5%	97.5%
Saskatchewan	38.3%	35%	21.7%	95%
Manitoba	33.9%	40.3%	21.6%	95.8%
Ontario	46.9%	34.1%	16.6%	97.6%
Quebec	45.8%	18.9%	33%	97.7%
New Brunswick	68.7%	26.9%	1.9%	97.5%
Nova Scotia	72.7%	20.5%	5.2%	98.4%
P.E.I.	66.8%	26.1%	6.3%	99.2%
Newfoundland	82.1%	14.4%	0%	96.5%
Yukon/N.W.T.	not reportable			
Canada	49.2%	30.5%	17.5%	97.2%

Table from *You Bet I Care Report:* Centre Resources and Expenditures (1999) Notes. Reprinted by permission of Child and Family Canada.

1. Information for the Northwest Territories and the Yukon is not reportable because of small sample size.

2. Quebec's phase-in of $5.00/day fees will alter the current relative reliance on parent fees and government grants.

3. Newfoundland announced April 1998 that it will be spending $4 600 000 annually on improving and expanding licensed child care centres. When implemented, this should reduce reliance on parental fees.

care. Among the concerns identified by Doherty et al. (1995) with provincial/territorial funding approaches are:

- the fact that fee subsidies do not cover the actual cost of care
- the lack of accountability for the use of public funds used by subsidy recipients to purchase unregulated care
- the use of public money to support commercial care
- the fact that too many parents are on the waiting list for subsidized child care

As Chapter 1 makes clear, a significant barrier to high quality child care is staff dissatisfaction, usually expressed through high turnover. The most important cause is inadequate salaries, and after that poor working conditions, which are the result of underfunding in other areas. Average salaries for teachers range from $6.76 per hour in Newfoundland to virtually double in Ontario at $13.48. There appears little immediate prospect of improvement, and this is a major reason why every practitioner in the field needs to be aware of the routes to public advocacy (see Chapter 11, "Community, Resources, and Advocacy").

Regulation Through Licensing

Whether related to early childhood, banks, or broadcasting, regulation is designed to assure minimum levels of quality and accessibility for the entire population. Regulation takes place through legislation shaped by the policy priorities of a particular government. Policy makers will move only within the limits of perceived public opinion. In the last decade all levels of government responded to the voices of angry taxpayers who have called for cuts to government spending.

TABLE 2-3	Interprovincial Comparison of Day Care Centre Costs Per Month		
Province/Territory	**Infant**	**Preschool**	**Family Day Care**
Newfoundland	not available	$360*	
P.E.I.	$542	$412	same as centre
Nova Scotia	$500	$412*	$11–18 per day
New Brunswick	$380*	$360*	
Quebec		$477*	$440*
Ontario	$783*	$541*	
Manitoba	$573*	$368	$400
Saskatchewan	$325	$380*	$265
Alberta	$525	$438	$378
British Columbia	$679	$453	$25.90 (per day)
Northwest Territories	not available		
Yukon	$580	$533	$493
Canada	$531*	$455	

SOURCES: Working Paper; *Child Care in Canada (1999)* The Child Care Research and Resource Unit, University of Toronto and *You Bet I Care*: Centre Resources & Expenditures. Statistics reprinted by permission of The Child Care Research and Resource Unit.

Administrators of licensed programs are responsible for understanding licensing and other regulations pertaining to provision of services for young children. Directors must ensure all requirements are fulfilled in a timely manner. Regulation is administered by the provinces and territories and takes the form of licensing centre-based programs, family child care agencies, or homes. All provinces and territories have licensing standards, but they vary widely in scope. When regulatory systems are well designed and effectively administered, they can help assure an acceptable level of care.

Licensing standards provide a baseline for acceptable care of children. In programs operating below that level of service, a child is actually deemed to be in danger. Regulations deal with structural aspects of quality that are readily measurable (floor space, ratios, and group size) as reviewed in Chapter 1. Licensing standards set forth the public definition of accept-ability: regulated programs must meet at least this level of quality in order to legally oper-ate. While services need to address regulations, these alone cannot ensure an adequate standard of service delivery. A truer indication of quality is provided by process aspects of care such as teacher–child interactions. A licence gives a program permission to operate rather than indicating quality.

Many parents feel more secure placing their child in a licensed facility. Some agencies provide parents with information about the standards of quality they should be looking for when placing their child.

Regulations need to be clear, so everyone can understand them. Programs need to know what is expected from them, and government officials need to interpret and enforce standards fairly and consistently. A functioning system of regulation establishes standards of quality and applies those standards to programs. It specifies penalties and procedures for programs that do not meet the standards.

Although licensing regulations vary greatly from province to territory, most provincial regulations usually include the following:

- *Staff:* specifying qualifications, as well as medical requirements for staff and children.
- *Building safety:* detailing minimum fire and building safety standards, procedures for evac-uation, and storage of harmful materials.
- *Program:* ensuring that the daily schedule offers opportunities for activities that pro-mote children's development. See Chapter 4 for summary by province/territory.
- *Physical space:* the amount of space necessary both indoors and outside, levels of light, fencing, and provision of diaper-changing areas (in programs serving infants and toddlers).
- *Equipment:* detailing the amount appropriate to the ages and numbers served, and speci-fications for equipment, such as cribs meeting Health Canada's product safety standards.
- *Record keeping:* outlining policies and procedures, financial statements, and health records for children and staff.
- *Nutrition:* requiring that children's meals meet Canada's Food Guide recommendations and are prepared safely.
- *Behaviour guidance:* prohibiting certain kinds of discipline and encouraging positive guidance strategies.
- *Ratios/group size:* specifying the number of staff required for the number of children served, in order to protect the safety of the children.

An operation can be licensed when it meets the basic criteria in these areas. Licensing has traditionally looked after the safety and protection of children, though other important areas such as record keeping, staff qualifications, and personnel policies must also be determined before a licensed setting can become operational.

The granting of a licence to a facility means that the province or territory also assumes responsibility for monitoring the centre or home to check compliance with standards. This can vary from unannounced spot checks to scheduled visits. Doherty-Derkowski (1995), among others, views lack of adequate monitoring as a contributing factor to poor quality child care. Adequate monitoring involves appropriately trained monitors, who have a thorough background in child development and early childhood, assessing the quality of care in the program. The range of enforcement available ranges from granting conditional licences and the removal of licences to fines and prosecution. In extreme cases, such as child abuse, flagrant lack of safety precautions, or outright negligence, a centre or home may be closed immediately and its administrator, owner, or provider faced with criminal prosecution.

Centres and homes are relicensed annually in some provinces such as Nova Scotia, Ontario, Manitoba, and British Columbia and every three years in others such as Prince Edward Island. There is a trend in governments to reduce the frequency of licensing and monitoring visits to cope with funding restraints.

In some centres, overworked or poorly trained staff may be unaware of how to meet particular regulations. Very few programs are actually ordered closed if they do not meet standards, since it is usually felt that parents and children are better served if government officials work in a consultative capacity to improve weak programs. In such a case, the centre is usually given a provisional licence, listing improvements that need to be made by a specific date. During this time, officials and/or consultants work closely with the administrator to bring the centre up to minimum standards. If a condition is not met then the operator may lose his or her licence to operate.

No regulatory system guarantees quality, and many child care facilities meet only the minimum standards required by their province or territory. Others operate at a higher level. The minimum set by regulation should be considered the beginning of high quality care, not the end goal. In any case, it should not be forgotten that about 10% of the total number of children in care receive care in a licensed or regulated setting (including regulated home child care).

McLean (1994) reported that provinces and territories vary in how they apply sanctions, how frequently a program is visited, and the number of programs for which each inspector is responsible. Since regulations are only as strong as the system of enforcement, there is some concern about the effectiveness of our licensing system.

There continues to be much change in provincial legislation concerning child care. For current information, consult your provincial or territorial office. Addresses are found in the Appendix to this chapter.

An administrator may find himself or herself working with local and provincial/territorial regulators at the same time. At times, the regulations from the various bodies are not totally compatible. It is the role of the operator to ensure that the program is in compliance. If the program is not in compliance, the operator runs the risk of having to delay the opening of a new program, pay fines, or in rare cases having to close down a program for failure to meet a licensing requirement.

THE ROLE OF LOCAL GOVERNMENTS

Like the provinces and territories, local governments have both a regulatory and a financial role in child care. The only province where municipalities play a significant role is Ontario.

Local Regulation

As part of the licensing process, regulated programs must comply with some local ordinances. The local or municipal government generally sets requirements in the areas of fire, safety, health and sanitation, building codes, and zoning bylaws. A centre must meet all these standards before a program can accept children. Each ordinance may be administered by a different department of the local government, requiring separate visits from inspectors.

The local fire department will require that an early childhood program have fire extinguishers, alarms, fire escapes, and a procedure in place for fire drills. Local health and sanitation authorities will inspect food handling, water, toilets, sewage disposal, and hand washing and diapering procedures, as well as plans for meeting the needs of children who are ill. Local health departments may also set requirements for immunization and the monitoring of health checks for both staff and children. Building codes cover such areas as approval of the type of structure being used for a child care centre, and the local department of building safety will be concerned with plumbing, electrical wiring capacity, and other related factors. The local zoning agency will be aware of the building and safety requirements.

Anyone setting up a child care centre needs to be knowledgeable about these regulations, and how to meet them. Often a consultant works with interested parties to assist them in this area (see for example Chapter 5, "Physical Environments").

Municipal Funding

Municipal involvement in child care is discretionary. As a result, there is a lack of provincial consistency in service provided. In many cases, local governments do more than ensure that facilities meet local bylaws. They may, for example, be responsible for determining the rules for making subsidies available to individual families, and administering payment of those subsidies. Needs assessments and eligibility will vary from jurisdiction to jurisdiction, and so there is no guarantee that a family with subsidy moving from one municipality to another will continue to receive subsidy. Even within the same province, different cities may not be using the same guidelines or income cut-off points in their needs assessment. Thus a family receiving subsidy in one part of a province may no longer qualify if they move to another area.

Provincial subsidy funding may be directed to local governments through a transfer of payments for child care. Here, funding limitations have made severe inroads. Provincial and municipal social service budgets pay for welfare as well as child care, and with the downloading of other costs, the provision of subsidies for child care has often had to take a back seat. A number of local governments have reduced the dollars allocated to child care. Expansion of necessary child care services becomes impossible as municipalities and provinces are limited in their funding, and it is becoming increasingly difficult to meet needs and costs for existing services.

Municipally Operated Child Care

Some municipalities operate their own child care services. Others enter into purchase-of-service agreements with existing centres, finding it cheaper to buy subsidized space than operate a centre. Some local governments do one or the other, some do both, and a few areas still offer no services at all. Alberta and Ontario municipalities play a larger role in providing direct funds for child care.

When a municipality embarks upon purchase of services, it contracts with a community child care centre to provide subsidized spaces. This may mean the local government enters into an individual contract with a centre, either non-profit or for-profit, to enable parents receiving subsidy to use a certain number of its spaces. Often a local government will purchase services in geographical areas where parental needs have been seen to exist. The contracting procedure is analogous to letting a tender for road repair, where the municipality shops around for the best price.

Sometimes local governments use a purchase-of-service agreement to raise the quality of child care. This can be done by imposing requirements additional to those required by the province, such as specifying that a centre must be on a clear licence and not a provisional one, or that all staff members must have particular qualifications. A purchase-of-service agreement may also be directed at specific groups of children, such as those needing infant/toddler care, school-age child care, special needs care, or home child care.

MILESTONES IN POLICY AND LEGISLATION

Since 1970, numerous commissions and task forces have studied child care services in Canada and made recommendations. What is needed now is for some of these recommendations to be turned into action. Put most simply, the proper care and education of young children affects national productivity in two ways: productivity goes down if parents are worried about the care of their children, and future productivity depends on future producers—today's children.

Below are some milestones in the development of child care in Canada since 1850. As an early childhood educator, it is crucial that you understand the roots of child care policy, keep up with current legislation, and make contributions for continuous improvements to child care in Canada. Among a few important questions to ask yourself are:

- What will be societal and governmental priorities in supporting new child care services?
- Will new services be funded privately, by government, or through a combination of both?
- Will these new services be accessible and affordable to all parents and children in need of them?
- How can I lobby for quality child care services for children and their parents?

Milestones in Legislation

1850   The earliest child care centres are established in Montreal.

1873   Kindergartens are established by the City of Toronto Board of Education as part of the public school system.

1885   Factory work by children under 12 became illegal in Quebec.

1889   Hester How (Toronto) allows students to bring younger siblings to school to reduce student absenteeism.

1890   Ontario's first recorded day care centre, called The Creche, opens in Toronto; it is also operated as an employment agency for domestics.

1910   Infants' Hospital in Vancouver opens an infant and preschool centre for working mothers.

1914   Jost Mission Day Care is founded in Halifax during World War I.

1916   The Creche (founded in 1910), organized jointly by the Associated Charities and the City of Vancouver, is placed under the jurisdiction of the provincial health department. This move puts British Columbia ahead of the other provinces in terms of government intervention and support for day care services.

1920   Introduction of the Mothers' Allowance Act of Ontario provides welfare benefits to single mothers, enabling them to stay at home to care for their children.

1924   Dr. Hinks, a leading figure in the early mental health movement, and Dr. Blott, head of the psychiatry department at the University of Toronto establish the St. George's School for Child Study (later the Institute of Child Study) headed by Dr. Blatz, the founder of Canada's early childhood education movement.

1930   Mother's Allowance is given to two-parent families on relief.

1937   British Columbia licenses child care centres, becoming the first province in the country to do so.

1942   Dominion-Provincial Wartime Day Nurseries Agreement enables any provincial government interested in establishing day care facilities to cost-share with the federal government. Ontario and Quebec are the only provinces to take advantage of this agreement. The other provinces maintain they have no need for day care.

1945   Quebec decides to close wartime centres. Institute of Child Study (Toronto) develops the Day Nursery Act, then administered by the Welfare Ministry. In Ontario a substantial public campaign keeps the centres open.

1960s   Insufficient number of licensed child care spaces and the high cost of day care are issues for parents as more women begin to enter the workforce. By 1967, women make up 20% of the Canadian workforce.

1966   Canada Assistance Plan (CAP) is passed by Parliament. Child care is included among social services for which the federal government agrees to pay half the cost of provincial subsidies for low-income families.

1970s   The Royal Commission on the Status of Women calls for government recognition and expansion of high quality child care services, stating that women will not achieve full equality without government involvement in child care.

1971   Introduction of the first tax deduction for child care.

1981   The census reports that mothers in the workforce outnumber those staying at home with their children. Fifty-two per cent of mothers participate in the workforce, and women make up forty-two per cent of the total workforce.

1983   Canada Assistance Plan sets out specific minimum and maximum income limits for eligibility in its new policy guidelines.

1984   The Liberal federal government commissions the Task Force on Child Care, chaired by Katie Cooke. Its mandate is to examine the need for child care services and parental leave in Canada, and make recommendations on the federal government's role in the development of a national child care system.

- Federal election year. For the first time, all three major parties make child care a campaign issue. The newly elected Conservative government promises a national child care program.

1986   The Task Force on Child Care chaired by Katie Cooke releases its report. Its principal recommendations are that: a publicly funded, universally accessible national system of licensed group and family child care should be developed over 15 years.

1987   Statistics Canada reports that the participation rate in the workforce of mothers with children under the age of 16 has increased to 65%.

- The Ontario government publishes "New Directions for Child Care," stating that it "recognizes child care as a basic public service, not a welfare service." This approach represents a fundamental shift in the way government views child care.

- The federal government proposes its National Strategy on Child Care. Included are a $5.4 billion day care program to take effect over seven years, child care tax deductions for receipted child care expenses, a research and development fund and a commitment to a national child care act.

1988   Statistics Canada identifies the country's ten worst-paid jobs. Day care workers are at the bottom of the list, behind housekeepers, zookeepers, and farm labourers.

- The federal government announces its Canada Child Care Act. Since it is a federal election year, there is not enough time to pass the act. The Conservative government wins the election and begins a second term.

1989   The reelected federal Conservative government announces it will reconsider the Canada Child Care Act, as too many interest groups are critical. The act does not reappear.

1990   The federal government limits annual increases to 5% on Canada Assistance Plan payments to Alberta, British Columbia and Ontario (the "cap on CAP"). This is a radical departure from the original open-ended agreement, and signals a change to the notion of universality.

1991   Federal revisions to Unemployment Insurance grant parents an additional 10 weeks of maternity benefits, which may be taken by either parent.

- The 1989 United Nations Convention on the Rights of the Child is ratified by Canada.

1992   The Canadian National Child Care Study releases its report as "Parental Work Patterns and Child Care Needs." This study provides a comprehensive review of the child care arrangements and needs of Canadian families with children from newborn to 12 years of age. It confirms that most Canadian children have two working parents.

- The federal government releases its report "Brighter Futures: Canada's Action Plan for Children." There is no mention of a national child care system or policy.

"Child care is now considered a last priority ... I had the privilege to be [its] killer."

—Benoît Bouchard, federal (Conservative)
Minister of Health, February 29, 1992

1993   A federal election replaces the Conservative government with the Liberals under Jean Chrétien. Although child care is not a major election issue, the incoming government does make a commitment to steadily increase the national total of high quality spaces available, when the economy improves.

"Child care remains a priority of this government [Liberal], as it addresses the two main objectives I have set for my department: getting people back to work and the reduction of child poverty."

—Lloyd Axworthy, federal Minister of
Human Resources Development, 1994

1994   The federal Liberal government initiates Social Security Review.

1995   The federal government announces Canada Health and Social Transfer (CHST) and Human Resources Investment Fund.

- The federal government offers provinces and territories $630 million for joint investment in child care (50–50 cost-shared).

1996   The Canada Assistance Plan ends in March to be replaced by block transfers to provinces.

- The federal government announces that it is abandoning its plans for federal/provincial cost-shared spaces.

1998   The National Child Benefit was implemented to build a cooperative approach between federal and provincial governments to address child poverty.

2001   Will the National Children's Agenda move forward children's issues and eradicate child poverty as promised by the House of Commons in 1989, the year it ratified the United Nations Convention on the Rights of the Child?

IN CONCLUSION

In 1996 an estimated 3.5 million children need child care while their parents are employed or attend school. This fact that reminds us of how essential is our role as early childhood educators. We must be the best that we can be when parents entrust such an important portion of the child's life to us. Good child care is an investment in healthy children. It contributes to child development; it reduces child poverty; it supports parents; and it contributes to economic growth. We need to advocate the designation of funding to make quality child care more available and affordable. To achieve major funding for child care involves the shifting of public opinion toward the value of quality child care. Currently the conservative ideological conceptions view child care as belonging in the private realm—a family matter. As educators, we need to increase our understanding of the foundations of social policy and its implications for our work.

ACTIVITIES

1. Would you make any changes to your province's or territory's legislation for child care? If so, discuss what would you like to see changed and explain why.

2. Construct your own "milestones chart" for legislation and other relevant facts, for the last 24 months. Discuss what has been happening nationally, provincially/territorially, and locally. What changes would you like to see in child care during the next 24 months?

3. Write to your local provincial member for the latest publications from his or her party concerning child care.

4. Outline who parents should contact to apply for child care subsidies or financial assistance in your local government. Where are these officials' offices located? Are they easily accessible?

5. Make a list of the steps you would take to license a child care centre in your province or territory.

REVIEW QUESTIONS

1. Identify significant milestones of the child care movement in Canada.

2. Identify the responsibilities of the provincial and territorial governments for child care.

3. Name two acts that had a major impact on the role of the federal government in funding child care.

4. Identify the key components of regulation.

5. What are key points we need to communicate about the importance of quality child care to the public and government?

FURTHER READING

Baker, M. (1995). *Canadian family policies: Cross-national comparison.* Toronto: University of Toronto Press.

Doherty, G., M. Friendly, and M. Oloman (1998). *Women's Support, Women's Work: Child Care in an Era of Deficit Reduction, Devolution, Downsizing, and Deregulation.* Ottawa: Status of Women Canada.

National Council of Welfare (1999). *Preschool Children: Promises to Keep.* Ottawa: Minister of Public Works and Government Services Canada.

APPENDIX: PROVINCIAL LEGISLATIVE OFFICES, REGULATIONS, AND EARLY CHILDHOOD ORGANIZATIONS

Alberta

Department Governing Early Childhood Programs
Ministry of Family and Social Services
Director, Day Care Programs
Alberta Family and Social Services
7th Street Plaza
10030—107th Street, 8th floor
Edmonton, Alberta
T5J 3E4

Provincial Act Governing Child Care or Most Recent Amendment
• Alberta Day Care Regulation 333/90
• Social Care Facilities Licensing Act amended 1994

Provincial Organizations and Addresses
Alberta Association for Young Children
Avonmore School, Room 31
7340–78th Street
Edmonton, Alberta
T6C 2N1

Alberta Association for Family Day Home Services
11411–54th Avenue
Edmonton, Alberta
T6H 0V8

British Columbia

Department Governing Early Childhood Programs
Child Care Team
Ministry for Children and Families
P.O. Box 9700, STN Prov. Govt.
Victoria, British Columbia
V8V 9S1

Provincial Act Governing Child Care or Most Recent Amendment

- Community Care Facility Act, Chapter 57, 1988
- British Columbia, Benefits (Child Care) Act, 1997
- British Columbia, Benefits (Child Care) Regulations, 1997

Provincial Organizations and Addresses
Early Childhood Educators, British Columbia (ECEBC)
3rd floor, 210 West Broadway
Vancouver, British Columbia
V5Y 3W2

Western Canada Family Day Care Association
c/o 9527–120th Street, Suite 212
Delta, British Columbia
V4C 6S3

Manitoba

Department Governing Early Childhood Programs
Department of Family Services
Child Day Care
114 Garry Street, Suite 102
Winnipeg, Manitoba
R3C 1G1

Provincial Act Governing Child Care or Most Recent Amendment

- The Community Child Day Care Standards Act (Chapter C158 of L.R.M., 1987)
- Manitoba Child Day Care Regulations 62/86

Provincial Organizations and Addresses
Manitoba Child Care Association, Inc.
364 McGregor Street
Winnipeg, Manitoba
R2W 4X3

New Brunswick

Department Governing Early Childhood Programs
Office for Family and Prevention Services
Department of Health and Community Services
P.O. Box 5100
Fredericton, New Brunswick
E3B 3N6

Provincial Act Governing Child Care or Most Recent Amendment

- Family Services Act, Chapter C–2.1, Part II. Community Placement Resources, 1983
- Family Services Act, Regulation 83–85, under Family Services Act Order-in-Council 83–457 (consolidated to June 30, 1985)

- Day Care Facilities Standards, Department of Health and Community Services, June 1, 1985

Provincial Organizations and Addresses
Early Childhood Coalition Petite Enfance is currently undergoing restructuring.

Newfoundland

Department Governing Early Childhood Programs
Family and Rehabilitative Services
Department of Health and Community Services
Confederation Building, West Block
P.O. Box 8700
St. John's, Newfoundland
A1B 4J6

Provincial Act Governing Child Care or Most Recent Amendment

- The Day Care and Homemaker Services Act, 1990
- Newfoundland Regulation 63/93
- Child Care Services Act, 1999
- Child Care Regulations, 1999

Provincial Organizations and Addresses
Association of Early Childhood Educators of Newfoundland and Labrador (AECENL)
P.O. Box 21462
St. John's, Newfoundland
A1A 4J7

Family Home Child Care Association of Newfoundland and Labrador
20 Carroll Drive
Mount Pearl, Newfoundland
A1N 3B1

Northwest Territories

Department Governing Early Childhood Programs
Early Childhood and School Services
Department of Education, Culture & Employment
Government of N.W.T.
500—4920 52nd Street
Lahm Ridge Tower, 3rd floor
P.O. Box 1320
Yellowknife, Northwest Territories
X1A 2L9

Territorial Act Governing Child Care or Most Recent Amendment

- Northwest Territories Child Day Care Act, 1988 (1), c. 13. (as amended by SI–101–87[1], c. 13)

- Child Day Care Standards Regulations, 1988 (pursuant to Subsection 39 [1] of the Child Day Care Act)

Territorial Organizations and Addresses
Currently there are no active child organizations in the N.W.T.

Nova Scotia

Department Governing Early Childhood Programs
Prevention and Day Care Services
Department of Community Services
P.O. Box 696
Halifax, Nova Scotia
B3J 2T7

Provincial Act Governing Child Care or Most Recent Amendment

- Day Care Act and Regulations, 1990 (Chapter 120 of the revised statutes)

Provincial Organizations and Addresses
Certification Council of Early Childhood Education of Nova Scotia
1200 Tower Road
Halifax, Nova Scotia
B3J 1C2

Child Care Connection NS
1200 Tower Road, Suite 100
Halifax, Nova Scotia
B3J 1C2

Ontario

Department Governing Early Childhood Programs
Child Care and Community Services Branch
Ministry of Community and Social Services
4th Floor, Hepburn Block
80 Grosvenor Street
Toronto, Ontario
M7A 1E9

Provincial Act Governing Child Care or Most Recent Amendment

- The Day Nurseries Act, 1990 (reprinted 1998), amended by the Services Improvement Act 1998
- Ontario Regulation 262, 1990 (amended 1998, 1999)

Provincial Organizations and Addresses
Association of Early Childhood Educators, Ontario (AECEO)
40 Orchard View Boulevard, Suite #211
Toronto, Ontario
M4R 1B9

Ontario Coalition for Better Child Care
500a Bloor Street West, 2nd Floor
Toronto, Ontario
M5S 1Y8

Home Child Care Association of Ontario
c/o Network Child Care Services
756 Ossington Avenue
Toronto, Ontario
M6G 3T9

Prince Edward Island

Department Governing Early Childhood Programs
Department of Health and Social Services
P.O. Box 2000
Charlottetown, Prince Edward Island
C1A 7N8

Provincial Act Governing Child Care or Most Recent Amendment

•   Child Care Facilities Act, R.S. P.E.I. 1988, Chapter C–5

•   Child Care Facilities Act Regulations (including any amendments to December 31, 1990)

•   The Welfare Act 1988

Provincial Organizations and Addresses
Early Childhood Development Association of P.E.I.
81 Prince Street
Charlottetown, Prince Edward Island
C1A 4R3

Quebec

Department Governing Early Childhood Programs
Ministère de la Famille et l'Enfance
600, rue Fullum
Montréal, Québec
H2X 4S7

Provincial Act Governing Child Care or Most Recent Amendment

•   An Act Respecting the Ministère de la Famille et de l'Enfance and amending the Act Respecting Child Day Care Centres. Bill 145, 1997

•   An Act Respecting Child Day Care Centres and Day Care Services R.S.Q., chapter S–4.1, R.2., as amended 1998

•   Règlement sur les services de garde en garderie, amended September 1997

•   Regulation Respecting Home Day Care Agencies and Home Day Care, 1998

•   Regulation Respecting Child Care Centres amended 1998

•   Regulation Respecting Reduced Contributions amended 1998

Provincial Organizations and Addresses
Association de l'éducation préscolaire du Québec
Montréal, Québec
H2K 4L1

Concertations inter-régionale des centres de la petite enfance du Québec
438, rue Victoria
St. Lambert, Québec
J4P 2J4

Saskatchewan

Department Governing Early Childhood Programs
Child Day Care Division
1920 Broad Street
Regina, Saskatchewan
S4P 3V6

Provincial Act Governing Child Care or Most Recent Amendment

• The Child Care Act, Chapter C–7.3, 1990

• The Child Care Regulations 948/90, Chapter C–7.3, Reg. 1 Section 27, 1990

Provincial Organizations and Addresses
Saskatchewan Child Care Association, Inc.
510 Cynthia Street
Saskatoon, Saskatchewan
S7L 7K7

Yukon Territory

Department Governing Early Childhood Programs
Child Care Services Unit
Department of Health and Social Services
Government of Yukon Territory
P.O. Box 2703
Whitehorse, Yukon
Y1A 2C6

Territorial Act Governing Child Care or Most Recent Amendment

• Child Care Act, Statutes of the Yukon, 1990 (Bill 77)

• Child Care Centre Program Regulations, 1995

• Child Care Subsidy Regulations, 1995

• Family Day Home Program Regulations, 1995

• School-Age Program Regulation, 1995

Territorial Organizations and Addresses
Yukon Child Care Association
Box 5439
Whitehorse, Yukon
Y1A 5H4

THE PHILOSOPHY STATEMENT—A FRAMEWORK FOR SUCCESS

The philosophy statement of an early childhood setting is a general statement of beliefs and goals that puts into words what the stakeholders believe to be most important about educating and nurturing young children. The philosophy has a direct bearing on the development of the curriculum, budget allocations, staff hiring, scheduling of routines, degree of parent involvement, and use of community resources. It may be driven by a board of directors or it may be set by the owner or director of the program. It should be developed in consultation with staff and the users of the program. Ideally, it should also reflect community needs, and be evaluated on a ongoing basis. The philosophy should underpin all aspects of the setting's operation, whether it be centre-based or home-based care. A philosophy statement is so crucial that it is required by law in some provinces. This chapter will outline:

- *The importance of the philosophy statement*
- *How to develop a philosophy statement*
- *Implementing and assessing a philosophy*

It is important to understand that the philosophy statement defines the operation of an early childhood environment and thus is a living statement. Since a philosophy is a culmination of beliefs and goals in child care, it is necessary to be open to new ideas and constantly reevaluate, so that the philosophy is dynamic and continues to respond to the needs of the community.

In an early childhood setting, the philosophy statement is used to focus the direction and evaluation of the curriculum, hire staff, write informational brochures, and recruit potential families. An explicit statement of philosophy is needed to guide and support curriculum and policies, and establish a basis of common understanding between staff and parents. The philosophy reflects assumptions about how children learn, and sets the priorities valued by the parents and staff. For example, if the focus is on content, then the staff may choose to teach such information as numbers and letters. If the focus is on a process-oriented environment, then staff members will facilitate children's interactions, ask them questions, reflect, observe, and evaluate the outcome of the curriculum.

A centre's philosophy needs to be readily available to parents and potential users of the service. It is generally available through the program brochure or flyer, and it should be a part of the setting's handbook. Administrators, staff, and board members should be able to talk with confidence about the philosophy's specific goals. It isn't enough to say, "Our basic objective is to do a good job and run a quality early childhood setting." These are good intentions but not sufficient for the daily operation of a quality child care environment.

THE IMPORTANCE OF THE PHILOSOPHY STATEMENT

The philosophy statement may be a few paragraphs or a few pages, but it is important that it be in writing, and available to all who are in contact with the setting. These include the administrator, home child care operator, board of directors, staff, parents and potential parents, training institutions, students, visitors, community agencies, and even the children themselves. In culturally responsive settings the philosophy should be translated so that the beliefs of the setting are clearly understood by all members of the community.

Parents who are approaching a setting for the first time should be able to use the philosophy statement to make informed choices about the care of their children. The philosophy statement provides the basis for initial decisions in choosing a child care service. If a particular family finds a program philosophy does not match their needs and values, they should be directed to a program that is better matched to their needs.

A clearly articulated philosophy statement guides the activities of the early childhood setting. It provides the framework for staff to set goals consistent with the direction of the philosophy and then plan and implement activities to meet these goals.

A philosophy statement provides a framework for decision-making regarding all aspects of the operation of an early childhood setting including program planning, equipment purchases and allocations for professional development. Click and Click (1990) state that "…clear goals allow coordinated planning for all parts of a school or child care centre. They are essential to the development and maintenance of a quality program" (p. 77).

Bertrand (1990) describes the significance of the philosophy statement to the Board of Directors. "The philosophy of a child care centre serves as a starting point,

- to build board and staff commitment

- to determine goals and objectives that guide the board of directors in managing and leading the centre's operations

- to make decisions"

The philosophy statement is a benchmark that provides direction and guidance for the child care centre. Research indicates that it is not the specific direction that is important, but rather, the fact that a direction is established and agreed upon (Bertrand 1990).

A philosophy draws together many strands—an understanding of child development, current research, personal beliefs and values, trends in parenting styles, and general societal expectations. All these areas are continually evolving. As the philosophy becomes part of the daily life in a setting, it should be continually reevaluated and adapted, so that it becomes a living statement fitting the desired practices and the needs of those who use it.

The need for a philosophy of early childhood education also has a personal dimension. In the same way that each environment needs a spelled-out philosophy, each practitioner needs to think through and continually reevaluate his or her own personal philosophy of early childhood education.

Examples of How a Statement Functions

The following example shows how one line in a centre's philosophy statement evolved over time in response to the needs of its clientele. Name changes reflect changing trends in early childhood education, and time changes reflect the needs of people living and working in the community.

Year	
1965	"The Day Centre will be open from 8:30 a.m. to 5 p.m. to meet the needs of student parents and working parents and their children."
1980	"The Early Childhood Centre will be open from 7:30 a.m. to 6 p.m. to meet the needs of student parents and other working parents and their children."
1990	"The Early Childhood Development Centre will be open from 6:45 a.m. to 6:30 p.m. to meet the needs of parents and their children."
2001	"The Child Care Centre will maintain 24-hour flexible care for infants, toddlers, preschoolers, and school-age children of working parents."

The philosophy statement serves to direct the action and behaviour of the staff, and allows caregivers to ensure they are comfortable with the rationale for the curriculum. In the previous example, only caregivers comfortable with flexible 24-hour care would apply for jobs with the Child Care Centre in the year 2001. When a philosophy is in place and the staff works toward its goals, then programming and related activities and experiences will be directed to helping children develop and learn in a particular manner. Individual staff members must be committed to the philosophy, if this focusing effect is to happen.

The next examples show how different approaches to learning can derive from the same statement of philosophy. Each approach is positive, but each illustrates a different emphasis.

Philosophy Statement:	
"Staff are committed to providing curriculum to assist in building children's confidence and self-esteem."	
Setting 1:	**Setting 2:**
Most of the children are from families that appear confident of their literacy skills. The staff is committed to providing a wide arrangement of dramatic play opportunities for children to widen and strengthen their social interactions and knowledge. They also believe in child-initiated play, under the protective eye of the teachers. All day staff members make special efforts to speak with the parents as they drop off and pick up their children, to keep them up to date on progress toward the common goals in the statement of philosophy.	Most of the children are from families with limited educational backgrounds. The opportunity to attend a year or two of head-start type programming would be beneficial, and would help prepare the children for the school system. The staff is committed to providing carefully selected activities for the children to widen and strengthen their social interactions and knowledge. This staff believes in more teacher-directed play and activities. For example, special play activities will be set up to build skills and knowledge in the use of telephones. Parent meetings are held regularly to explain the goals in the statement of philosophy, and how they are being met at the centre.

HOW TO DEVELOP A PHILOSOPHY STATEMENT

A philosophy statement is developed when a new setting is opening, or any time that changes are wanted in the operation of an existing one. It provides a collective understanding of goals so that board, supervisor, staff, parents, and student teachers all work in the same direction. The board or owner is responsible for monitoring the implementation of this collective understanding, as he or she is ultimately responsible for the content of the philosophy.

The statement must express a series of goals. For example, one goal in a high-quality early childhood program is likely to be the fostering of a positive self-concept. To meet this goal, staff and parents need to work together to help children develop confidence in their abilities. In another example, staff might present many opportunities for children to chant or sing together, giving them a sense of accomplishment without singling out individual strengths or weaknesses. They might also fill the room with children's artwork or projects. They can demonstrate the value of the child's culture by providing opportunities for parents, grandparents, and others to participate with the children in reading stories from their childhoods, or in preparing food for the children.

Another goal may be that children learn to play and work together cooperatively and harmoniously. In such a setting, an early childhood educator would not get a group of children ready for outdoor play by saying, "O.K. Let's see who can get out the door the fastest and grab a tricycle." Instead, he or she could say, "When you are ready, you may go out. Remember to share the tricycles." As the basis for the setting's policies, program, and procedures, a philosophy needs to be concrete, operational, and measurable.

The statement can be developed from the top down, the bottom up, or as a collaborative effort. Parents and key stakeholders should have an opportunity to participate, and the philosophy should express the relationship between setting and community. Most often, a collaborative model is used, because this gives everyone ownership and thus a solid reason to uphold the philosophy. The time it takes to discuss, clarify, and reach consensus about the philosophy of an early childhood setting is worth the investment. All stakeholders should be involved in the process; parents, staff, managers, and community representatives. As feedback and research information is collected, staff should have an equal opportunity to participate in shaping the setting's philosophy. Through this process, common directions can be established.

This process requires a significant investment of time as diverse opinions are discussed and negotiated. The value of the results are best characterized by Click and Click (1990), "The decided advantage in this method of goal determination is that users of the goals (staff) are more likely to want to carry them out. With input comes an inducement to implement those goals" (p. 78).

Steps in Developing a Philosophy Statement

Many early childhood educators have found it useful to develop their own personal philosophy statements to guide their individual practice. The process of developing a personal philosophy is in many ways similar to that of articulating a setting's philosophy. Steps important for the development and implementation of a statement include research and dialogue with peers, colleagues, and parents, and integration of the philosophy in the program development. The following describes the activities required to develop a philosophy statement through a process of consultation and consensus.

Research

Anyone preparing a statement must have a clear understanding of different theories of child development and learning. A first step is to research the contributions made by such theorists as Johann Pestalozzi, Frederick Froebel, Jean Piaget, John Dewey, Arnold Gesell, Susan Isaacs, Maria Montessori, and Benjamin Spock. Such research gives the statement substance. Following a review of existing theories of learning and development, you can integrate your findings with your own values and beliefs.

Example: After reviewing several educational philosophies, you may take an eclectic approach and select a number of key ideas from different theorists/practitioners, add your own ideas, and begin to build your own philosophy. You should reevaluate it as you gain more experience and work in a wider variety of environments.

Consultation with Peers and Colleagues

It is important to get feedback from others. Share and discuss ideas with colleagues, college faculty, supervisors, parents, licensing officials, and other practitioners in the field. Invite the active participation of the families in your setting. Input from parents can be solicited through a variety of methods including parent questionnaires, discussion at parents' meetings, or questions posted for parents' response when picking up or dropping off their children. Formulate questions that will elicit feedback about individuals' beliefs and values. Open-ended questions that enable participants to explore their beliefs about quality child care will provide input for questionnaires, informal discussions, posters, and focus groups. Answers should be solicited in a climate that respects and values the input and ideas of all participants. Some may prefer to provide feedback in a more private, confidential manner.

Prioritize

Once all of the research and feedback has been gathered, it is important to get a sense of what people believe is most important. This can be accomplished by asking participants to select and/or rank the statements that they believe to be most important. This phase of development can be difficult. It is important to provide a structure for this process that maintains the momentum of this activity. Grouping items that are similar will prove helpful.

Drafting the Philosophy Statement

As priorities are established, common threads will appear. Use these to begin to draft a statement that will constitute your setting's philosophy. Use terminology that is appropriate for the audience that will be reading and implementing this document. Begin by using language that captures the main ideas. Revise statements to reflect people's reactions and suggestions. Continue this process until the statement is completed, remembering that the goal is to develop a philosophy that is acceptable to all participants.

These consultations widen the base of knowledge and experience supporting a statement of philosophy.

Example: Your early childhood setting has just hired a new staff member whose background is Mexican. He shares his knowledge and ideas with the centre, including the fact that

Take time to discuss the philosophy, and ensure that it is consistent with the values of parents.

he thinks the setting's lunch menus are limited and bland. Based upon staff discussion, the centre reviews its existing philosophy and decides to make a change. The old philosophy states: "Health is a primary concern for all. Good nutrition is essential to maintaining good health." This is changed to: "Health is a primary concern for all. Good nutrition, and providing a wide range of food opportunities reflecting many cultures, is essential to maintaining good health and a sense of pride and well-being."

Implementation

A philosophy statement should be a living document. Once the development process is completed, the next step is to operationalize the beliefs and values contained in the document to guide behaviour and practice.

This involves "translating" the beliefs and values in concrete terms. Examples of standards of practice should also be provided. For example, the philosophy of an early childhood setting may identify that "partnership with parents" is an important belief. The standards of practice that operationalize this belief could include the following examples:

1. Staff share the daily events of the setting with parents through a variety of methods that bring their child's day to life.
2. Parents' involvement in the program is actively recruited. This involvement may mean that parents join the children for certain activities, lend items, share special talents or skills, act as resource people, etc.
3. Evaluation feedback is solicited on an annual basis.

Staff Evaluation

The expectations used in evaluation should emerge from the setting's statement of philosophy and the job descriptions used to hire staff members. These job descriptions should reflect the setting's philosophy. Home care providers would follow the same procedures for self-evaluations. When evaluations are implemented and effectively used, they can facilitate self-growth and build confidence. Used improperly they can create mistrust and poor morale.

Example 1: As the new director of a setting, you ask each staff member to list his or her perceived strengths and weaknesses. You then use a list of questions to interview the staff. At the end of these two exercises, you have solid evidence that the staff as a whole has a major area of weakness around professional development, even though the centre philosophy states that the professional development of staff should be supported. No staff member has been to a professional conference in five years, and three staff members have never been to a conference at all—not even as students in training! The staff has been feeling professionally isolated. You present these results to the board, which recommends funds for professional development, and works with you to strengthen the commitment to professional development in the philosophy. Staff are given a list of conferences and workshops and are encouraged to discuss these opportunities at the next staff meeting. A two-year plan is made for staff professional development. Three staff members will attend conferences within the next four months. Morale, productivity, and enthusiasm begin to skyrocket!

Example 2: Mrs. Ng, a home care provider, finds she is planning the same menus week after week and has overheard the children say, "Oh no, not this again!" She feels professionally isolated. She sees an advertisement in the newspaper about a Dairy Association workshop called "Menu Planning: Feeding Children Well." She attends the workshop and receives handouts that are full of new ideas for menu planning, as well as providing different suggestions for children's hands-on food activities. The workshop participants exchange addresses and agree to meet again, informally, next month at Ai Suko's home. Mrs. Ng finds she now has the opportunity to make like-minded friends, belong to a group, and exchange new recipes and ideas. She feels more self-assured about her work, is not so tired at the end of each working day, and enjoys being with the children more. Her morale, productivity, and enthusiasm are improving as well.

Being Open to New Information

As a program operates from year to year, the philosophy should be reassessed to make sure it continues to reflect current thinking on the development of children, and the emerging needs of the parents and community it serves.

This is equally true in the development of a personal philosophy. As an educator in the field, you should continue to consider and assess your own views, alongside new information you gather from practice in the field. You can acquire new information from courses offered through continuing education programs, educational journals, and membership in professional organizations.

Example 1: Several early childhood education students feel children should sleep at home in their own beds at night, and find it difficult to accept that their field placement will embark upon flexible child care in the fall. On the weekend these same students go to a party. At 2 a.m., when they call a taxi to take them home, they find the driver has an infant in a child car seat in the front. The taxi driver apologizes because her child care arrangements have broken down. How is a single parent in her position to keep her job?

The students hadn't considered a dilemma like this. As they think this experience over, they see a real need in their community for flexible child care—not only for taxi drivers, but for waiters, hospital staff and many others.

Example 2: A school-age program is held in an inner-city community centre. This program used to be the sole user of the building during weekdays, and children often went unaccompanied to the toilets. The neighbourhood's needs changed and now several groups are using the building. The staff realize that the children's security and safety are a primary concern, and they rethink the toilet procedure. In a group discussion with the children, it is agreed that an adult will now accompany the children to the toilet area and remain nearby.

IMPLEMENTING AND ASSESSING A PHILOSOPHY

Specific goals and objectives in the statement of philosophy set the direction of the program and determine how the activities are carried out. The supervisor and board are responsible for how these goals are achieved.

Staff members must feel comfortable with the philosophy and the way specific goals are to be achieved. In order to give it their full support, staff members need a philosophy compatible with their own, and involving them in the development of the philosophy statement gives them a stake in it. Here are examples of a successful and an unsuccessful fit between staff member and program philosophy.

The program philosophy stresses positive support, non-punitive guidance, and the value of play for children, along with professional development for staff.	
Teacher 1:	**Teacher 2:**
The substitute teacher is very pleased to be called so often by the school-age centre. This is her fifth year working part-time there. It's an enjoyable place to work, and she feels she is being paid to do the thing she likes best—interacting with children in an enthusiastic environment.	When she was hired, the new staff member said she agreed with the centre's philosophy. However, her own upbringing had been abusive, and she had not enjoyed her training because of her difficulty in guiding the children's behaviour. During her three-month probation in her new job, she realized she disliked working with children and their parents. Her colleagues helped her obtain career counselling to find another career.

When you talk with prospective parents, make them aware of the philosophy statement, and take time to discuss the philosophy. Make sure that they understand it, and that it is consistent with their values and traditions. For example, is the setting sensitive to cultural distinctiveness? Are all staff members—including cook, secretary, janitor, etc.—sensitive to the presence of children from different religious beliefs? Are vegetarian meals and snacks available? Such discussion will ensure a better fit between parents and staff, who work together in the interest of the children.

The philosophy statement also provides a basis for understanding between the setting and training institutions. Training programs, and the students they place in the early childhood setting, should be aware of the staff's philosophy and be prepared to follow it. In order for this to happen, field placement agencies should provide an orientation process, or the setting must be prepared to provide one during each placement.

Methods for Monitoring and Assessing a Philosophy

Evaluation of the philosophy statement, and of the way it reflects and guides the aims of the centre and needs of the general community, should be regular and ongoing. Therefore continuous review of a setting's philosophy will help guide future strategic planning. Such review or evaluation should be built into the program, usually on an annual basis. The review should include research, observations, and suggestions from staff, parents, and the board of directors (and sometimes from the children as well), to see whether the work of the setting still reflects the statement of philosophy, and whether program goals and objectives are being met. While input from outside consultants can be beneficial, the responsibility remains primarily in the hands of the supervisor, the board of directors, and the staff. If a philosophy is to be responsive to parent needs, parent feedback must be a part of the process.

Children need the security of consistency in routines and activities planned by staff in order to have a sense of security in their lives. Staff need direction from a clear statement of philosophy in order to maintain continuity and consistency in their work. Parents need to know what they can expect from the setting, how they can contribute to it, and what is expected of them. The setting needs to explain to the community what it stands for and how it operates.

The evaluation of a philosophy statement should take into account:

- the structure of the program
- the environment in which the program operates
- the changing needs of the community
- the way in which the program is funded

Evaluation can range from developmental checklists of children to complex research processes. After discussing a number of child development theories and methods of evaluation, Evans (1975) concludes that empirically based evaluation methods are probably most appropriate. This is because philosophy statements, and their resulting policies and programs, often assume a life of their own as staff continually reevaluate their role and mission.

While recognizing the value of evaluation, early childhood educators often feel they lack the knowledge, time, or funds required to do it adequately. Consultants can be useful here. Assessment tools have also been developed that can be useful as well as time-saving—for example, Jorde Bloom's *A great place to work: Improving conditions for staff in young children's programs*; Harms and Clifford's *Early childhood environment rating scale* (also available: *Infant/Toddler, Family home day care,* and *School-age care* environment rating scales); and the National Academy of Early Childhood Programs' *Guide to accreditation.* Validated instruments can often be used successfully after a minimum of staff training. The areas measured must be consistent with your setting's philosophy—any tool is valid only if it measures what the program views as quality.

Evaluation time should be made a priority. It is necessary to budget adequately for evaluation, because costs exist both directly, as in the purchase of materials, and indirectly, as

Children need consistency in routines in order to have a sense of security in their lives.

in staff time. The program should also budget for and commit itself to program development, training, and staff development.

IN CONCLUSION

The philosophy statement is a general statement of beliefs and goals. It outlines how these beliefs and goals govern the teaching and the general approach to the children. It has a direct bearing on curriculum development, budget allocations, staff hiring, scheduling of routines, degree of parent involvement, and use of community resources. The steps for its development include research, consultation with peers, colleagues, and parents, and integration of the philosophy into the program development. Evaluation of the philosophy statement, and the way it reflects and guides the aims of the setting and needs of the general community, should be regular and ongoing.

ACTIVITIES

1. As an early childhood educator, begin to develop a "living" statement of philosophy. Write down your philosophy (one to three pages) and include: objectives of the program, methods the program will use to meet these objectives, and theories that support the statement of philosophy. Discuss it with peers and at least two other professionals (director, staff, or board member) working in your community.
2. Compare four statements of philosophy, including one from the centre where you are doing a field practicum. Consider each philosophy, write what you like about each, and look for omissions that should be included.
3. Write out an ideal philosophy for the following components in centre-based care: school-age child care, respect for environment, and respect for culture.
4. Collect two statements of philosophy for either centre-based or home care-based settings in your community. Visit these settings. Look for examples of how goals, values, and beliefs are implemented in the programs. What do these philosophies have in common? How are they different?
5. Monitor the philosophy statement of a setting where you are doing a practicum, by making journal entries of specific events and structures that support or do not support the philosophy. Discuss these entries with your cooperating teacher and faculty advisor, and bring them to class for discussion.

REVIEW QUESTIONS

1. Why is a philosophy statement important?
2. What are the most important steps in developing a philosophy?
3. How do you implement a philosophy?
4. How does the philosophy have a direct bearing on the development of the curriculum, budget allocations, staff hiring, scheduling of routines, degree of parent involvement, and community resources?
5. What are the techniques and tools for ongoing evaluation of a philosophy?

FURTHER READING

Ayles, T. and S. Becker-Griffin (1990). *Daily operations manual with supplement on finance management.* Toronto: Umbrella Central Day Care Services/Child Care Initiatives Fund, Health and Welfare Canada.

Ayles, T. and S. Becker-Griffin (1990). *An A–Z handbook for boards of directors of non-profit community-based child care programs.* Toronto: Umbrella Central Day Care Services/Child Care Initiatives Fund, Health and Welfare Canada.

Bertrand, J. (1990). *Childcare management guide: A comprehensive resource for boards of directors.* Toronto: OCBCC (Ontario Coalition for Better Child Care)/Ottawa: Canadian Advocacy Association.

Click, P. and D. Click (1990). *Administration of schools for young children.* Albany, NY: Delmar.

Harms, T., E. Jacobs, and D. White (1996). *School-age care environment rating scale.* New York: Teacher's College Press.

Harms, T., D. Cryer, and R.M. Clifford (1990). *The infant/toddler environment rating scale.* New York: Teacher's College Press.

Harms, T. and R.M. Clifford (1989). *Family home day care environment rating scale.* New York: Teacher's College Press.

Harms, T. and R. Clifford (1980). *The early childhood environment rating scale.* New York: Teacher's College Press.

Sciarra, D.J. and A.G. Dorsey (1996). *Developing and administering a child care center.* Albany, NY: Delmar Publishers.

Taylor, B.J. (1993). *Early childhood program management—people and procedures.* New York: Merrill.

APPENDIX: SAMPLE PROGRAM STATEMENT FROM THE *ONTARIO DAY NURSERIES MANUAL*

Philosophy

Day Nursery X attempts to provide a positive learning environment for your child that enhances his or her level of development. Through play experiences and the guidance of specially trained staff, your child will be exposed to situations that will stimulate:

1. curiosity, initiative, and independence;
2. self-esteem and decision-making capabilities;
3. interaction with and respect for others;
4. physical activity that develops gross motor skills;
5. communication skills; and
6. fine motor development.

Program Development

Programs are reevaluated regularly to reflect changes within the Day Nurseries Act and ideologies on early childhood education. Workshops are also offered for both staff and parents to review program content. At regular intervals throughout the year, a newsletter will be sent informing you of these workshops, as well as topics of interest, events, and nursery news. You are invited to contribute to these newsletters.

Ages of Children

Day Nursery X has facilities to accommodate the following children:

1. 10 infants, 16 weeks to 18 months
2. 15 toddlers, 18 months to 2 1/2 years
3. 24 preschoolers, 2 1/2 years to 5 years

Days and Hours of Operation

Both full- and part-time care are provided 52 weeks each year.

1. Full-time care is offered between 7:00 a.m. and 6:00 p.m., five days a week
2. Part-time care is offered:
   a) four days a week, or less
   b) 7:00 a.m.–11:30 a.m., five days a week
   c) 1:00 p.m.–6:00 p.m., five days a week

Admission and Discharge Policy

An interview will be arranged to familiarize you and your child with the philosophy and surroundings, and to answer questions and complete admission forms prior to enrollment. A non-refundable registration fee is also required, and can be paid at this time. For the first week you are encouraged to stay with your child at the beginning of the day in order to reassure him/her and minimize fears until you and your child become more comfortable.

Written notice of permanent withdrawal must be given two weeks in advance. If notice is not received, full program fees will be charged. A permanent space cannot be guaranteed if you wish to temporarily withdraw your child. Therefore, your child will be placed on a waiting list. Day Nursery X may terminate services if policies are not followed or fees are not paid.

Arrival and Pick-up

Young children depend on regular routines for their own sense of security. We recommend that you establish fixed hours to pick up and drop off your child. When your child arrives, notify a member of the staff as to your child's presence. Similarly, when picking up your child, enter the building and make sure the staff knows you are leaving. Unless otherwise arranged, children will not be released to any person other than those specified on the admissions form.

Parking

A drop-off area is provided for cars. However, if you anticipate staying at the day nursery for any length of time, kindly park at the facilities located within easy walking distance of the nursery.

Specialized Services

Day Nursery X is an approved integrated centre for handicapped children. In addition to participating in the daily routine, individual programs for developmentally or physically handicapped children are conducted by a qualified resource teacher.

A program has been arranged with the neighbourhood swimming pool for supervised lessons twice a week. Parents who are interested in enrolling their children in this activity should notify the supervisor.

Nutrition

A nutritious midday meal and morning and afternoon snacks will be provided. Children's special dietary needs and allergies will be posted in the cooking and service areas. Weekly menu plans will be posted for the current and following week to assist you in menu planning at home.

Health and Administration of Drugs

The Day Nurseries Act stipulates that prior to admission, each child must be immunized as recommended by the local medical officer of health. Day Nursery X also requires that a medical certificate confirming a complete medical assessment be submitted at this time. Regulations require daily outdoor play for each child. Therefore, it is our policy that children too ill to play outside remain at home. If a child becomes ill during the day, temporary care will be provided until you can be contacted and your child taken home. Day Nursery X will administer both prescription and non-prescription drugs to children, in accordance with provincial legislation. This requires that parents provide:

1. written authorization, including the dosage and times any drug is to be given; and
2. medication in the original container, clearly labelled with the child's name, name of the drug, the dosage, the date of purchase, and instructions for storage and administration of the drug.

Medication is not to be left in the cloakroom area. Kindly give it directly to a program staff member.

Clothing and Possessions

Your child should be dressed in clothing that is appropriate for physical activity, the weather, and the season. A second set of clothing should be kept at the nursery in case of accidents. Also, all clothing and toys should be labelled with your child's name.

Discipline

Children are disciplined in a positive manner at a level that is appropriate to their actions and their ages in order to promote self-discipline, ensure health and safety, respect the rights of others, and maintain equipment.

Spanking or other forms of corporal punishment are not permitted.

Methods of discipline are discussed at staff meetings, and consistent disciplinary measures are agreed upon. A workshop on discipline is planned, so that parents and staff may exchange ideas.

Parental Involvement

Daily contact with parents and staff will be supplemented by individual interviews, group meetings, and workshops. You are encouraged to participate in the daily program and visit your child in your free time.

Field Trips

Throughout the year, trips are made to special places of interest. A notice will be sent home in advance of the excursion informing you of the destination, time, and date. It will also include a permission slip to be signed and returned. You are always welcome to accompany us.

Holidays/Sick Leave

Day Nursery X observes the following statutory holidays: New Year's Day, Good Friday, Easter Monday, Victoria Day, Canada Day, Civic Holiday, Labour Day, Thanksgiving, Remembrance Day, Christmas Day, Boxing Day.

In addition, each child may be absent for two weeks' vacation/sick leave a year, where payment of fees is not required. There are no refunds for any additional days missed. Written notice of an intended vacation is required at least one month in advance.

Fees

Monthly fees are required on the first day of each month. Fees can be paid by cheque or money order. A late fee may be charged if payments are not made on time. Monthly receipts will be given for income tax purposes. Subsidized services may be available to eligible families. Further information may be obtained from the supervisor.

Fee Schedule

Full day	$
Half day	$
Infants	$
Toddlers	$
Preschoolers	$

Fees for children in part-time care may be negotiated.

SOURCE: Revised *Ontario day nurseries manual*. March 24, 1988, pp. DN-0202-02, 1–5. Toronto: Ministry of Community and Social Services. Used by permission.

MAKING CURRICULUM WORK

Curriculum is a key dimension of quality care, as discussed in Chapter 1. As the person who monitors the implementation of the program philosophy, the supervisor ensures that the development, implementation, and evaluation of curriculum is consistent with the philosophy of the early childhood setting. This chapter will discuss curriculum under the following headings:

- *What is curriculum?*
- *Three major positions on child development*
- *Developing curriculum—where to begin*
- *Developing curriculum—the supervisor's role*

WHAT IS CURRICULUM?

Curriculum can be defined in several ways. Different definitions illustrate different points of view on what an early childhood program should be. Those designing curriculum, whether boards of directors, supervisors, community members, staff, consultants, or some combination of these, should choose the definition that best reflects the philosophy of the setting and the needs of the children and families who use it.

Some define curriculum as "what happens" in an early childhood setting (Schwartz and Robison 1982). In this definition, the child chooses his or her activity, while the teacher provides an environment rich with possibilities and supports the choices the child makes. Such a program is child-centred. Rather than setting out the day's activities ahead of time, teachers plan a variety of activities to fit a range of developmental levels and interests.

In another approach, Seaver and Cartwright (1986) use the term "curriculum" to refer to "activities deliberately selected and systematically implemented by staff." This definition implies a more teacher-directed program, which sets out goals and objectives, and views the activities as a way to reach them. The goals may be short- or long-term, general or specific. While they provide an overall structure for the program, they are general enough to allow staff some flexibility in adapting plans to children's needs and interests.

A more formalized curriculum for children may consist of a detailed set of written plans, or a syllabus that identifies what is to be taught and the sequence in which it is to be presented. Such a plan will generally specify learning outcomes and how to evaluate them.

Finally, "emergent curriculum" is another conceptual model for responding to the needs of young children. Emergent curriculum is grounded in the power of play; it is not a curriculum formula. It views young children as active rather than passive learners. It is a planning process that responds to the individual needs and interests of young children within a specific environment. The teacher's "planning" emerges from the daily life and interests of young children. Within this model, children's ideas form the foundation for additional experiences shaped by the early childhood educator to build on the child's initial interest.

If staff lack consensus about what curriculum is, the program will lack consistency, thus diminishing its effectiveness in supporting the growth and development of young children. The definitions discussed above would result in programs that differed sharply from one another, in the extent to which the activities are preplanned, the role of teachers, and the specific expectations for children. The process of defining curriculum can serve as an excellent starting point for the development or revision of a program philosophy. The discus-

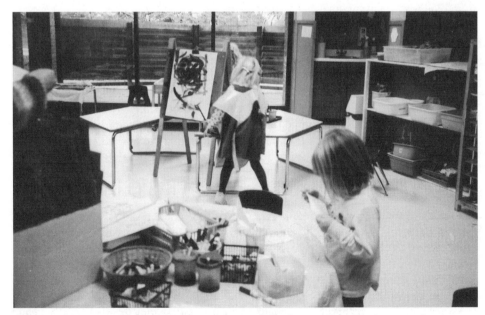

Quality programs provide choices and encourage independence and the development of autonomy.

sion can help staff clarify their beliefs about the role of early childhood programs in the lives of young children and their families, enabling them to work more effectively.

What Is Good Curriculum?

Curriculum development involves a number of decisions, each with different implications for how the program is constructed. Ask ten individuals to describe a good program for young children and you will probably get ten different answers, although there will be common elements. Consensus is often difficult to reach, but a shared understanding is essential to the provision of high quality child care.

Several professional organizations have developed position statements with guidelines for early childhood curriculum. The Association for Early Childhood Education, Ontario (AECEO), the Canadian Child Care Federation (CCCF), and the U.S. National Association for the Education of Young Children (NAEYC) have each produced statements that provide guidelines for good early childhood programs. The NAEYC has also produced a position statement on developmentally appropriate practice that provides comprehensive guidelines for quality programs for young children.

These documents share common elements, and the following list represents a synthesis of these shared ideas. A good early childhood curriculum:

- provides opportunities for the child's active participation
- provides experiences that contribute to all areas of a child's development: emotional, social, physical, and cognitive
- is developed based on the program's philosophy or program rationale
- reflects both individual and group developmental needs and interests
- provides a balance of quiet and active experiences
- challenges children to think, explore, solve problems, and discover
- provides choices and encourages independence and the development of autonomy
- reflects the values of parents and the community
- is based on observations and records of each child's interests, strengths, and needs

As discussed in Chapter 3, a philosophy should reflect a collective understanding of how children grow and change, forming the basis for commitment to common goals. The philosophy provides the basis for curriculum development, so there needs to be consensus regarding the philosophy for the centre before the curriculum is developed.

THREE MAJOR POSITIONS ON CHILD DEVELOPMENT

You will already be familiar with the three major theoretical positions on how children develop and learn. We will briefly review them here, since each theory has different implications for the teaching/learning process and thus forms the basis for a particular kind of curriculum design.

Staff in a setting that is developing its curriculum may have different understandings and beliefs about how children develop and learn. They can work to achieve consensus in one of two ways. The first is to "start from scratch" and brainstorm, sharing their beliefs about child development. Common elements can then be identified and compared with the three major theories in an attempt to find a match. Identifying the theory that best fits the staff's beliefs will provide a foundation for curriculum development and evaluation. The other approach is for staff to examine the major theoretical positions to find the one that best reflects their views of early childhood. Either way, staff must articulate their beliefs and reach agreement, or the result will be patchwork curriculum design and an inconsistent program.

The Maturationist View

Maturationists view the development of the young child as the result of biological and genetic factors. Development is determined by heredity, and change is the result of the natural unfolding and maturing of physiological structures. Children enter each new stage of development as they mature.

If this theory is used as a framework for curriculum design, the responsibility of the early childhood educator is to provide an environment rich in possibilities and allow the child to choose her or his own experiences. The child needs to be "ready" for experiences, and the teacher's role is to match children with activities that are developmentally appropriate. Maturationists believe it is unlikely that a teacher's planned activities will shape a child's development, although they may help it unfold as it should.

The Behaviourist View

While maturationists believe that change is determined by biological factors within the child, behaviourists ascribe change to environmental forces outside the child. They view the child as a "blank slate" (you sometimes hear *tabula rasa,* which is Latin for "blank slate") whose development can be molded. Learning is a continuous hierarchical process. As learning accumulates, it forms the basis for the acquisition of more complex ideas. Reinforcement strategies play a key role in development, as they can be applied systematically to shape desired behaviours.

Behaviourist programs for young children are teacher-focused. The teacher makes key decisions related to the teaching/learning process, deciding what is to be learned and how. He or she uses reinforcement systematically to shape learning, and thus children acquire skills through deliberate stimulation and reinforcement.

The Cognitive-Developmental View

Cognitivists see the child's development as the result of interaction between internal and environmental factors. Children are viewed as intrinsically active, constructing knowledge of the world through interactions with their peers and environment. According to cognitivists, children progress through a series of developmental stages, each qualitatively different from the other. These stages are sequential, and are characterized by different ways of thinking and reasoning. The child sees the world quite differently from one stage to another.

In this view, children are active participants in their learning who "construct" knowledge. Educational experiences should provide opportunities for children to explore and experiment, and the educator's understanding and knowledge of the world has little impact on the child. The teacher doesn't explain—instead, the child discovers. It is the teacher's responsibility to provide challenges and experiences that foster discovery. This requires both an environment rich in possibilities, and a teacher who is trained to assess cognitive development and interact appropriately.

Common Principles of Child Development

Despite their differences, the three theories agree on several basic developmental principles that affect curriculum design across the board:

- Development follows a predictable sequence.
- There are individual differences. While the sequence of development is predictable, timing is flexible.
- Behaviour becomes increasingly differentiated and complex.
- There is a genetic component to development.
- There are critical periods in development.

DEVELOPING CURRICULUM—WHERE TO BEGIN

There are a number of possible starting points for designing curriculum, from creating a design specifically tailored to the needs and interests of the children in your care, to selecting something prepackaged. Written plans are useful in providing direction to the program, a framework for organization, and a guide for interactions with children. Planning formats include long-range, weekly and individual activity plans.

Long-range plans should be flexible, to accommodate later fine-tuning and adaptation to children's learning needs and interests. They provide information about upcoming activities

Early childhood programs should be designed to respond to the developmental needs of young children.

for parents, and enable staff to collect the appropriate resources. While such plans are useful in providing a general direction to the program, they can also be adapted to respond to unexpected opportunities.

Weekly plans identify the major activities of each day and provide a framework for planning specific activities. Planning may be based on specific developmental goals and objectives, a thematic approach, or regularly scheduled activities such as story time, music, and outdoor play.

Individual activity plans can be particularly useful for beginning teachers, as they provide guidelines for interactions and the evaluation of planned experiences. They may include items like objectives for the activity, materials required, directions on how to proceed, and an evaluation to be completed afterwards. See the Appendix to this chapter for an example.

Regardless of format, it is important that planning responsibility be clearly articulated in job descriptions, and that time be allotted for it.

Licensing Requirements and Regulations

As discussed in Chapter 2, each province and territory sets licensing requirements for day care, specifying minimum standards, health and safety requirements, space minimums, and staff qualifications. These may be specified in the legislation or outlined in accompanying regulations. They must be considered in planning curriculum.

These regulations do not provide guidelines for optimal programming—rather, they state the minimum of what is acceptable. Some advocates of high quality care argue for the establishment of national standards, while others would rather see individual provinces develop improved standards.

Alberta

The program should meet the developmental needs of children and provide a variety of indoor and outdoor activities. In addition, the program should be flexible and provide for rest, toileting, nourishment, and rigorous and quiet activities for groups and individuals.

British Columbia

The program must include a comprehensive and coordinated set of activities for the development, care, and protection of children, based on individual developmental needs. Activities that provide for physical, intellectual, language, emotional, and social development are defined by a set of program standards, the "Program Standards for Early Childhood Settings."

Manitoba

Every person is required by the regulations to promote the "physical, social, emotional, and intellectual" development of children. The program should include daily individual and small-group activity, physical, cognitive, language, and social activity, and both child-initiated and adult-directed activities. Outdoor play must be provided on a daily basis. Sleeping and toileting should be provided according to the development and capability of each child.

New Brunswick

The setting must provide a positive, stimulating atmosphere and structure conducive to the total development of children. In addition, the program is required to provide a support service to family. A written daily program is required. Children unable to walk are to be separated during play period. Children under six are to be separated during play period. Children attending the centre for more than seven hours are to have up to two hours' outdoor activity.

Newfoundland and Labrador

A flexible program suited to the age and developmental needs of children is required. The program should provide experiences designed to facilitate intellectual, perceptual, and language development. Activities should encourage creative expression and allow for freedom of choice. Outdoor play and a rest period must be provided each day. Efforts should be made to provide children with male identification figures. Television is to be used only for viewing educational programs.

Northwest Territories

The daily program should facilitate children's intellectual, physical, emotional, and social development. Activities should be developmentally appropriate and reflect the cultural and ethnic background of the children. Children with special needs should be integrated into the daily program as much as possible. Community services may be used to enhance the quality of the program.

Nova Scotia

The daily program should facilitate and stimulate intellectual, physical, emotional, and social development appropriate to the developmental level of children. Activities designed to encourage language development should be included. Facilities may be licensed to provide a day care program for young children with special needs.

Ontario

A written statement outlining the philosophy, program, and method of operation is to be discussed with the parent prior to admission, and reviewed annually. The program should be varied and flexible, as well as appropriate to developmental levels. It should include group and individual activities, active and quiet play, and activities that provide for the development of fine motor, language, cognitive, emotional, and social skills. Children in each age group should be separated for indoor and outdoor play. The program should provide a rest period for children. Outdoor play should be provided for two hours a day, weather permitting.

Prince Edward Island

The program should foster a sense of self-worth, respect family values and involvement, and further the comprehensive development of the child. The program is required to plan for the integration of children with special needs. Outdoor activity should be provided according to the child's developmental needs, with a minimum of one hour in winter and two hours or more in summer.

Quebec

The applicant for a day care permit must undertake to provide children with day care and a program of activities to promote their physical, intellectual, emotional, social, and moral development.

Saskatchewan

The environment must be supportive of the normal development of the individual child. Periods of rest and sleep, according to the age and needs of children, are required. Young children with special needs should be integrated into the "regular" program.

Yukon Territory

Programs must provide a planned, but flexible, daily schedule for rest, toileting, and nourishment. Activities should be age-appropriate and designed to facilitate cognitive, perceptual, and language development. Opportunities for creative expression and decision making should be provided. Young children with special needs should be integrated into the program "as much as possible."

Meeting the Challenge of Diversity

High quality early childhood programs provide care and education for the whole child, and recognize a multiplicity of family types, religions, ethnic groups, cultures, gender, age, and abilities. It can be challenging to address the totality of such diversity in programs designed for young children. There are a number of curricular approaches to addressing diversity, which include the global education approach, social cooperation, cross-cultural education and anti-bias curriculum. Early childhood educators must be knowledgeable about these approaches, the issues related to inclusion, and the theories that support meeting children's diverse educational needs.

Biases and stereotypes are still pervasive in our society. Children need to be empowered to resist biases because they limit children's development and their view of the world. Early childhood educators need to ensure that children develop to their fullest potential in a manner that responds to their individual needs and is respectful of the diversity of others. Children need to be supported to grow to be compassionate, caring, and whole humans in a world of differences.

Supervisors should ensure that activities provided for young children are grounded in an inclusive perspective. While staff need to accept primary responsibility for their own growth and development, the supervisor should provide leadership in ensuring that staff have knowledge of multicultural education and inclusive approaches to working with young children. As a first step, staff need to be aware of their own cultural beliefs, biases, and feelings toward children with special needs, so they can work toward addressing their own professional development needs.

Cultural Diversity

Early childhood programs should include developmentally appropriate materials and activities that reflect cultural diversity. These activities should be integrated into the fabric of the program, not set apart.

For many early childhood educators this approach will be new, requiring the development of new skills, for example, dealing with racist incidents involving young children. The supervisor can be a catalyst for this growth by helping identify professional development needs and providing the necessary resources.

Parents may be challenged by this new approach and should be involved in the early stages. Questionnaires designed to identify the cultural heritage of families will help to sensitize parents to the need for a program that reflects cultural diversity. When the feedback is summarized and shared with parents, the results may be surprising. Some parents may want to contribute to the new focus by providing resources; for others, sharing information about their cultural heritage will contribute to a new sense of partnership with their child's setting. A resource that is useful in this context is Kenise Kilbride's *Multicultural early childhood education: A resource kit* (1990).

Developmental Diversity

As more children with special needs are integrated into early childhood settings, supervisors and staff need to adapt curriculum and centre environments to meet the resulting wide range of developmental needs. Both the nature of the special needs and the number of children with them need to be considered in designing curriculum.

Age Groupings

Finally, the ages of the children in the early childhood setting will of course determine the types of activities provided. A space designed for infants and toddlers is dramatically different

The curriculum should provide experiences that support all areas of the child's development: emotional, social, physical, and cognitive.

from one designed for preschoolers or school-age children. From the size of the space to the type of play materials, the differences reflect the developmental needs of each age grouping.

DEVELOPING CURRICULUM—THE SUPERVISOR'S ROLE

Working with Staff

A key part of the supervisor's role is to provide leadership to staff. For example, he or she may plan a meeting to consider the merits of implementing a new approach to program planning, and encourage staff to examine the possible benefits from a number of perspectives. The supervisor creates the structure within which staff members discuss their values and beliefs about how children develop.

The supervisor must be a curriculum specialist with the skills necessary to design and implement a high quality program. These skills enable her or him to provide staff with concrete goals.

Chapter 6 discusses the developmental stages of early childhood educators as defined by Lillian Katz (1972). The staff in a centre will be at different stages in their understanding of curriculum—some may be recent graduates and thus relatively inexperienced, while more experienced staff may be in a creative rut, relying too heavily on old lesson plans. The supervisor must work with staff as individuals, and support their skill development by providing support and access to resources where they are needed.

To support professional development needs, the supervisor should:

- support staff members in their own professional development plan
- motivate staff, recognizing and building on their strengths
- provide in-service workshops
- enable staff to attend conferences or workshops providing opportunities for specific skill development related to curriculum design
- provide time for staff to visit other settings noted for their programs, and to network with other resources in the community
- model ongoing self-evaluation and commitment to lifelong learning

Since these activities will require financial support, the supervisor must ensure that funds are budgeted for professional development to ensure staff growth and renewal. He or she may need to convince the board or owner of the importance of providing the necessary funds.

Developing curriculum takes time. If staff are to develop a high quality program, the supervisor must provide planning time for these activities. She must implement strategies to relieve staff from classroom responsibilities for two hours or more per week, to give them the opportunity to work as a team in developing curriculum. Substitute staff may need to be hired.

On a more basic level, the supervisor must ensure staff have input into the ordering of supplies and resources to support a high quality program. While early childhood educators are experts in locating free materials such as wood scraps and "beautiful junk," they still need an adequate supply of paint, scissors, construction paper, etc.

In consultation with staff, the supervisor must structure a process for evaluating the curriculum, both formally and informally. Through this process, the supervisor plays a role in ensuring that high curriculum standards are maintained and that the needs of children and parents are met. Criteria for a high quality program such as those outlined by the Association for Early Childhood Education, Ontario, the Canadian Child Care Federation, or the U.S. National Association for the Education of Young Children should be part of a framework for program evaluation.

Working with Children

The supervisor may sometimes substitute for a staff member or, on small programs, may work with the children on a regular basis. For instance, she or he might assume responsibility for a particular curriculum component, such as planning science activities. In this way, the supervisor can get to know the children and assess the program from the staff's perspective, while simultaneously acting as a role model for them.

In some larger centres, the supervisor may only have a little time to do this, while in others it may be possible to alternate half-days teaching and administering. This may also vary depending on the province or territory—for example, in British Columbia most supervisors do double duty as regular teaching staff.

The supervisor is also responsible for structuring a process to assess the children's progress, and ensuring that this is an ongoing part of the centre's activities. In consultation with staff, the supervisor should structure an assessment process, create timelines for assessment, and monitor implementation.

Working with Parents

Parents need information to understand the rationale for the activities their child is involved in, the more so since their own early childhood experiences were likely quite different. For example, a parent may not understand a particular centre's approach to toilet training. The supervisor must help them understand the centre's activities, providing informal opportunities for sharing information, formal interviews, orientations, and newsletters.

The early childhood staff can help parents interpret the value of their children's experiences by explaining how children learn through play. In addition, parents will need infor-

A balance of quiet and active experiences is important.

mation in order to understand what is meant by "developmentally appropriate practice." One of the primary ways for parents to develop an understanding of these concepts is through their real-life experiences in early childhood settings.

As discussed in Chapter 10, there is a wide range of strategies that can be implemented to facilitate parental involvement. As one approach, parents can be encouraged to observe the program in action. The staff can subsequently talk to the parent about their observations while helping them to interpret the experience within a developmental context. In the course of debriefing the experience, the supervisor can also help the parent to identify gaps in their understanding and provide information and/or resources that will supplement the parent's understanding of early childhood programs.

Program Evaluation

Evaluation should be a collaborative process leading to a shared commitment to continuous program improvement, and validating the successful aspects of the program. For evaluation to be successful, all staff need to support the process, and share responsibility for ongoing program improvement.

The supervisor plays a key role in leading the evaluation process, ensuring that a collaborative approach for gathering and analyzing information is in place. She needs to ensure that the process is trusted by staff, and that information is shared openly and honestly. In addition, resources such as time, assessment tools, and in-service training are required to support the process.

The standards for evaluating the program need to be identified. *The early childhood environment rating scale* (Harms and Clifford 1980) and the *Child care inventory* (Abbott-Shim and Sibley 1986) each provide a useful framework for evaluation. There are four versions of the environment rating scale developed by Harms and Clifford and their associates: for infants and toddlers (1990), preschoolers (1980), school-age (1996), and family home day care (1989). Alternatively, staff can develop their own standards, using the philosophy and goals of the centre for reference. Regardless of the mechanism, standards must be measurable.

Procedures for gathering information may include observations, interviews, surveys, standardized tests, and a review of program records. To ensure its validity, information must be gathered from different sources. These include children, parents, staff, administrators, students, and other resource persons.

As the evaluation team analyzes its information, it should refer back to the program philosophy in order to establish priorities for change. The team needs to establish an action plan, with possible solutions to the identified problems as objectives. This plan should be monitored to see if it is reaching its objectives, and should be modified as necessary.

Evaluation should be an ongoing process. It may be useful to "start small" and choose a specific focus for evaluation in order to ensure success.

Developing high quality curriculum for young children is not easy. It requires time, energy, and teamwork from a knowledgeable staff who are committed to the process, and a supervisor who can provide the necessary leadership.

IN CONCLUSION

The supervisor ensures that the development, implementation, and evaluation of curriculum is consistent with the philosophy of the early childhood setting. There are a number of definitions of "curriculum" that differ in the extent to which activities are preplanned, the role of the early childhood educator, and the specific expectations of children. While approaches to the curriculum may vary, quality programs share common elements which include: a balance of quiet and active activities, activities that contribute to all areas of a child's development, and opportunities for the child's active participation. Theories of child development also have different implications for the teaching/learning process. In addition, each province and territory sets licensing requirements for child care that must be addressed in planning curriculum. These requirements are minimum standards only.

Finally, this chapter identifies that activities for young children need to be grounded in an inclusive perspective, given the diverse background of young children and their families. Supervisors need to provide leadership in ensuring that staff have knowledge of multicultural issues and inclusive approaches to working with young children. Through working with staff and parents, the supervisor ensures that high curriculum standards are maintained and that program evaluation is a part of the regular cycle of activities in early childhood settings.

ACTIVITIES

1. Select two program evaluation tools. Implement an assessment of an early childhood environment using each tool, and compare the results.

   a)   Which tool provides the most useful results? Explain.

   b)   Which tool is easiest to use?

   c)   Are the results similar?

2. In an interview, a parent is concerned that his child plays all day and asks, "When are you going to start teaching?" How would you respond?

3. You are hired as a supervisor in an established early childhood program. There has been little staff turnover; the newest staff member has been working in the centre for five years. You soon realize that there are some problems with the program—the staff seem to be in a rut, and appear to put little energy into curriculum development. What would you do?

REVIEW QUESTIONS

1. How is curriculum defined?

2. What is emergent curriculum? How does this approach differ from other approaches to designing curriculum?

3. Identify several of the key characteristics of high quality early childhood curriculum.

4. What are the three major theoretical positions on how children develop and learn?

5. Identify three formats used to plan curriculum.

6. What role do licensing requirements play in designing programs for young children?

7. Why is it important for programs to be grounded in an inclusive approach?

8. How can the supervisor support the professional development needs of staff?

9. How can the supervisor and staff support parents' understanding of early childhood curriculum?

10. Describe the steps involved in program evaluation.

FURTHER READING

Association for Early Childhood Education, Ontario (1988). *High quality child care statement.* Toronto: AECEO.

Bredekamp, S. (ed.) (1987). *Developmentally appropriate practice in early childhood programs servicing from birth through age 8.* Washington, D.C.: National Association for the Education of Young Children.

Brown, J. (ed.) (1982). *Curriculum planning for young children.* Washington, DC: National Association for the Education of Young Children.

Canadian Child Day Care Federation (1991). *National statement on quality child care.* Ottawa: CCDCF.

Jorde Bloom, P. , M. Sheerer, and J. Britz (1991). *Blueprint for action: Achieving centre-based change through staff development.* Mt. Rainier, MD.: Gryphon House.

Schwartz, S. and H. Robison (1982). *Designing curriculum for early childhood.* Boston, MA: Allyn and Bacon.

Seaver, J. and C. Cartwright (1986). *Child care administration.* Belmont, CA: Wadsworth.

Spodek, B. (1970, October). "What are the sources of early childhood curriculum?" *Young Children.*

APPENDIX: ACTIVITY PLANNING SHEET

Activity:

Date of Activity:

Number of Children:

Ages of Children:

GOALS FOR CHILDREN	OBJECTIVES FOR CHILDREN
Write broad general aims for the children. Use words such as *develop, enhance, increase,* and *expand.*	The objectives should be related to the goals. Each objective should refer to specific, short-term tasks and skills in which the children will be engaging.

PROCEDURE
List the procedure in a step-by-step format. Be specific in describing the introduction, implementation, and conclusion of the activity. Also include a plan for transitional activities. Identify open-ended questions to be asked.

EVALUATION
1. Describe the children's response to the activity. 2. If you were to implement this activity again, describe the changes you would make to improve the experience.

PHYSICAL ENVIRONMENTS

This chapter provides a systematic approach to the organization of physical space both indoors and outdoors, while considering the needs of individual and groups of children and their families. Creative and effective design arrangements for new centres and renovated settings must provide safe, efficient and desirable environments for children and staff. This chapter examines:

- *Developmental considerations when designing space*
- *A systematic approach to the use of existing space*
- *Designing new environments*
- *Planning outdoor space*
- *Ensuring safe and healthy settings*

Early childhood programs depend on carefully planned physical environments to be successful. The arrangement of space is one of the most critical factors in assuring quality programs for children from infancy to school age.

The physical environment must be developmentally appropriate for children, provide security, ensure safety, be aesthetically pleasing, and be supportive and convenient for the staff.

Throughout the history of child care, early childhood educators, parents, volunteers, and student teachers have worked in various physical settings to provide inviting and stimulating environments for young children to explore and manipulate. For many years, church basements, apartment complexes, old houses, and community centres were renovated to accommodate child care programs. While staff need to be creative in the use of all environments for children, more recently centres have been opened that were designed as child care centres.

The role of the supervisor is to work closely with the staff and parent boards to monitor and evaluate the creative use and care of the physical environment. Centres built for the specific purpose of operating child care centres certainly have an advantage over renovated settings, however, the challenge for staff and the supervisor is to provide safe, effective, and appealing space to meet the changing developmental needs of individual and groups of children.

DEVELOPMENTAL CONSIDERATIONS WHEN DESIGNING SPACE

Foremost when considering how to arrange the environment to ensure a quality program is to know and understand the developmental needs of the children. Many centres now have programs for children ranging in age from four months to twelve years. This presents a considerable design challenge. Future as well as the present use of the centre should be contemplated in case the ages of children needing care in the centre should change.

As demographics change, centres are faced with shifting enrollment demands. Centres must have the ability to change space flexibly, quickly, and easily in order to respond to parental, political, or social factors. For example, the range of programs that school boards may offer for young children may depend on financial and space restrictions that evolve at the provincial and regional/municipal levels of government. Centres will need to plan for space that is adaptable, flexible, innovative, and responsive to the changing climate in early childhood.

Developmental needs are a key factor in design of space.

Focus on Safety

Later in this chapter we address the need to provide a healthy and safe environment for children of different age groups. Nonetheless, it is necessary to emphasize the importance of planning for safe environments prior to discussing the specific safety issues involved.

Health and Welfare Canada continues to stress the importance of safe environments for children, both at home and in alternative care settings. Too often we take safety for granted and are surprised when situations arise that might have been easily prevented.

These general rules will help you to be ever alert to potential hazards for young children. Your role is to generalize these guidelines to every aspect of the environment, and to ensure that the safety of every curious and adventurous child is guaranteed. In addition, a way of monitoring all aspects of providing a safe environment must be in place on a routine basis.

Guidelines for Safety

- Are all toys, equipment, and materials safe, in good repair, non-toxic, and suitable in size and shape?
- Is large equipment such as toy and book containers, adults' storage containers, outdoor play equipment, and so on solidly placed so it cannot fall on young children?
- Are all physical barriers for children secure and in good repair, with gaps in crib slats and wooden fences no more than 6 cm apart to avoid a head or neck injury?
- Eliminate and monitor for loose-fitting clothing, drawstrings, loose threads, curtain pulls, scarves, mitten strings, skipping ropes, or any possible variation of these that might cause injury while children are at play indoors or out.
- Are all centre chemicals and washing and cleaning materials under lock and key at all times?
- Are water-play activities and water areas under close supervision, and removed or securely covered when not in use?
- Are all electrical outlets covered, and cords to electrical appliances out of reach of the children, in every area of the centre?
- Eliminate and monitor for plastic wrappings, balloons, and other materials that children could suffocate on.

The Health and Safety Checklist at the end of this chapter provides the tools you will need to set up a regular monitoring system. Prevention through planning is the best method of ensuring safety.

Safety standards for outdoor play space provide excellent safeguards for young children. The Canadian Standards Association standards ensure that all aspects of outdoor play equipment meet the code for safety, and CSA standards must be used when designing or renovating early childhood outdoor playgrounds and equipment.

Designing Space for Infants

We know from extensive research and experience that infants need an environment that makes them feel secure, and stimulates them through varying levels of challenge. Infants in group care usually range in age from four to eighteen months. This developmental range is very wide, requiring careful planning for the youngest infant to the most active sixteen- to eighteen-month-old.

One of the many benefits for infants grouped together in this age span is the opportunity for the younger ones to experience varied social interactions. Younger children imitate and respond to their older peers, who enjoy helping and comforting the younger ones.

Young infants need secure and comfortable places to view and interact with their environment. Very young infants need to be protected from beginning walkers, and it is equally important for the older infants to have space to practise their developing skills. Infants also have different individual needs and temperaments. Some require orderly, quiet environments, while others seem to do best in environments that are busy and highly stimulating. A range of options needs to be available.

As demand steadily grows more and more centres are incorporating care for infants. Studies by Wach and Gruen (1982) underscored the importance of understanding environmental factors such as noise, overcrowding, and spatial arrangements in supporting positive and negative responses in children. As space becomes more and more expensive to build and renovate, we must increase our ability to use what we have effectively and flexibly. Space for infants must offer:

- an environment where supervision is optimal and easy
- quiet areas and spaces to be alone either with an adult or readily seen
- areas that encourage and support small group social interactions
- room to allow for a wide range of movement
- areas to stimulate the senses
- opportunities to offer change, challenge, novelty, and enjoyment

A centre should reserve one particular area for infants. Space for infants can be defined by large, stable dividers or by full walls or half-walls of tempered glass. Keep in mind that there are many times when safety requires keeping all the infants together. Large foam-covered areas with low foam walls provide a space where older infants can interact with younger ones. This division will ensure the physical separation necessary to keep them safe, while allowing crawlers to get about and allowing stumbling new walkers to try out independence. Flexibility in design is needed to meet all the needs of this age group.

There are many specific requirements to keep in mind for a physical space for infants:

- an array of sensory areas that are aesthetically pleasing
- space where staff can carry non-mobile infants about to explore their environment
- ample floor space for mobile infants to experiment with their bodies through toys and material
- play areas that allow for hiding, imitating, grasping, banging, dumping, and filling up
- spaces that encourage young children to move in and out of social interactions with their peers
- serving areas that are easily sanitized, with convenient appliances
- feeding areas with tiled floors to allow finger foods and quick clean-up
- places where infants can pull themselves up safely and be sufficiently cushioned when they tumble or fall

- a division between the non-mobile and mobile areas, that promotes exploration while also ensuring safety

- permanent sleep rooms with individualized beds that promote security and permit individualized schedules

- adult-height change areas with large sinks where staff can wash children comfortably

- individual storage areas for each child's clothing and personal belongings

- accessible and handy storage for bulky diapers, extra toys, and materials

- counter space for parents to change outerwear, fill out daily forms, and share information about the child with the teachers

- easy access to the infant playground with storage for triple strollers and other outdoor equipment

The physical care of infants is demanding. An effective arrangement of space allows staff to focus more of their caregiving time on pleasant teacher–child interactions. If space is poorly laid out, staff become frustrated and time spent with the children is reduced and often less productive.

Parents are often anxious about leaving a very young child in group care. Their confidence in the centre will be increased if the physical environment is thoughtfully laid out, safe, aesthetically pleasing, and conveys an atmosphere of respect for individual and family diversity.

Designing Space for Toddlers

What a fascinating group of active young learners—move equipment aside and give them space! They want to use their bodies to do just about everything. They push things, fill and empty wagons and buggies, pails and purses, as they practise and refine their skills. Toddlers are doers who need the security of some defined space and the flexibility of large areas. This sensory-motor stage leads them into testing every skill over and over again. They test their bodies by climbing stairs, hills, and slides. They prefer large toys, moving them around with maybe a stuffed animal parked under one arm. In their mind there is nothing they can't do!

How do we design space to incorporate what we know about toddlers? Much of what we said about infants also applies to toddlers—for example, they need change areas, easily cleaned surfaces, and convenient storage areas. Unlike infants, toddlers are mostly very mobile—moving, adjusting, rearranging, piling, organizing, knocking down, and rebuilding. A centre needs space where they can accomplish such energetic tasks.

Washrooms in or adjacent to the playrooms foster self-help skills and peer toilet training. Low sinks, where they can wash their own hands and get a drink, further foster these skills. Not only are these facilities necessary for the young child but they are also critical for the staff to support and encourage their beginning efforts.

Toddlers need space without sharp corners and without cluttered areas to experiment with their bodies. They like to sprawl and spread out their toys, with little interest in putting them away. Low cupboard areas encourage little ones to put away their toys and make more space to clutter all over again. Toddlers like to pick up large objects and carry them around, unconcerned that the objects may be as large as they are themselves.

It may be possible to build ramps, slides, and different levels into the playroom for the sensory-motor toddlers. Stairs that take toddlers to safe platforms where they can look down at the adults give them a feeling of power. A space under the platform allows others to read books quietly and be by themselves, or with one or two others. Open areas for walking about, pushing buggies, and pulling wagons are as important to consider indoors as outdoors. Such different levels can become a permanent part of the room, to be used in a variety of ways. At the same time, leave enough open space to allow you to adapt the environment quickly to meet changing developmental needs.

Safety is a fundamental consideration for all ages in child care centres, but toddlers are most vulnerable. Infants are dependent on adults to get around, and preschoolers have learned some basic safety rules, but for toddlers the understanding of what is safe is often secondary to curiosity and the drive for independence. Space for toddlers must be secure, padded whenever possible, and free from obstacles that impede their play and interaction with their world.

Designing Space for Preschoolers

The developmental needs of preschoolers also cover a very broad age range. In most provinces this group includes children from two-and-a-half to five, or until they are eligible to attend either junior or senior kindergarten. Initial decisions about arranging physical space to facilitate children's optimum growth will depend on the philosophy of the centre. Will preschoolers be family-grouped or age-grouped? part-day or full-day? and so on. Once these decisions are reached, environments can be planned more effectively.

Problem Solving and the Development of Self-Concept

Preschoolers need ample opportunity to become independent problem solvers involved in their environment. A positive self-concept is reinforced when children are given opportunities to

Positive self-concept is reinforced through choice making.

make choices, time to carry them out, and a planned environment to feel safe and comfortable in. Staff must also consider the changing and developing needs of each individual in the group, as well as the needs of the overall group—therefore activities and experiences with varying degrees of difficulty must be provided.

Opportunities for problem solving or divergent thinking are important during the preschool years, so the environment should provide a wide range of choices. A developmental curriculum for preschoolers usually results in a variety of learning centres, each with its own characteristics and properties. Placing learning centres in close proximity to one another allows children varied opportunities to test and transfer their learning.

Educators set the stage for learning by providing activities with a range of ease and difficulty in each of the learning areas. For example, the science area can have many simple materials for the beginning manipulator to explore, as well as more complex materials to challenge others. Such blending of resources throughout the playroom encourages social interaction, peer assistance, and more in-depth and varied questions from the children.

The layout of the room should reflect program goals and expectations, giving behavioural cues to the children. When space is totally open and provides no clear guidelines for the children to follow, play spills over from one area to another. This may encourage children to develop some level of skill in conflict resolution, but it tends to inhibit the concentration of play involvement and to increase the number of negative interactions.

Layout of Play Area

Children need clear definitions between play areas. This defined space enables children to concentrate both on the task at hand and on the social interactions with their peers. This results in more productive play. Social skills develop slowly in young children, and they need to be protected and supported by being involved in smaller groups to optimize successful interactions. Larger group times may also be part of the schedule but are often more teacher-directed than the free play child-directed activity times. This is an important consideration for children in all care settings—as adults we also do best when our interactions are limited to reasonable numbers of other people at one time.

The arrangement of space dictates the level of teacher involvement needed to help children remember the expectations for inside play. Clear pathways, or traffic patterns that lead from one area to another, must be visible from the child's eye level so they can move freely and independently. This physical layout and space definition helps children understand that some want a quiet space to reflect, while others are always ready for new playmates. All developmental areas should be clearly accessible and defined so children have opportunities to choose many different experiences. For example, if something like the block area is hidden from easy view, some children may miss its fabulous play potential. At the same time, this activity must provide sufficient space and clear definition from other activities.

Open, undefined space tends to lead to chaos, running, and a high level of noise and confusion. There are certainly times when children need this open space, but it is best considered outside or with a special activity or event.

Dramatic play is critical during this developmental stage, and requires large amounts of space. Dramatic play can take many forms, from creative movement to representations of daily living that children try out over and over to help them make sense of their world. Settings that can be duplicated in play with the help of a few teacher-supplied props include parent workplaces, outdoor camps, shopping malls, pet stores, libraries, and many others.

Defining play space effectively is a difficult task, especially for the beginning teacher. Each group of children brings new and different needs, which take time to understand and incorporate into the environment. What worked with one group may not work with another. As children become more competent in their play, educators may want to involve them in the set-up of the room. A very confident teacher is often more willing to provide this experience for the children. Planning with the children, defining goals and expectations, and physically involving the children in the room arrangements, can be a valuable and rewarding experience for both children and staff.

Independence and Self-Help Skills

The development of independence and self-help skills continues to be important during the preschool years. Washrooms should be conveniently located so that children can go on their own with minimal guidance. That way, visual supervision by staff tends to replace physical assistance, fostering independence in the child while giving staff more time for creative work. Similarly, children's personal items and clothing should be located close to the playrooms in order to enhance their self-help skills. Windows in the playroom walls looking out to the coat area allow for supervision while increasing the children's sense of independence.

Designing Space for School-age Children

Within the last ten years, the ages of children housed in child care centres has changed to include infants and toddlers at one end of the age scale to school-age children at the other. This great developmental range means that supervisors face many challenges in assigning staff and using space, equipment, and financial resources wisely.

Canadian children enter formal schooling between the ages of 3.8 and 6 years, depending on the province or territory, and children between 3.8 and 12 are considered school-age

Dramatic play helps children make sense of their world.

children under some board of education definitions. However, school-age children are generally defined as 5- to 12-year-olds. Depending on individual needs, child care centres may enrol these children before school, at lunchtime, after school, or after or before kindergarten.

Staff-to-child ratios are generally lower than those required for younger children, but space requirements are higher. School-age children need many and varied opportunities for gross motor activities, sturdy equipment that is developmentally appropriate, space for large-scale projects, opportunities to change equipment, and greater emphasis on recreational activities.

Developmentally, older children require increased opportunities to plan their own activities, structure their own schedules, and participate in group decision making and project development. They are developing their own hobbies, interests, and life skill activities, and require both space and time to work in groups, as well as quiet, reflective areas to do homework or just be private.

Since school-age children spend all or part of their day in school, they need different kinds of experiences in the child care centre. Ideally, recreational programming should be a primary consideration. While it may be possible to install basketball hoops or provide cooperative games, most centres rapidly come up against their own limitations. Older school-age children love hockey, baseball, and other team sports, but incorporating these into the program may be difficult. Any alternative sports require dedicated space as well. Many school-age programs are housed in schools, and may be allowed to use the gym or playground. In other cases, recreational space can sometimes be found in a nearby community centre or church.

Quiet areas for relaxation, reading, and doing homework should be set away from the noise of more rambunctious play. Often, the space used by school-age children is used by other ages during the day, so locked portable cupboards are required to keep school-age materials secure.

A SYSTEMATIC APPROACH TO THE USE OF EXISTING SPACE

It is often difficult to analyze the present use of existing space, especially if your program has been running for some time and the staff is used to doing things in a certain way. A systematic approach to analyzing your centre's physical environment will speed up the process, give you a rationale for your plans when you present them to staff, and ensure that you take all aspects of the program into account. If you change one room or area at a time without having an overall plan, you will not get the most efficient and effective use of the space in the long run.

Systematic Analysis Step by Step

1. Review your statement of philosophy and your centre's overall goals

- What are you trying to accomplish with the children, parents, staff, and the local and professional community you belong to?
- What have the staff agreed about how children best learn and grow?
- What do the staff agree upon as developmentally appropriate practice for young children?
- Do your staff have a good understanding of the developmental needs of each of the age groups in your centre?

- How do the staff want to involve parents?
- What are the staff's long- and short-term goals?

Once you have reexamined your philosophy and overall goals for the centre, you can begin to assess how the physical environment can best meet these needs.

2. Look at your present or anticipated enrollment

What are the ages and number of children in each group? We have seen how the setup of the physical environment can support developmentally appropriate practices. A review of the developmental needs of the children served by a centre is essential in your analysis of the best use of an existing environment.

3. Evaluate the existing physical space

Go through your centre with measuring tape and graph paper in hand, and actually measure each area that is presently part of your centre. Don't be satisfied with rough estimates for each area. If you are lucky there may be a set of plans you can work from, but this is often not the case. Completing this exercise has several advantages:

- It helps you to develop a clear idea of spatial relationships. You may think you know what an 8 x 12 metre room looks like, but you may be surprised when you actually measure out the space.
- It helps you to develop a clear visual image of your overall centre, and the size of each area in relation to other areas.
- You begin to get the "big picture" and become more methodical in your thinking about how best to use your space.

4. Draw a plan of your centre

This doesn't have to be a masterpiece in design and layout. Decide on a scale, make it an easy one, and lay out your centre according to the measurements you have taken in each area. Scale your space large enough so that you can sketch in shelving units and equipment, using a constant scale so that eventually you can move your equipment around in your rooms as you try out different arrangements.

5. Establish priorities

Develop several lists to be considered in your planning. The first list would include the things that are impossible or extremely difficult to change in your present setting—kitchen and bathrooms, windows, and structural considerations such as bearing walls.

The next list would contain the areas where you need additional information before you can make a decision. Costs might well be a determining factor; or if you share space with another organization, you need to examine how your changes would affect them.

Develop a list of the areas you can change. You may find that a consideration on one list should be moved to another. For example, you may have wanted to move a wall and make a large room out of two small rooms, and then had to give it up when you found out the wall was a bearing one and could not be moved. Upon further examination, you discover you can open the two rooms up with a large archway, which solves your supervision problem and still leaves the bearing wall with sufficient strength. Don't eliminate possibilities before looking at a range of ways for solving the same problem.

6. Move to the "what if" stage

"What if we moved the staff room into the storage room, found some storage in another area of the centre, and used the staff room as the extra space we need off the playroom? This location for the staff room would provide more convenient access to the playroom, and the storage area tends to be a 'throw it in and close the door' kind of room."

"What if we moved the coat cubbies to the other end of the hall, and left this end open in order to divide the children into smaller groups for circle time?"

"What if, what if ..." You have now opened your mind up to new possibilities you may not have been aware of before. Staff can have input into how the centre might be laid out as they experiment with the various arrangements on the scaled drawings. The more you stimulate ideas, the greater the possibilities. The old response, "Yes, but we tried it that way once and it didn't work," may be heard for the last time. Often that response was born from the fact that staff didn't relish the idea of lugging equipment from one end of the room to the other and back again while a final decision on its resting place was decided. There's no way to avoid physically moving the equipment, but after the staff have become involved and excited about the new physical arrangement, only one move will be required to put it into place.

By scaling your equipment to size in your drawing, you can try out many possible arrangements of space. Make scale cardboard templates of the equipment, furniture, storage areas, shelves, and so on. Now you can begin to get an idea of the possible ways to use your centre without actually lifting the equipment around. Careful attention here saves much time and difficult work, and avoids the trap of "Just leave it there—I'm not moving another thing."

7. Consider health and safety issues

Careful review of all health and safety conditions is critical. This should take place both before you lay out the room arrangement and after you complete it.

As you consider changes in your existing set-up, examine your local licensing regulations to make sure you are not overlooking some fire regulation. You may need to arrange a visit from the fire department to ensure that you are not interfering with the fire exits. Sometimes rules change so that you gain more flexibility in the use of some areas.

Sometimes the opposite is the case, and you find you are inadvertently breaking some new regulation.

You need to consider such things as play areas near drafty doors and windows, and washrooms that cannot easily be supervised. The floor surface in each area is a health and safety issue. Carpets that can't be cleaned easily may collect dirt and dust, causing health problems, particularly in children with allergies. Surfaces that become slippery when wet can be a hazard. Protecting a carpeted area from messy activities such as painting by putting down plastic may create a safety hazard. A safe traffic pattern must be established in each area to prevent accidents and protect children who are using the floors for play.

While it is the responsibility of every staff member to be alert to health and safety issues, one person should be assigned the task of completing a checklist of such issues on a regular schedule. Otherwise some areas of the centre may get overlooked. A checklist is the best method to use to feel confident that each area of the centre has been examined for health hazards or safety concerns.

Any areas identified as potential hazards should be noted and an action plan put in place. The list should also indicate when the correction would take place and the date of the next inspection. Educators have too many details to keep in mind to trust the health and safety aspects of the centre to memory. A systematic way of monitoring potentially dangerous health and safety issues leaves staff more able to supervise with ease and freedom. A sample checklist is given in the Appendix to this chapter.

8. Determine accessibility and proximity

When existing space limits access from one area to another, staff have to come up with creative solutions. For example, what if there are no sinks near the creative area? Portable sinks could be used, as long as they are kept sanitary. It reduces tension to have water nearby, rather than watch a three-year-old trail a thick path of goop and finger paint across clean floors and rugs.

The developmental needs of the children will dictate the kinds of activities you make available. A few suggestions might help you decide the proximity and accessibility of one area to another.

The planning and provision of learning areas seems to be the most commonly used approach in implementing a developmental curriculum. There must be space for:

- science and nature activities
- cognitive experience, fine motor development, and quiet games
- creative endeavours
- the development of gross motor skills
- listening centres for music, and for enjoying stories and other language experiences
- privacy and quiet reflection
- sensory experiences and exploration
- imaginative and dramatic play
- experimentation
- blocks with many properties

9. Don't forget empty space

While consideration must be given to the curriculum areas listed above, it is also important to evaluate the amount of empty space available to the children in each room. Each province has guidelines setting the minimum space to be provided for each child. In your space planning you need to include open or empty space for children to use.

Kritchevsky et al., in *Planning environments for young children* (1983), discuss the need to include areas of empty space in proportion to the group size. It would appear that the larger the number of children, the higher the proportion of empty space needed by each child. It is recommended that one half of the space available in the room should be uncovered surface.

Kritchevsky et al. also refers to dead space, usually occurring in the middle of the playroom without visual or tangible boundaries. Often such space invites running and less constructive play requiring more teacher intervention.

10. Consider the proximity of one activity to another

Once you have laid out your room on paper, cluster the activities by considering the kind and amount of space they need. Then think about their proximity to other activities. For example, large blocks and dramatic play take far more space than cognitive games. Activities of the first kind need space for construction, rearrangement, and finally tearing down, while the latter require less movement. Activities that are alike should be clustered together, providing opportunity for children to transfer their learning and practise their skills on a number of different materials and media.

Traffic flow or pathways must be organized so children see and use them effectively. Learning centres must be protected by some kind of partition so that activity does not get disrupted when other children pass by. At the same time, it is worth remembering that children painting can get inspired by the activities they see in another section of the room.

Other Considerations in Redesigning Space

The surface of the floor in each area is also a consideration. A corner area may seem appropriate for a quiet book place, but it may be the only area where the creative activities can take place, because of limited options in floor surfaces.

Areas with natural light may also influence decisions about where certain activities need to be placed. After you have listed the learning centres and curriculum areas you wish to include, you may find that natural lighting is required for some of them. Ventilation in the room becomes even more important if you house pets. The nature and science area may require sunlight for some part of the day. Fish tanks should not get direct sun, while some experiments require it.

Aesthetics must also be addressed. Pictures, mobiles, plants, and artwork can help create a warm, soothing environment. Attractive surroundings including a variety of textures allow children opportunities for sensory experiences. When the centre is arranged to provide children with opportunities to touch and explore, they can be encouraged and expected to help care for their own environments.

A chart could be developed to organize the many variables related to the use of space. This chart would be helpful in other ways as well. It should include:

- the various activities included in the curriculum
- aesthetic considerations
- equipment and materials needed, and their relative size
- pathways and desired traffic patterns
- the desired amount of open space
- noise considerations
- areas with natural and artificial lighting
- doors and windows in the room
- location of washroom and coat cubbies

Each centre has its own strengths and drawbacks. Systematic analysis will help you make the best use of any environment.

Environmental Health Considerations

Recent research has begun to look at health hazards that may exist in indoor environments. These are particularly an issue if you have a sealed space (that is, without windows that open) with a central air supply. Rapidly growing young children may be particularly sensitive to indoor environmental hazards.

Noxious vapours can be given off by new carpets, paint, and cleaning agents. Common areas need to be disinfected, but do not use cleaning agents that are harsh or leave a lingering odour. Carpets and curtains can hold dust and moulds that are circulated through air conditioning and heating systems, feeding sickness and allergies. Humidifiers may be necessary in winter, but avoid bacteria build-up by making sure the humidifier is cleaned out regularly.

An area that is still controversial concerns children's sensitivity to the electromagnetic fields (EMFs) given off by electric cables and appliances. Recently a kindergarten was closed in Toronto because of unacceptable EMFs originating in power cables running under the floor. Again, rapidly developing young children are seen as being most sensitive, and jurisdictions as far apart as Sweden and New York City have recently passed rigorous standards limiting the strength of EMFs to which children and pregnant women can be exposed. That old computer you leave running in the corner for the children to play on may be emitting fields far above the New York school board limit.

Exercise common sense: keep children well back from electrical appliances and away from transmission lines. If you are concerned, your local hydro authority may come in to measure fields in your centre. These measurements should reflect the actual situation at your centre, so make sure they are not done at times when electrical use is low.

DESIGNING NEW ENVIRONMENTS

While early childhood educators often become expert at the adaptation of existing space, the best way to make sure a child care centre meets all the requirements is to design a new one. Helping design a new centre can make people anxious, but it is certainly exciting to put a vision of what young children need into the reality of new physical space.

Sometimes altering or adding to an existing space appears to be a quick and simple solution to a long-standing problem. "If only we could add to the storage area it would solve all our problems." The solution may be just that simple. But the systematic approach is just as necessary when considering an expensive addition. No change, or expansion, is without cost. Look at what you want to achieve in the overall scheme of things before you make a final decision on building or altering space. You may find that there is need for extra space, but you may also discover versatile uses for it that were not part of your original thinking.

Although architects and other professionals are becoming more and more knowledgeable about the needs of young children's environments, you are the expert on what children, staff, and parents need. Just as a doctor must describe to an architect what kinds of activities go on in her or his office, an early childhood educator needs to describe, in full detail, what goes on in a quality child care program, and what the environment requires in order to be successful. A great deal of preliminary work is required from the staff to clearly lay out and fully explain the activities, routines, daily schedules, and space requirements. The architect needs a clear picture to design a space to meet well-defined needs. Below are some guidelines on how to communicate your needs to the architect.

Translate the Centre's Philosophy and Goals into the Physical Requirements

Once you are clear about what you want to accomplish in your centre, you will have to translate these needs into terms an architect can understand. For example, if increased independence in self-help and personal hygiene is one of your long-term objectives for the children, the physical environment could encourage this goal by providing child-size personal cubbies and washrooms easily accessible from the playroom.

If your goals stress parental involvement in the centre, this must be reflected in a design providing places for parents to engage with the centre. The final design must reflect your written philosophy about how you feel children best learn and grow, and the role parents should have in that process.

Describe the Needs of Staff and Parents

Comfortable staff and work areas must be included when centres are being designed or redesigned. Staff need work areas that are separate from the lounge section. A staff lounge area allows time to relax and send the staff back to the children more refreshed and enthusiastic. Space to prepare curriculum materials and complete reports enable staff to complete these tasks that are important to develop a quality program for the children. This work area should have proper storage to house large rolls of paper, containers of paint, wonderful junk, and all the other supplies will enable staff to prepare their materials efficiently. Consideration of individual storage areas could be included so that staff are encouraged to develop their own personal resources and store them in individually safe spaces. A small kitchenette will reduce the volume of traffic in the kitchen, particularly during the hectic noon-

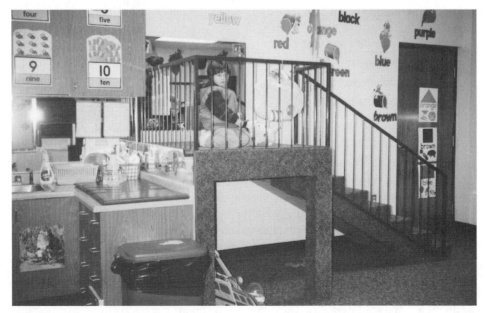

Design space for increased independence.

hour schedule. Adult washrooms should be included adjacent to the lounge area, along with closets for bulky winter outerwear.

This kind of staff space will keep the centre organized and free of clutter. Centres can't provide office space for each individual staff member, but a common room to be scheduled for parent interviews or to discuss the progress of student teachers will meet this need. Depending on the size of your centre you may have a reception area, a supervisor's office, or both. Whatever the case, they should be located near the entrance, accessible to parents as they enter the centre. A space to keep an ill child who is waiting to be picked up is also required by some licensing bodies, and a location near the supervisor's office is advisable.

Parents' areas are also important. As outlined in Chapter 10, we are gaining more and more information and are convinced about the benefits of parent involvement. The more parents feel comfortable with the staff and the children's environment, the easier it seems to be for children to settle in and learn from their new experiences. If there is space designed to increase parental involvement, then parents will spend more time in the centre and become familiar with the staff and the program. Bulletin boards providing current information, a coffee area with books and articles, and private space to meet with the staff all encourage parents' increased involvement.

Interpret the Regulations of the Local Licensing Body

This could be a simple or a more difficult task depending on the complexity of regulations governing your province or territory. Most regulations mention the following areas:

- requirements of the local health, fire, and zoning authorities
- teacher–child ratios
- age groupings
- group sizes and room capacities; square metres per child, both indoor and outdoor
- curriculum planning and daily records
- staff qualifications and training
- use of indoor space
- playground requirements
- health and safety regulations
- amount and types of toys and equipment
- administrative procedures
- regulations regarding the physical plant

Reading the regulations is one thing; clearly understanding their implications is another. Your role is to make sure all parties involved in the design agree about what they mean. A regulation may require one toilet and sink for every 15 preschoolers, but not specify the location. It is up to the child care professionals to think about where the toilets should be placed. Regulations typically refer to minimal requirements that are just that—minimal. It is cheaper and less disruptive to determine the centre's growth needs at the time of construction than it is to rip up areas later.

The regulations take time to incorporate into your overall planning and should not be taken lightly. When you are designing a new centre, the preliminary plans are usually sufficient to get approval in principle from your licensing body. The licensing body should be able to provide you with other helpful information to assist in the development of your centre. Understanding the procedure to follow is the most important aspect for us to consider here, since regulations vary so greatly across the country.

Incorporate Health and Safety Features

A hazard-free environment offers more opportunities for children's free use of the space without anxious staff overseeing their every move. Children must be protected from such hazards as poisonous substances, hot tap water, slippery floor surfaces, uneven rugs, electrical outlets, sharp edges, and unsafe windows and stairs. When planning your space, keep flexibility of use in mind alongside the purpose of a specific area. For example, area rugs over tile do not work with young children. The ends become frayed, children like to lift them and slide under, and sometimes they become a safety problem. In areas where children are going to play on the floor, wall-to-wall rugs are safer.

A single-storey centre is safest, if the land site makes it feasible. Stairs require the enforcement of safety rules easily forgotten by young children. The relationship of the playground to the building is another safety feature. Direct access from indoors to the playground will ensure that children do not stray when one of the eyes in the back of the teacher's head is blinking. Parents should be able to go directly to the playground to pick up their child.

The location of swings and creative climbers must also be clearly considered from a safety point of view. Space to walk easily and safely around each piece of equipment is essential. Hills for tobogganing must be placed so that they point away from the building, and away from fences and other pieces of equipment. Consider too the effect of seasonal variations on the playground. The author was visiting a centre and was taken to see a newly constructed playground. It looked very attractive and contained the variety and scope of equipment that encourage gross motor development. The area also included some nice areas, which might stimulate social interaction. The playground contained a hill with good ascent for slipping and tobogganing. In fact, it appeared to be an exemplary set-up. But by midwinter the supervisor was at her wit's end: what looked like a well-considered playground turned out to be a disaster when ice formed. The gently sloping hill changed into a slippery nightmare only bobsledders could use. The speed the children came down at took them directly into the fence. No amount of salt and sand seemed to make a difference, and the staff spent the rest of the winter slipping and sliding on the hill to retrieve children eager to give it another run.

More and more regulations are coming into place for playground safety. Keeping up to date on playground requirements and daily inspection procedures must be in place. While it is supervisors' responsibility to ensure daily inspection reports are completed, every staff member must be acutely aware that all safety factors are in place each day before the children enter the playground as well as while they are using the space and equipment.

The location of parking for the parents is another safety consideration. Little feet too tired to move from the snack table suddenly spring into action as parents struggle to get them and their precious belongings into the car. Safety bumps and clearly marked traffic patterns all assist in making dropping off and picking up safer.

Look at everything with a critical eye. Think of how the building, the equipment, or any other aspect of the program might become a hazard for young hands, bodies, and minds.

Ensure the Design Allows for
Flexible Enrollment and Programming

When you are designing a new centre you usually have a given number of children in mind. The number in each group is often determined by the staffing ratios established by the licensing regulations governing your area. For example, if the staff–child ratio is 5:1 for toddlers, and your maximum group size is 15, then you may plan for a group of 15 toddlers. You may decide that 10 toddlers in a group is a better overall size, but after further consideration you conclude that three staff makes for a safer situation. Economics and safety may together determine your final decision to have 15 in the group.

If your staff–child ratio is 8:1 for preschoolers and your maximum room size is 24, you have another decision to make. Do you have two groups of 16 children with two staff in a room, to make a more appropriate group size for young children, or one group of 24?

Developmentally appropriate practices and the philosophy of your centre should be the most important considerations in your decision, although the financial viability of your centre will also play a role. Further growth may also be a factor for the board to consider.

Long-term plans may involve a phase-in schedule.

Once you have determined the beginning capacity and age groups you are starting with, consider the flexibility of the space in terms of its use by various ages. Let's say that your beginning capacity is 10 infants, 15 toddlers, 32 preschoolers and 15 school-age children. Registrations are coming in, and you find that your predictions are being matched for the infants, toddlers, and preschoolers, but there are only one or two requests for school-age care. Now what?

Back to the "what if" principle. What if we give the parents of the two school-age children the option of incorporating their after-kindergarten children into the oldest preschool program for the half day, and use the school-age room for the extra toddlers requesting care? Good idea! If we have included the necessary requirements for flexible use in our design, we are ready to accept the second group of toddlers. Keep in mind that many of the physical features necessary for one program can have another use with a different age. For example, change areas with large sinks in the toddler room would make very useful creative areas with an older age group. When a checklist of needs for each area has been prepared, another column can be added for alternative use of the area with other ages. This procedure can be followed throughout the centre.

Flexibility is a smart insurance policy against unpredictable changes. Enrollment may suddenly change, after remaining consistent for several years. Another centre may open or close in your area, the board of education may do a pilot project, or new adult education programs may increase the demand for a particular age group. Whatever the case, flexible programming is important to meet the needs of the families in the community, and it makes good sense from the point of view of economics.

Explain the Need for Accessibility,
Proximity, and Clustering of Activities

This is a big undertaking and encompasses almost every other consideration discussed to this point. What activities do you want to cluster together? How do you ensure safety for the children? Where should the support services be located? What about staff, parents, and entrance areas?

One way to begin to get a handle on this task is to decide which activities go together and why. Activities and activity areas related to the children themselves make the first cluster. You can visualize the clusters by drawing circles containing related activity areas (see Figure 5–1).

- playrooms, storage of toys, supplies, beds, etc.
- washrooms
- gross motor area, indoor/outdoor storage
- coat cubbies, personal storage
- dining area
- playground, indoor/outdoor storage

Activities related to the provision of services require another cluster. Draw another circle and include the relevant areas. (Don't worry at this point if you are not entirely sure what should be included in a particular cluster. Fine-tuning comes later, but for the moment you want all areas included.)

- kitchen
- pantry
- sleep room (if separate from playrooms)
- laundry room
- janitorial room
- storage for extra toys, equipment, supplies
- seasonal storage

Cluster staff areas in a third circle:

- lounge
- supervisor's office
- reception area
- work area and supply area
- interview room
- personal space and resource storage
- kitchenette
- adult washroom
- area for a sick child

Make a fourth circle for the inclusion of parent needs.

- lounge
- information area
- meeting room

Keep in mind that the point of this exercise is to look at what you want to include in your centre, and how each area relates to others. Each centre will have a different set of priorities and needs that will guide the layout.

You may want to take one area out of a certain cluster and put it into another. For example, you may decide the staff washroom should be clustered with the children's area so that

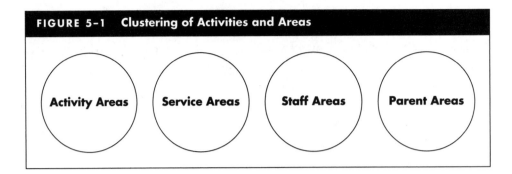

FIGURE 5-1   Clustering of Activities and Areas

staff can use it readily. Or you may want the washroom required for the school-age children to double as a second staff washroom near the children's area.

After the activity areas are grouped in circles, bring the circles together, overlapping the ones you think should relate to one another most closely. For example, you will want to locate the playground, gross motor room, and indoor/outdoor storage close to one another. A washroom easily accessible from the playground is essential for supervision and the avoidance of unnecessary untidiness from messy and snowy boots. Playrooms should be close to one another to allow flexibility of use, easier supervision in times of emergencies, and versatility of programming. Access from one room to another allows multiple use, so that different groups of children can share space, age groupings can reflect changes in enrollment, and curriculum can be adjusted as needs of the children change throughout the year.

The philosophy of the centre will dictate some further decisions about how you cluster areas together. The reception area, supervisor's office, or both should be near the entrance for easy parental access. The parent area or areas should be easy to reach from the entrance, and should invite parent involvement. The staff room may have to be placed away from the supervisor's office, since there is only so much space in one area.

Other Considerations

Planning to reduce noise

Young children are easily stimulated and react to the activities around them. Some activities require concentration, which is easily broken by the sudden screech of excitement when a last block is finally balanced on the top of the pile. You do not want to discourage this productive sound, but you also want an atmosphere where children can "get into" an activity requiring quiet concentration. Hence the dilemma!

Experts from other professions are contributing to the design of child care centres, studying areas such as the impact of noise on adults and children working together for long periods of time. New solutions include special acoustic strategies not considered in the past, with a combination of more familiar architectural concepts. Children react to noise around them in varied ways. Some are able to ignore it, some become louder in their play as the noise level accelerates around them, and some react very negatively to various levels of sound. It is important to include an acoustical expert in the planning of a centre in order to implement solutions specific to each site.

Storage areas

Although it may seem obvious, the provision of adequate storage needs to be emphasized when preparing final plans for building or alterations. Storage space is critical for beds, indoor/outdoor gross motor equipment, seasonal material like bicycles, wagons, holiday decorations, and so on. The goal is to reduce clutter and ensure a safe environment as much as possible. Equipment is bulky, and having varied ages of children in a centre means that you need a variety of choices available throughout the year to provide a high quality program. A lack of proper closed storage makes child care impossible, both aesthetically and practically. Stress the need for storage to ensure safety, organization, and accessibility. As you continue to work with children you will see how important it is to have proper storage as a high priority.

Maintenance

Children play hard and are not as much in control of their bodies as adults may sometimes like them to be. Surfaces must be durable and washable. Tiled floors should be of good quality for the heavy washing they will need. Rugs should have good underpads and be of sturdy fabric that can be sanitized. Wall surfaces must be durable. One of the best solutions is to have attractive arborite glued on the walls, with wood trim. This may be more expensive initially, but in the long run it is economical. Cautions and concern for maintenance is essential, and the time and effort spent in carefully planning children's areas will be rewarded financially and aesthetically.

Further features to keep in mind

Other specific features that require attention include:

- washrooms in, or directly adjoining, each playroom and playground
- adult-size sinks in each playroom
- closed storage for curriculum toys, games, supplies, beds, and equipment in each playroom
- access from one playroom to another
- consideration for multi-purpose areas
- a minimal number of doors and corridors
- glassed areas to create an impression of spaciousness
- in the group areas, separation for learning centres and space for privacy or solitary play
- entrances that are aesthetically pleasing and comforting to the child (open and airy), avoiding long halls and corridor-like cubbies
- storage that is accessible from both indoors and outdoors for gross motor equipment
- exits for parents from the centre or the playground
- service entrance to pantry from outside
- direct access to the playground from as many playrooms as possible, for indoor/outdoor programming in good weather
- parking for staff
- parking for parents that is convenient and safe for children

PLANNING OUTDOOR ENVIRONMENTS

Outdoor space needs to be organized as much as indoor space. Many of the principles discussed for indoor environments can be applied to playgrounds or outdoor space. Developmental needs for each age group should be reflected in the playground layout to enhance children's social, emotional, cognitive, and physical growth.

Canada's four seasons bring new challenges, learning potential, and the excitement of discovery for children. While some children prefer to be inside, many blossom and thrive in the space and freedom presented to them outdoors. Children have a greater sense of vitality and discovery outside even when they are burdened with a bulky winter snowsuit—running, experiencing different sounds and using language in new ways, and enjoying less structured opportunities for self-expression.

Safety

Playgrounds must be safe for use by any age group. Smaller, more vulnerable children need to have adults check and recheck the safety of the playground. People passing by may inadvertently throw something over the fence that could harm infants and toddlers. Gates and fences must be checked constantly to ensure that children cannot hurt themselves or escape to an unsafe area. Outdoor areas require extra vigilance. It is important to emphasize again that a system for inspecting the playground should be made each day in order to ensure safety for the children and staff.

Proximity

The cubby area, a washroom, and playrooms need to be close to the playground. This is crucial for infants and toddlers, and highly desirable for the preschoolers. The school-age children have developed sufficient self-help skills that priority should be given to the younger children to access these areas more readily. When playrooms and outdoor areas are close to one another, staff can extend inside play to the outside as weather allows, while maximizing staff supervision.

Playground Equipment

As Esbensen (1987) states, the quality of playground equipment and its location, together with the surface type and the condition of the playground, can present safety hazards for young children. All equipment must include such safety features as adequate handrails, child-size steps, soft and absorbent landing areas, clear boundaries for safe traffic flow, recessed bolts that protect small hands and fingers, and locations that make supervision possible from many angles. The playground layout should allow staff to be in assigned areas so that each adult in the playground can assist children readily and quickly. Because of the complexity and size of the gross motor equipment, it is usually best to open areas as staff are available to supervise them, rather than trying to supervise too large or complex areas. Safety is the critical factor that determines whether or not children should use the equipment.

Incorporating equipment that children and teachers can enjoy together may help achieve this goal. Safe, comfortable swinging or stationary benches, picnic tables, low dividing walls, and other environmentally attractive seating areas can be incorporated into the playground design.

Private companies involved in the design and layout of safe and effective playgrounds are now available to consult with child care centres. Once staff have an overall idea of what they want to achieve in their outdoor area, professionals can assist with the location, quality, design, and maintenance of equipment and surface areas including asphalt paths, type of fencing for the given area, recommended landscaping, natural mounds, levels, building overhangs or covered areas for wet days, storage space, and so on. The final design is critical, given the expense, the relative permanence of the playground, and its importance in meeting the centre's developmental goals.

Some staff naturally enjoy the playground activities while others prefer to be indoors. However it is important (and, in most cases, required by law) that children spend parts of the day outdoors. Attractive, comfortable space that is safe and convenient to supervise will entice "indoor" staff to want to be outdoors more, and increase the amount of time they stay outside.

Playground Space—Designated Areas

The size and shape of the playground will probably be determined by how much space is available. Provinces and territories have minimum requirements—for example, Ontario requires 5.6 square metres per child. Other factors to be considered include ages and number of children in the centre, the location of the playground in relation to the centre, what play areas are to be incorporated, use of surrounding land, nearby traffic and noise from outside, and the ratio of open to closed space.

Experts support the notion that dividing a playground into areas or zones helps children define space in a way that encourages particular types of play, and supports positive social interactions. The specific layout of designated spaces will be determined by the goals of the centre. Clearly defined areas, with boundaries easily understood by the children, would

Quality and location of equipment are important.

contain space for quiet reflection, social/dramatic areas, large gross motor or physical play areas, and creative/cognitive space. Walsh (1988) simplifies the description by calling them open areas, active areas, and quiet areas.

It is important to highlight the importance of open space outdoors. While gross motor equipment such as swings, slides, and a complex climbing apparatus is important, open space allows children to engage in self-directed activities. These experiences can change from day to day as children use props with increasing creativity and imagination. When staff encourage children to participate in many opportunities to problem solve, be spontaneous, and make decisions, the outside environment will provide open space for these goals. It is always easier to provide movable equipment and materials that allow children to use open space constructively, than it is to change permanent structures.

IN CONCLUSION

This chapter is an introduction to the complexity of early childhood education environments. Try to capture a sense of a child's perception of the world, and incorporate this point of view into the environment. Designing a centre is a procedure where new challenges are raised by every task solved. The information in this chapter will hopefully encourage you to continue to search for new and innovative ways to meet the needs of children, parents, and staff through the physical set-up of your centre.

Designing space for young children requires knowledge of child development, a professional philosophy about how children best learn and grow, and a good understanding of how to design and implement curriculum in an appropriate environment.

Outdoor play is a central part of the curriculum.

Environments for young children must ensure their safety, contain developmentally appropriate toys, materials, and equipment, and be aesthetically pleasing to both children and adults. In order to accomplish these goals, centres must be designed to allow close proximity of playrooms, washrooms, eating and sleeping areas, and outdoor space.

The needs of staff and parents must also be considered in order to plan and design appropriate space for them.

Obtaining information from licensing authorities and interpreting the regulations is an important first step in ensuring that all health, safety, legislative, and local requirements are met.

Programs must be designed to allow maximum flexibility in order to meet the changing needs of parents and the community, and to remain financially viable.

ACTIVITIES

1. Visit a centre and observe one program for half an hour. Draw the floor plan of the room you observed and answer the following questions:

    a) What was the traffic pattern in the room, and how did it affect the children's involvement and behaviour?

    b) What was the noise level in the room, and what effect did it have on the children?

    c) What was aesthetically pleasing in the room, and what would you have changed?

    d) Did the room include sufficient open space for the number of children in the group?

2. Talk to one or two early childhood educators who have been working with children for several years. Find out what areas of the physical design in their centre have facilitated their ability to present curriculum and have enhanced teacher–child interactions, and what areas are a hindrance.

3. What would you list as the three most important areas to include in the centre's physical design for each of the following age groups: infants, toddlers, preschoolers, and school age children?

4. Spend an hour in a playground. Make a list of the important developmental needs of the children using that playground. List the areas in the playground that help meet those needs.

REVIEW QUESTIONS

1. Why is it important to design flexible and adaptable environments for young children in group care?

2. Describe safety precautions that must be in place in order to ensure the well-being of young children.

3. What are some of the most important developmental considerations in planning space for:

    a) infants

    b) toddlers

    c) preschoolers

    d) school-age children?

4. List the steps involved when using a systematic approach to the use of existing space.

5. What areas might be included in regulations that affect the development and regulation of a centre?

6. Explain the need for accessibility, proximity, and clustering of activities.

FURTHER READING

Esbensen, S.B. (1987). *The early childhood education playground: An outdoor classroom*. Ypsilanti, MI: High Scope Press.

Frost, J.L. (1992). *Play and playscapes*. New York: Delmar Publishers.

Kritchevsky, S., E. Prescott, and L. Walling (1983). *Planning environments for young children: Physical space*. Washington, D.C.: National Association for the Education of Young Children.

Lovell, P., and T. Harms (1985). "How can playgrounds be improved? A rating scale." *Young Children* 40 (3): 3–8.

Sciarra, D.J. and A.G. Dorsey (1996). *Developing and administering a child care center*. Albany, NY: Delmar Publishers.

APPENDIX: HEALTH AND SAFETY CHECKLIST

HEALTH AND SAFETY CHECKLIST
Inspection completed by _____ Date _____
Summary of concerns from last inspection _____
_____
_____ Date of last inspection_____

INSPECTION AREA	YES	NO	COMMENTS
INDOORS			
Surfaces that are easy and quick to disinfect			
Floors that provide warmth and comfort			
Rugs secure to prevent tripping			
Non-slip floor surfaces			
Rounded or padded corners			
Climate control and draft-free environment			
Good ventilation with all systems working			
All areas are well lighted			
Acoustic and noise levels are appropriate			
Safe, locked storage for hazardous materials			
Controlled systems for food storage and refrigeration			
Sanitary diapering procedures posted			
Sanitary food handling procedures posted			
Hand washing procedures posted			
Electrical outlets at children's level have dummy plugs when not in use			
No electrical or phone wires at children's level			
Furniture is stable, washable, not peeling or chipped, without toxic paint			
Safety glass in doors and windows, securely fastened			
Child-size furniture and equipment to avoid accidents			
Equipment and toys have no protruding edges and are in safe working order			

INSPECTION AREA	YES	NO	COMMENTS
Science and nature materials are non-toxic and safe			
Toys and equipment are stored safely when not in use			
Toy shelves and cupboards are stable			
Water-play is changed after use			
Sand is disinfected regularly			
Woodworking equipment is organized and safely stored			
Pathways in rooms are uncluttered, at child's eye level and easy to follow			
Toilets and sinks are at children's level			
Step stools used are wide, strong, and stable			
Faucets used by children are temperature-controlled			
Paper towels are readily available for children to use			
Children can access paper cups and a drink of water easily			
Kitchen is out of reach of children			
Dangerous equipment in kitchen is well out of reach of children			
Storage areas are uncluttered and have safe passages			
All areas of centre are cleaned daily (floors, washroom, kitchen, counters)			
Intensive cleaning is completed on a regular schedule (walls, doors, windows washed)			
Staff areas are organized and uncluttered			

OUTDOORS

	YES	NO	COMMENTS
Playground can be accessed safely from building			
The entire playground is visible			
Playgrounds have clear and safe pathways			
Grounds are clean, garbage-free, and well maintained			
Fencing in all areas is at least 1.25 metres high			

INSPECTION AREA	YES	NO	COMMENTS
Fences are in good shape, latches working and secure			
Bushes and tree limbs are strong and sturdy			
Surfaces are free from holes and protrusions			
Sandboxes are covered or inspected for debris			
Equipment is confined to designated areas			
Drainage is working well			
Washrooms and drinks are readily accessible			
Gross motor equipment is well anchored			
Equipment is free of holes, gaps, and rough edges			
Equipment has no protrusions that clothes can catch on			
Equipment has space between each area			
Equipment is easy for staff to supervise			
Equipment is developmentally appropriate			
Children are protected from sun, wind, and cold			
Surfaces under equipment have good cushioning			
Water play areas are changed at least daily			
Plants, shrubs, etc., are non-poisonous			
Swings are checked to ensure safety			
Slides have no pinch points or protrusions			
Riding paths are in good shape			
Wood on equipment is smooth and splinter-free			
Bolts and screws are recessed			
Riding toys are checked for safety			

ALL CONCERNS OR PROBLEMS WERE REPORTED TO THE SUPERVISOR ON _____

BY _____

STAFFING—
THE KEY TO
QUALITY

This chapter examines an employer's roles and responsibilities in relation to staffing, and then discusses professionalism in early childhood education and how it can be enhanced. It is essential that every staff member understands personnel policies, procedures, and issues. The key points are:

- *Defining a competent early childhood educator*

- *Early childhood education as a profession*

- *Stages of professional growth*

- *Methods of enhancing professionalism*

- *Supporting staff development: the supervisor's role*

If you ask an experienced early childhood educator what is the single most important thing determining a quality environment for children, you will probably get an answer like "Teachers are the key to quality—the teacher can make it or break it." The importance of staff in early childhood settings can't be overemphasized. Doherty-Derkowski, in *Quality matters: Excellence in early childhood programs* (1995), reviews research studies, conducted over 15 years in a number of countries, confirming the critical role that committed and knowledgeable staff can play.

DEFINING A COMPETENT EARLY CHILDHOOD EDUCATOR

If asked what qualities, personality traits, values, beliefs, knowledge, and skills are most important in working with children, most of us would identify warmth, sensitivity, energy, knowledge of children, or patience, to name a few. However, there is a lack of agreement about what makes a competent early childhood educator.

Current research demonstrates that program quality is strongly related to staff education and training: Whitebrook et al. (1990), Doherty-Derkowski (1995). In a high quality early childhood program, qualified staff use specialized skills to meet the needs of the group as a whole, while remaining focused on the needs of each individual child and family. The kind of specialized knowledge gained through teacher preparation includes a foundation in the theory and research on child development, and in the development of appropriate individualized, concrete, and experiential programs for young children.

Whitebrook (1990) found that working with young children requires skills and knowledge that are provided through formal education and training programs. Formal training alone does not guarantee high quality programs, but several studies indicate that the standard of care improves when staff are educated in child development and early childhood education. This is shown through the children's increased social interaction with adults, development of pro-social behaviours, and improved language and cognitive development.

As the field of early childhood education expands and diversifies, the specific training needs for early childhood educators are being reexamined. Since staff should have specialized training for the age group they work with, the span of the ages of children served in early childhood programs may affect the length, content, and structure of teacher education programs. Some experts in the field hold the view that early childhood education extends to age eight or even twelve, whereas others concentrate from birth to five.

One proposal for teacher education suggests a three-year diploma, with all students participating in a common core program for the first two years. In a separately streamed third year, students could choose an area of specialization such as working with children with special needs, administration of early childhood settings, or could specialize in an age group such as toddlers or school-age children. This model is unlikely to be implemented widely, since there is pressure to reduce education costs. A different model offers the year of specialization as a post-diploma program. Many provinces have developed articulation agreements between two-year college and four-year university programs in order to provide a continuum of teacher preparation opportunities and to facilitate professional growth.

Apart from formal education, competent early childhood educators must have the appropriate personal characteristics for working with young children. Among the qualities of a good early childhood educator are a high energy level, patience, warmth, nurturance, openness to new ideas, a tolerance for ambiguity, flexible thinking, and maturity. Peters (1988) would also add positive self-concept, along with positive attitudes and expectations about children's achievements. Bernhard et al. (1995), in *Paths to equity: Cultural, linguistic, and racial diversity in Canadian early childhood education,* state that staff who have graduated from postsecondary courses must demonstrate the ability to have respectful interactions with families whose backgrounds differ from their own.

We know intuitively that these are important qualities. It is more difficult to concretely demonstrate their impact on the quality of children's experience, although attempts have been made to clearly and systematically determine what qualities make an effective teacher. Individual staff members can be evaluated through observing their interactions with children, parents, and staff, and monitoring their implementation of curriculum.

It is important for the early childhood educator to receive broad-based professional training in such areas as human growth and development, program planning, working with adults, interpersonal communication, and behaviour management. A field placement experience is a critical factor that enables the application of theory into practice. In this experience, a student may practise and develop skills with the guidance of a cooperating teacher. Field placements provide the opportunity to learn to interact effectively with young children as well as to work as part of a team. More specialized knowledge and skills may be added around the core curriculum, as required. For example, many educators are increasingly aware of the need to address the area of employee rights on the job.

Another important area is appreciation of diversity. College and university programs are infused with the philosophy of diversity, allowing students to graduate with an understanding of the breadth of human culture, an appreciation of issues such as bilingualism and second-language development, and an ability to respond proactively to bias and prejudice. Some provinces, such as Ontario and British Columbia, have firmly addressed this area of need. In the paper *Early childhood education program standards* (1996), the College Standards and Accreditation Council mandated that all early childhood graduates must demonstrate the ability "to act in a manner consistent with principles of fairness, equity, and diversity to support the development and learning of individual children within the context of family, culture, and society." In order to keep pace with rapid changes in the field, educators must be prepared to participate in professional development throughout their careers.

EARLY CHILDHOOD EDUCATION AS A PROFESSION

Many believe the quality of early childhood environments is influenced by the level of professionalism in the field of early childhood education. Educators need recognition of their professional role. Increased recognition of educational qualifications, better salaries, and improved working conditions usually accompany professional status, and these are clearly warranted and appropriate goals for which to strive. They are also crucial conditions to ensure that the profession attracts and keeps good and experienced caregivers. Early childhood educators are familiar with the impact of low wages, high staff turnover, and inadequately trained staff. Unionization and advocacy have evolved as significant avenues to improve these areas.

The differing perspectives of unionization, advocacy, and professionalism need not be mutually exclusive. Regardless of the approach taken, professionals require and deserve working conditions that enhance competence. Professional growth requires opportunities for learning new skills, and time for planning and acquiring appropriate resource materials.

As discussed in Chapters 1 and 2, legislation and regulation, although critical, have limitations in ensuring quality environments. Many aspects of professional behaviour that cannot be regulated have a direct impact on the quality of care the child receives—such as the quality of interactions between child and caregiver.

Professionalism refers to a combination of competence in a particular field of knowledge and identification with a group of colleagues who can collectively define and support quality practices. Recognition of educational responsibility is crucial—many people are unaware that early childhood education has a distinctive professional knowledge base that informs practice. Many have researched what is needed to move the field toward professionalization, including Griffen (1994) and Spodek et al. (1988). Elements to include in considering the professional nature of early childhood education are discussed in the next section:

* specialized knowledge
* standards of practice
* entry to practice and continuing competence
* a code of ethics and accountability

Specialized Knowledge

Specialized knowledge in early childhood education is derived from developmental psychology and many other fields. A great deal of knowledge exists about how to care for and educate young children from birth through age 12, and research demonstrates that those who apply this knowledge provide better care and education for young children. Developmentally appropriate practice endeavours to base decisions about best practices for young children on child development research and current knowledge of learning. This offers a body of specialized knowledge to early childhood educators.

Professional judgment involves assessing events, weighing alternatives, and estimating the potential long-term consequences of decisions and actions based on that knowledge. Our choice of courses of action is based not only on common sense, but also on specific expertise acquired through professional training and ongoing professional development. Practitioners must continually challenge and evaluate professional judgments and practices to ensure that they are based on the best available information. The knowledge base of the field has expanded greatly over the last decade, and it continues to grow as the needs of children and families increase in complexity. Early childhood educators need to upgrade their knowledge through reading, courses, conferences, and discussions with colleagues.

Standards of Practice

Professional standards, based on the best available knowledge and practice, are useful to the profession in establishing its own benchmarks of quality beyond the requirements of legislation and contribute to the quality of early childhood settings. Professionals adopt standards of practice to ensure that members apply uniform procedures and principles in response to typical situations using their best professional judgment. Occupational standards also protect the public interest by ensuring that all practising professionals are working safely and ethically within a minimum set of guidelines. Standards of practice can be used to guide professional preparation programs, certification principles, and as a basis for job descriptions.

Practising professionals are committed to performing at the same high standards consistently, without allowing personal matters or moods to affect their work or their relations with children, coworkers, or employers. Regardless of the setting, young children deserve to be cared for and to be educated by adults who possess the appropriate knowledge and skills. The process of professionalizing creates greater consensus among practitioners on the meaning of critical terms and concepts. Greater consensus supports working toward shared goals.

The Canadian Child Care Federation published occupational standards based on broad consultation in the field for practitioners working with children and administrators in both centre-based and family child care agencies as well as family resource programs. The standards are based on what practitioners do and the skills and abilities required to facilitate a child's well-being and development in addition to supporting families. These standards are part of the National Framework for Quality Assurance.

Entry to Practice and Continuing Competence

A major characteristic of a profession is that all practising professionals have a minimum level of knowledge, experience, and qualifications prior to entering the profession. Qualifications for early childhood educators are determined by provincial and territorial regulations. At present the requirement is primarily an ECE diploma, although many provinces do not even require this level of training. Prolonged formal training ensures that early childhood educators learn the knowledge base and techniques necessary for informed and effective performance before they begin work, and continue to learn throughout their career. A variety of instructional formats can be used for training, such as internships, field work, in-service workshops, professional literature, and conferences.

Our Child Care Workforce: From Recognition to Remuneration (1998) examines human resources issues associated with employment in child care in Canada. In chapter six, it specifically details some of the challenges in defining skills required by early childhood caregivers, gaps in skills along with issues in postsecondary education and professional development opportunities. The report provides recommendations for addressing these concerns.

The purpose of continuing competence is to ensure that practising professionals are made aware of and educated about new knowledge in both their own and other disciplines. In many professions, the individual must fulfill a specified number of professional development hours each year in order to maintain registration in the professional body. For example, a certified social worker is required to fulfill 75 hours of professional development over a five-year period.

Code of Ethics and Accountability

To claim to be a professional is to declare publicly that one adheres to goals and values that go beyond immediate interests. In order to attain true professional status, practitioners need to adopt a common code of ethics. One of the hallmarks of professionalism is its recognition of and adherence to a code of ethical conduct. Such a code embodies guidelines for behaviour, and facilitates decision making when a practitioner faces an ethical dilemma. The protection of vulnerable children demands that all individuals working with children conform to the highest standards of ethical conduct. Professionals not only agree to operate according to a high standard of behaviour, but they also agree to monitor the conduct of others in the field.

The process of developing a code of professional ethics may begin by describing the standard predicaments that caregivers confront in the course of their day-to-day work. Early childhood educators are faced daily with dilemmas. Many of these situations do not have easy solutions but can be supported with defined professional ethics. Ethics may be defined as the way a group of associates specify their responsibility to their clients, to one another, and to the community in which they work. How practitioners collectively express their commitment to children, parents, colleagues, and community is guided by statements found in a code of

EXAMPLE STANDARD

Caring for Children—Occupational Standard One

Protect and promote the psychological and physical safety, health, and well-being of each child being cared for.

1. The practitioner is able to maintain a sanitary environment that minimizes the risk of infection or food contamination through:
   - developing and implementing effective procedures to maintain the required level of cleanliness and sanitation;
   - encouraging an awareness among children of good health and hygiene practices through modeling and a variety of learning experiences; and
   - being able to recognize symptoms of common childhood diseases and take appropriate action.

2. The practitioner is able to maintain a hazard-free environment that minimizes the risk of accidents or injury through:
   - developing and implementing effective methods of ensuing that, at all times, the building, the outdoor play area, the furniture, the toys, and the equipment are in good repair and safe for use by the children;
   - ensuring the safe storage of medications and all potentially dangerous materials;
   - providing supervision that is appropriate for the children's developmental levels;
   - developing and implementing effective procedures for emergency situations; and
   - assisting the children to develop safety awareness through instruction, modeling, and reinforcing safety concepts.

3. The practitioner is able to promote children's health through:
   - providing snacks and meals that are nutritious and balanced and take into account cultural preferences within the parameters of Canada Food Guide, or, in situations where families are responsible for snacks, encouraging and assisting parents to follow the Canada Food Guide;
   - monitoring children's physical status on a daily basis and reporting concerns about possible abuse or neglect as required by and outlined in current provincial or territorial legislation;
   - developing and implementing procedures to identify and monitor children who have allergies or chronic medical conditions that require special precautions or care and ensuring that such precautions are taken and/or the requisite care is provided; and
   - developing and implementing a specific procedure for administering medications.

4. The practitioner is able to protect and promote children's psychological health and well-being by:
   - providing an environment that conveys a sense of order, routine, consistency, and continuity;
   - setting realistic expectations and clear limits and using positive and developmentally appropriate approaches to guiding children's behaviour;
   - providing experiences that are appropriate for the child's developmental level and responding to each child's efforts to grow and acquire skills in a positive manner;
   - noting, accepting and respecting children's expression of their feelings, whether positive or negative, and the underlying message that is conveyed through body movement or facial expression;
   - supporting children in openly expressing their positive and negative feelings through a range of verbal, nonverbal, and culturally based communication strategies; and
   - providing activities that respect each child's individual ethnic and cultural heritage and encourage each child to feel proud of his/her heritage.

ethics. This statement represents what is right rather than what might be expedient. What is best is not always easy to determine, and a code of ethics is an important tool to guide staff in their daily decision making.

The journal *Young Children* examines a number of these challenging dilemmas in a series of articles starting in 1985 and continuing to the present. For example, early childhood educators may occasionally be forced to choose between a parent's and a child's needs. A code of professional ethics provides common principles for dealing with such dilemmas, principles based on the value of childhood as a unique stage of life, on knowledge of child development, on a valuing of family and cultural ties, and on helping individuals reach their potential through supportive relationships. Such a code is created through discussions with colleagues who reflect on challenges that occur regularly within the profession.

Penalties (fines, or suspension or termination of one's right to practise) may be levied against members of the profession who are incompetent or who fail to act in accordance with standards of ethical practice.

At this time there is no single code of ethics to guide practitioners in Canada. Early Childhood Educators of British Columbia (ECEBC), the Association of Early Childhood Educators, Ontario (AECEO), and Child Care Connection NS in Nova Scotia have developed codes for their members. The Canadian Child Care Federation is developing a national code of ethics in consultation with provincial/territorial affiliate organizations. This draft code is included at the end of this chapter.

A final component of professional ethics is altruism—ideally, members are expected to perform their services with unselfish dedication with an emphasis on social goals. From its beginning, early childhood education has been grounded on the principles of improving the lives of young children and families. On this criterion, early childhood educators rank highly, since their salaries could be said to be truly sacrificial and their concerns are with children and families. Since we are dealing with human lives, we have to be accountable—we have to care about what we do and how we do it.

The application of all these criteria to the field of early childhood education suggests it is on its way to developing into a profession.

STAGES OF PROFESSIONAL GROWTH

The idea of developmental stages is commonly understood and used by caregivers of young children, however the notion of steps of development among adults is not as readily considered. Glickman, Katz, VanderVen, and others have defined predictable developmental stages that early childhood educators go through. Individuals vary greatly in the length of time they spend in each stage:

- Stage I—Survival
- Stage II—Consolidation
- Stage III—Renewal
- Stage IV—Maturity

The authors describe an early childhood educator's typical behaviour at each of these stages, and identify specialized training and professional development appropriate to each level. Chapter 7 discusses the supervisory style and its effectiveness with staff at different developmental stages.

Stage I—Survival

In this stage, which usually lasts through the first year of teaching, the beginning early child-hood educator feels the impact of full responsibility for a group of young children. The care-giver's primary roles will be to provide hands-on care, assist with activities, manage behaviour, and contribute to centre maintenance. This experience is often jarring and anxiety-filled, and the individual typically experiences self-doubt and feelings of inse-curity. At this stage, the novice professional's main need is for support, encouragement, and guidance. Staff in the survival stage should not be expected to supervise students who are on field practicum.

Teachers in this stage need encouragement, insight into the reasons for children's behav-iour, and instruction in specific skills. On-site support and mentorship from other teachers are the most appropriate strategies to support staff in the survival stage of development.

Stage II—Consolidation

As they pass the survival stage, educators begin to exhibit some degree of confidence in their skill level and focus on specific tasks. They commence interpreting what is happening in their classroom and are eager to seek alternative approaches. During this step, they move their attention to challenging children or to situations that deviate from the norm. They learn by observing, modeling, and doing, and thrive in a supportive environment that encour-ages problem solving and sharing. They learn to structure physical environments and activ-ities in a way that reduces the need for external controls.

At this stage, educators benefit from more focused observations and feedback that iden-tify challenges, problems, and new classroom approaches. An administrator can provide encouragement to develop resources and form a support network.

As they develop further and master classroom fundamentals, teachers are ready to develop more challenging skills. They require exposure to new ideas to stay motivated and avoid burnout. In the later stages of the consolidation phase, individuals are ready for eval-uation systems that facilitate introspection and personal goal setting. Possible methods include self-administered checklists, video analysis, or a mentor approach. Such a mentor rela-tionship most often involves the supervisor or a lead teacher, along with regular opportunities to formally review issues that have arisen in the course of daily practice.

Stage III—Renewal

Early childhood educators in this stage have reached a professional plateau. After several years of teaching the same curriculum to children at the same age level, they may no longer feel challenged. They may search for stimulation, asking: "What's new in the field? Are there new areas of curriculum I haven't considered before?"

When this occurs, the early childhood educator has reached the renewal stage. Practitioners at this stage are interested in learning about new developments in the field. They often enjoy meeting with caregivers from other programs. Professional development opportunities that are particularly beneficial at this stage include attending conferences and workshops, taking a course, and active involvement in a self-assessment process.

Stage IV—Maturity

Mature educators view themselves as committed professionals. This step is reached by individuals at different points and represents a coming to terms with themselves and their profession. They have developed a philosophy of education and care, and recognize the critical nature of early learning. Mature teachers acknowledge the need for continual professional growth and self-renewal. They are committed to improving the early childhood profession, and see the role of sharing information as an essential part of this goal. They are often searching for the meaning of social, economic, historical, and political influences on society. Mature caregivers need opportunities to interact with others and participate in events where questions are addressed by others searching for similar insights.

METHODS OF ENHANCING PROFESSIONALISM

Although early childhood education is not yet a profession in the formal sense, competent practitioners seek out opportunities to improve their skills.

Self-assessment is an indispensable route to professionalism. It helps us to be accountable to others, and even more importantly makes us accountable to ourselves. This process of validating our accomplishments and identifying what we need to work on can lead us to feel more confident about our role. Supervisors and peers can assist us, by providing feedback on our strengths and supporting us in the areas we want to improve.

Certification and accreditation were mentioned in Chapter 1 as means of assuring quality in early childhood settings. Both methods incorporate self-assessment as part of the process. These programs can improve standards of practice and promote the professional image of early childhood education.

Certification is the awarding of a credential that identifies persons who possess the competencies needed for successful teaching. Voluntary certification recognizes the educational qualifications of early childhood educators in a variety of settings. Individual program policies may require that staff be certified. The qualifications required for certification stipulate that certified practitioners possess specified levels of professional competence. Eligible individuals voluntarily participate in the certification process to develop their skills and knowledge in the field.

There are three provinces whose provincial professional organizations offer voluntary certification: Alberta, Nova Scotia, and Ontario. However, only a small number of practitioners in each of these provinces are certified. There is a need for practitioners to promote recognition and valuing of the certification process as a step in becoming a profession. The process of certification varies among the different provincial organizations. Among the methods used to assess candidates are peer evaluation, self-assessment, a set exam, and development of a portfolio.

Another route is Prior Learning Assessment Recognition (PLAR), which allows experiential learning to be identified, evaluated, and equated with an amount of postsecondary credit. There is growing interest in PLAR as a mechanism for granting advanced standing to candidates with related work experience. This process is not a replacement for academic credit, but a mechanism for recognizing prior learning. Among the assessment measures used are the presentation of a portfolio, transcripts from other institutions, challenge examinations and performance evaluations. Early childhood educators with the right background will find that assessment of their experience will enable them to complete a diploma or degree more quickly.

The self-governance of a profession is carried out by professional bodies having the authority to regulate its members and their practice. The recognition of these groups is usually embedded in legislation. Some provinces are pursuing legislative recognition of early childhood educators. This process is intended to provide public accountability and a more respected status for those achieving it. Part of the process is a clear definition of an early childhood educator. The work done in defining occupational standards by the Canadian Child Care Federation is an important step.

Morris (1995) surveys the status of certification and licensing requirements across Canada. At the present time, the status of certification in Canada seems to be in a state of flux. There are no national certification standards for early childhood educators equivalent to those for kindergarten and primary school teachers. This discrepancy is probably rooted in economic interests as much as academic ones. Early childhood educators are more poorly paid, and some legislators fear that raising educational requirements would further increase the pressure for higher pay, thus increasing the cost of services.

Accreditation is another way that the public and other professionals can recognize high quality child care programs. While licensing implies meeting minimum standards, accreditation means performing at a high degree of excellence and meeting model standards. Accreditation is a process whereby a representative body, recognized by both the service community and the community in general, establishes standards for service. It is founded on the belief that for change to be real and lasting, it must be initiated by the early childhood organization. That program improvement results from a collaborative problem-solving approach involving administrators, staff, and parents in a systematic review of the program's strengths and weaknesses. In some models, excellence in settings is verified by visits and assessment by the body granting accreditation. A study of programs accredited by the NAEYC confirmed the positive impact of accreditation and also indicated that the process facilitated improvements to the program, which led to even higher quality (Herr, Johnson, Zimmerman 1993). There is a growing trend in the United States to tie government funding to programs with accreditation status.

Some of the benefits of accreditation include:

* improvements in staff development, communication, and morale

* measurable program improvements

* marketing: parents feel confident that they have made a good decision in choosing an accredited program for their children

Despite these potential benefits, there is no national child care accreditation in Canada, although such programs are standard in the delivery systems of other services such as hospitals and postsecondary institutions.

As the profession evolves, we are becoming more knowledgeable about theories of development and learning, and more skillful in applying these in our daily work with children. We are working on professional issues including ethics and standards of practice. We must continually strive to do our best for young children and families through informed, ethical practice. Further, we must be willing to share this perspective with others. Chapter 11, "Community, Resources, and Advocacy," provides a variety of strategies for public education.

As early childhood education comes of age, we are more aware of our specialized expertise and training. But we still have a way to go in developing our professional image, so the present is a critical time for practitioners to serve as advocates. As educators work

together on common goals they invest part of themselves in the process, and this investment contributes to our shared professionalism. This enhanced sense of collective purpose
is what makes educators willing to become involved in voluntary efforts surrounding the
improvement of child care.

In the words of one professional: "It is in this subtle area of private endeavour that a
profession, in its totality, achieves greatness. Sometimes it is called professional spirit. It is
the result of the association of men and women of a superior type, with a common ideal of
service above gain, excellence above quality, self-expression beyond motive, and loyalty to
a professional code beyond human advantage."

This is the commitment needed to realize quality early childhood experiences for every
Canadian child. The next section discusses how settings under the leadership of the administrators can maximize staff growth and provide high quality programs.

SUPPORTING STAFF DEVELOPMENT:
THE SUPERVISOR'S ROLE

A major challenge for supervisors of early childhood programs is to create an atmosphere
that enables staff as well as children to develop. Such an enabling environment contributes
to the development of relationships within the program, and should flow from the program
philosophy. To grow professionally, early childhood educators need to share ideas and
problems with other staff, and to receive appropriate in-service training.

Supervisors can explore different ways of expanding opportunities for staff to enhance
their knowledge base and develop new skills and competencies. It is important to provide
release time for staff to visit other early childhood programs. Professional conferences and
workshops provide opportunities for staff to receive new information and discuss practice-
based issues with colleagues. Such activities not only rejuvenate individual teachers, but
their benefits are often also felt in a ripple effect when new ideas and resources are shared
with other staff members.

Supervisors need to ensure that money and time are available for staff development.
Staff opportunities for continuous growth not only bolster morale, but also enhance the program's ability to foster children's healthy growth and development. Some programs provide
money for early childhood educators to take relevant courses through colleges or universities, and allow staff members time to complete their field placements and daytime courses.

There should be a bookcase in the staff room stocked with professional magazines, journals, and books for staff to read. Relevant articles should be circulated among staff, students,
and parents. Investing in these resources is an inexpensive way of enhancing program quality.

The administrator plays a key role in staffing, through the development of informed
personnel policies, through the hiring process, to ensuring that staff work at their optimal level.
Along with the board or owner, the supervisor has the following responsibilities:

- developing enlightened personnel policies
- developing effective recruitment and hiring procedures
- conducting regular staff performance reviews
- providing opportunities to staff for ongoing professional growth
- developing effective staffing policies and communicating them to staff
- ensuring the environment meets staff needs

Personnel Policies

A statement of personnel policies is a written document covering employer–employee relations. It spells out the conditions of employment. Personnel policies reflect the philosophy of the overall program and can serve to optimize human resources by being responsive to individual needs. These introductory comments provide an important framework for the policies and procedures that follow.

All information relating to employment should be located in one place, making it easier to find than if it is scattered on various memos, minutes of meetings, and bulletin boards. Descriptions of policies and procedures include: responsibilities, structure and reporting procedures for the organization, evaluation and disciplinary procedures, health and safety matters, and a description of the process to amend policies. This information is usually communicated to the employee at the time of hiring and made available through an employee handbook for reference.

A well-conceived employee handbook describes what types of behaviours are encouraged and discouraged, as well as informing employees about their rights and benefits. It should serve as a one-stop source of answers to any questions that might arise regarding one's employment. Policies and procedures must be in compliance with applicable laws such as the Employment Standards Act and regulations on parental leaves, minimum wages, and hours of work. When applicable, policies must conform to union requirements, which are generally spelled out in a collective agreement. Personnel policies should be precise, clear, comprehensive, and organized into logical sections. It is important that the interests of staff, children, and families are considered.

Personnel policies may be prepared by the administrator, an owner, or the board of directors of a non-profit program. In the latter case, there generally is a personnel committee with responsibility for staffing responsibilities.

A well-written set of personnel policies is an important cornerstone of an effective supervisory process. Policies set goals, clarify expectations, and establish ground rules. When the policies, procedures, and priorities of a program are communicated to the employees, they contribute to all staff performing appropriately. All policies should be supplemented with an effective orientation, ongoing professional development, and a supportive supervisory process.

Recruitment and Hiring Procedures

Given the importance of well-qualified staff, an employer needs to make all efforts to attract and keep them. A recruitment strategy that is well planned and implemented is essential. Start by looking for potential employees in logical places—community colleges and universities and members of professional organizations. Each setting should establish and follow the same general procedures regarding advertising, interviewing, and filling vacancies as they arise.

Job Description

The first step is to ensure there is a complete and concise description of the duties involved in the performance of a particular job. This document speaks directly to an employee about the specifics of her or his job. For this reason, a well-written job description can contribute to employee motivation and be an effective tool in the supervision of an individual employee.

Job descriptions serve as important mechanisms for reducing uncertainty, and in some cases conflict, for staff members. The document should be in tune with the centre's philosophy, and should include:

- *job title*—a simple description of the nature of the job
- *accountability*—to whom the person reports
- *job summary*—a brief description highlighting the general characteristics of the position. This summary is often quoted to job applicants.
- *job requirements*—education, experience, skills, personal qualities. Qualifications may be determined by the licensing standards and by union contracts.
- *responsibilities*—a more detailed statement of what duties the job entails. This section lists major tasks for which the employer tends to hold the employee accountable.
- *salary and benefit schedule*—the range of pay for the position
- *work schedule*—start date, hours of work

Once the job description is completed, the supervisor should meet with existing staff and review their skills and strengths as a team. This gives everyone an opportunity to have input into the recruitment process and assess what skills might complement the team, thus defining new job requirements that will help enhance the overall program.

A supervisor wants to develop a team that works together with a shared philosophy, where each member supports and complements the others. This not only provides a richer program for the children, but also provides opportunities for in-service training where staff can share their expertise and skills with one another.

A job description gives the broad outline of a position's responsibilities and relationship to other positions. Although it should not be restrictive, a job description should be specific enough to measure performance and give staff a clear outline of their responsibilities. In fact, it is usually a fairly general document that leaves room for more specific requirements that can be included in a job posting. For example, a job description might state that the candidate should be able to plan, prepare, and implement an overall development curriculum for toddlers. A sample job description is included in the appendices to this chapter.

Considerations in recruiting employees

Administrators should recruit early childhood educators who reflect the ethnic, cultural, and linguistic diversity of the families served. A professional must be prepared to meet the children's diverse developmental, cultural, linguistic, and educational needs. Staff who speak more than one language and who are culturally knowledgeable are an invaluable resource. In addition, a staff member should have an understanding of sociocultural and economic issues pertaining to a particular community. This knowledge can be used to support the family in the use and development of the child's home language and in the acquisition of English and/or French as a second language.

A second consideration in recruitment is gender. Some parents prefer programs with male caregivers because they want their children to have positive male role models. The report *Caring for a living* (Canadian Day Care Advocacy Association and the Canadian Child (Day) Care Federation (1992)) identifies that fewer than 2% of early childhood education staff are male. Part of this situation stems from societal beliefs that women have a natural ability to nurture children and that men do not have this instinct. Male staff can fill a special role for young children who grow up in single parent homes without a father figure. Yet men leave the field of ECCE at a greater rate than women. Some male caregivers reported that they were subject to subtle prejudicial attitudes from parents, female coworkers, and administrators. Misconceptions about men who work in early childhood settings include stereotypes: men may get romantically involved with coworkers; they are naturally athletic, able to repair anything mechanical, and lift heavy objects. There is a need for staff to examine individual attitudes and help increase parental awareness of the value of male staff members. It is most likely that economic reasons prevent men from entering the field of ECCE or cause them to leave more readily. Poor wages continue to be a pivotal factor affecting recruitment of desirable males and females.

Advertising and interviewing

The next task is to find a candidate who meets the identified requirements. A good match is critical, when you consider the time it will take for a new staff member to get to know the children, parents, coworkers, and the overall operation. Staff changes are very unsettling to children. If you hire someone and they don't work out, you will have spent a good deal of time and energy only to begin the process over again.

Post the job internally to ensure that present staff know about it and have a chance to apply. They shouldn't have to hear about a position from outside, and they may know of a good candidate to recommend. Many desirable candidates can be drawn from those who have completed student placements with the program or are currently working as casual staff.

Determine the interviewing team before the applications are reviewed. In non-profit programs, involve the board of directors (specifically parents), by getting one or two members to be part of the team. Many supervisors use a four-step process for hiring. The initial screening of résumés against the identified requirements and the first interviews narrow the

Children need nurturing male role models.

field, by determining how well the candidates' qualifications parallel the program's needs. In the second stage, several candidates are invited to participate individually in the playroom for a minimum of two hours, to allow the director and/or staff to observe their skills in interacting with children and with other staff. The third stage begins when staff, parents, and director discuss what they observed, and fourthly a follow-up session is held with the candidate to discuss and clarify observations.

It is critical to involve the staff member who will be working most closely with the new person. This contributes to building a compatible team. His or her role can include reviewing résumés or applications, asking questions and/or taking notes during the interview, and observing a candidate's playroom interaction style. A staff member who participates in selecting a candidate is likely to be more eager in facilitating the new member's integration into the staff team.

Finally the supervisor, along with the board or owner, makes the decision to hire. In a case where there are two equally qualified applicants, an additional question-and-answer period may be necessary. In a unionized setting, there will be specific rules to observe with regard to internal candidates and seniority.

You will want to cover these areas when you are interviewing a candidate:

- education, skill, and experience related to the position
- salary, benefits, start date
- attitude, interpersonal skills
- knowledge and understanding of child development
- ability to plan a developmentally appropriate curriculum
- methods used for guiding and supporting children's behaviour
- evidence of problem-solving strategies and conflict resolution style
- methods suggested for involving parents in the centre
- commitment to professional development

It is important that all applicants be asked the same questions. In addition, the interviewing team must be aware of human rights legislation, and know which questions are not permitted. Some programs adhere to equity hiring practices, where preference is given to qualified candidates who are a visible minority, aboriginal, have a disability, or, in the field of early childhood, to male applicants.

Time spent in planning a thoughtful and thorough interview process will ensure that both your interviewing team and the candidate have ample opportunity to exchange information in order to make a well-informed decision about job match. Remember, while you are interviewing a candidate, they are also interviewing your program. Effective hiring procedures result in greater compatibility between employee and program, a higher level of job satisfaction, and ultimately a higher quality program. Ensure that candidates provide references, and that you follow them up. Once employment is offered, Manitoba, British Columbia, Saskatchewan, and Ontario legislation requires a criminal reference check for all employees working directly with children. It is important to be cautious when hiring individuals who work closely with and influence young children. Children and staff can be safeguarded by screening out people who do not belong in the field.

Once you decide on a candidate, you present an offer that states the salary, the details of the benefit package, and terms of employment. This is usually documented in a written contract, which outlines: date of hiring, probationary period, evaluation process, pay for the period covered by the contract, benefits, and, where appropriate, the termination date as well as conditions for termination. This statement provides both the employer and employee with some security.

Staff orientation

Integrating new staff members takes commitment, determination, and patience. An effective recruiting and hiring process introduces new staff members to general aspects of the program such as philosophy, objectives, curriculum, program design, and level of parent involvement. A detailed orientation process is necessary when they start the job.

A handbook helps new employees become familiar with the administrative policies and procedures in the setting. Employees should be provided with a sense of the history and mission of the organization. At a minimum, personnel policies should open with a statement of the philosophy and goals of the program. It should provide information on:

- program philosophy and goals
- organizational structure—board of directors, staff reporting
- terms of employment—job descriptions, hiring procedures, compensation, discipline, termination, grievance procedures, resignation
- performance review process and probationary period
- benefits for employees—holidays, sick days, health benefits, insurance, staff development
- expectations of employees—behaviour guidance, reporting requirements, health and safety, parent/staff/child relations, attendance
- confidentiality

This list can be expanded to meet a setting's specific needs.

Current staff can help integrate new personnel by serving as mentors. Mentors can help provide a basic orientation on questions such as where to find the first aid kit. More importantly, mentors can introduce the new staff member to all employees. Mentors can be "safe havens" for new employees with lots of questions that they may feel foolish asking their supervisor. Other strategies include: pairing staff members for meetings or sending a group of staff to a workshop.

Allow for on-the-job orientation, where the new staff member can spend time discussing the staff manual and learning the specific responsibilities of the position. Strategies to assist parents in welcoming new staff include a profile in a newsletter or a welcoming introduction at a meeting. In the long run, time spent in carefully introducing new staff to the children, parents, and overall operation is time well spent. Remember, you are building a long-term relationship with your staff members. They will feel respected and valued by being part of this process.

Performance Appraisals and Staff Reviews

Many supervisors view performance appraisals as one of the most difficult, time-consuming, and emotionally challenging tasks they face. When they are carefully and consistently implemented, staff reviews can become the springboard for professional growth, program improvement, and staff motivation. Many programs use the job description as the basis for the performance appraisal (see sample performance tool in appendices to this chapter). The annual review provides an opportunity to reflect on staff performance, as well as to ensure the job description is updated to represent increased responsibilities. Supervisors can use the review process to identify strengths and needs, provide opportunities for addressing and reinforcing those areas, and develop the unique potential of each staff member.

In a supportive climate, the review process builds motivation, competence, and commitment to the organization. An effective staff development program can go a long way toward influencing and increasing professional development skills and self-esteem among early childhood educators.

All staff members need to know they are valued and respected for their work. It is a major challenge for a supervisor to create an atmosphere that encourages all staff to enhance their skills and participate in self-assessment, and that helps them plan experiences that result in better teaching. A supervisor plays a vital role by providing ongoing support for staff and by giving them open, honest, and regular feedback. While it is up to the individual to make the decision to change behaviour, this feedback on performance provides direction for change. It makes individuals aware of what they do well, and may help them improve their performance in areas that need attention. Such feedback need not be directive when it is based on an evaluation model where director and teacher work together to generate solutions and explore alternatives.

This appraisal model concentrates on a staff member's performance, rather than on her or his character traits—on how a person acts, rather than on some judgment of who they are. It is specific rather than global, and focuses on the future rather than dwelling on the past. Regular open communication will have a more enduring impact on an individual's self-esteem and overall performance than any specific resources that are provided to them. Jorde Bloom et al. (1991) provides a comprehensive look at supervision practices, within a perspective that acknowledges stages of employee development.

The administrator gives support and guidance to each staff member through performance appraisals.

The relationship between the supervisor and the caregiver is the most critical element in producing improved performance. The quality of the supervisor's skills, combined with the degree of trust between supervisor and staff, determines the success of the evaluation process. Effective supervisors use the appraisal process as an opportunity to promote trust and motivation in the program's most valued resource—its staff.

Evaluation can acknowledge superior performance, give feedback on the selection process, and provide a basis for career planning and professional development. By clarifying the expectations of the program, feedback is especially helpful to beginning teachers. The appraisal system used must fit the professional skills, maturity, and experience of the staff. A comprehensive approach to assessing staff performance will use a variety of formats to meet the needs of individual practitioners in each stage of their development. (Review the section in this chapter that discusses the four stages of professional growth.)

Staffing Policies and Communication with Staff

The following are some specific policies and procedures that are important for a supervisor to have in place. Equally important is effective two-way communication with staff through meetings and other structures.

Employee records

Provincial licensing guidelines usually require programs to maintain up-to-date records on each employee. Items often contained in the employee's file include:

* application materials such as transcripts, references, and résumé
* staff health records, which follow licensing requirements, including: a physical assessment stating that the individual is free from communicable diseases; a negative tuberculin test or a follow-up on a positive one; an immunization record. These should be updated at least every two years. Any on-the-job injuries should be documented, along with the treatment given. Records of frequent absences due to illnesses should also be included.
* employment record, including start date, leaves, salary levels, termination
* performance appraisal records
* disciplinary incidents documented as per personnel policies

Leave policies

A program's leave policy is intended to fulfill an employee's need for time off in a way that maintains a consistent staffing pattern. Among the types of leave policies an employer should consider are: vacation time, sick leave, personal leave, parental leave, leave without pay, bereavement leave, and leave for jury duty. It is important that policies reflect applicable federal and provincial/territorial labour laws. The federal government provides maternity and parental leave under the newly named Employment Insurance Program, but leave from employment is governed by provincial legislation. Programs may have a great deal of latitude in the development of some policy areas, while legal conditions apply in certain areas, such as maternity leave, or jury duty.

Grievance procedures

Close contact with each employee, periodic scheduled evaluations and immediate feedback can prevent grievances. Dealing with situations early can mean easier and quicker solutions to problems. An astute administrator can recognize signs of dissatisfaction and should immediately set out to identify its cause.

At the heart of every grievance procedure is the fundamental question about the rights and responsibilities of employment. A grievance procedure is a written statement informing employees that they have the right to express complaints and a right to expect the employer to review and respond to the complaint. One area of concern is the interpretation of personnel policies. No matter how clearly policies are written, there are always situations that do not fit the existing policies and will require a judgment call. Secondly, there may be an employee–supervisor conflict. A grievance procedure explains how an employee can appeal a decision or action of a supervisor to a higher level in the organization. Generally, if an employee is not satisfied with an administrator's decision, the employee may appeal to the board of directors or owner.

The first step in resolving a situation is to speak directly to the person involved. Most problems can be solved this way. The next step is to contact the supervisor. All involved have the right to see that grievances reach a logical conclusion.

Staff meetings

There are numerous ways in which staff can communicate, and one of the most critical is the staff meeting. In most organizations, workers spend considerable time in meetings of one kind or another. Yet despite their importance to the functioning of the environment, few staff speak favourably about meetings. They often view them as a burden and a waste of time. In early childhood programs, they are the primary vehicle for decision making and problem solving. Meetings with staff should be held as often as it is productive. It is essential to plan each meeting and create an agenda. Determine what is to be accomplished (solve problems, receive reports, plan strategies, give direction to or provide an opportunity to develop staff skills, clarify issues, share information). Circulate the agenda to the staff ahead of time so they can make a meaningful contribution to the meeting.

There are no ideal meeting times that meet the needs of every setting. The time and frequency of meetings vary depending on the amount of business to be carried out. It may be better to schedule weekly or biweekly meetings that are brief and productive than to make them longer and less frequent. It is important that meetings start and end on schedule. Good time management is important to enable as much as possible to be accomplished. Productive meetings not only contribute to a sense of accomplishment, but they can also serve to promote cooperation and feelings of collegiality. Follow up the meeting with brief notes on topics, decisions and any action to be taken. These notes provide clarification, are helpful for future reference, and inform those who were absent. There are tools to assess the effectiveness of staff meetings—see Jorde Bloom et al. (1991).

Staffing concerns

From time to time situations occur that need to be resolved. The areas tend to cluster around a few issues: concerns about coworkers who make the job difficult, or are perceived to lower the program quality because of poor teaching skills; problems with staff or volunteers who are unprofessional; or staff concern that the supervisor does not manage people effectively.

Solving problems is hard. Rarely does one quick, easy answer suffice. Often the problem is complex and multifaceted. The more severe the problem, the more complex, time-consuming, and difficult the solution. In most cases, you may have to use an individualized approach and be persistent.

However, every problem does have a solution. Requesting an individual meeting with the person involved to discuss concerns and problems is an important first step. In order to prevent problems, it is essential to establish positive relations with coworkers and to treat them with respect. Work with your supervisor to develop personal goals to strengthen interpersonal skills. There are some very helpful suggestions to aid staff in resolving concerns in Saifer's *Practical solutions to practically every problem: The early childhood teacher's manual* (1990).

Termination

There must be just cause and due process in the termination of an employee. Conditions for termination should be clearly defined in the employee handbook. Periodic reviews with staff can provide an opportunity to deal with problems before they become too severe. Discipline involves both written and verbal action. The written documentation may eventually lead to termination. The employee should be informed of the infraction, given warning, and told the consequences of continued unsatisfactory performance. The supervisor should consider the evidence carefully, determine the appropriate consequences, and be prepared to follow through if the infraction reoccurs.

The supervisor should inform their superior of the problem and the intended actions. The board of directors or the owner may interview the employee. All information is recorded and kept, and each party should have a copy of it.

Ensuring the Work Environment Meets Staff Needs

Early childhood education is both physically and emotionally demanding. The supervisor is responsible for making sure policies, practices, the physical environment, and organizational values are responsive to staff needs.

Children need environments where they feel secure and free from anxiety. Minimal staff turnover and stable staff–child groupings build security for the children and allow for consistent application of the program philosophy. High staff turnover adversely affects both the children and staff morale, which in turn further affects the children and their program.

A number of surveys, such as Whitebrook et al. (1990) and *Caring for a living* (Canadian Day Care Advocacy Association and the Canadian Child (Day) Care Federation 1992), as well as current studies, show that early childhood educators stay in the field longest when they have appropriate training, wages commensurate with their training, and good working conditions.

Employees in early childhood environments are entitled to the same legal rights as other workers. Both federal and provincial laws protect workers with respect to minimum wage, overtime pay, and a variety of working conditions. Supervisors, owners, and boards of directors must be aware of these laws and ensure their personnel policies reflect current legislation.

A good deal of attention in the field has focused on how the physical environment of early childhood settings can be made responsive to children, but little attention has been paid to adult needs. The general layout and design of space can help or hinder staff in carrying out their jobs, and can powerfully influence moods and attitudes. Staff must have the proper equipment, materials, and resources to do their work effectively. This aspect of early childhood settings is discussed in detail in Chapter 5, "Physical Environments."

The supervisor must be concerned with potential health hazards in the workplace. The Canadian Pediatric Society (1997) cites the following health hazards in early childhood education: increased risk of illness; toxic substances in art supplies and cleaning agents; back problems from heavy lifting and frequent bending; physical strain from using furniture in an environment designed for children; poor lighting; high noise levels; and stress. Another major health hazard comes from the common tendency among early childhood educators to ignore their own health needs, because they lack extended health benefits and time off, and because they feel responsible for meeting children's needs first.

With the support of the board of directors, the program supervisor is responsible for creating a program environment sensitive to the needs of adults as well as children. These issues can be addressed by:

- ensuring that personnel policies are responsive to staff needs, including such features as a staff health plan
- creating a positive healthful environment
- assisting staff in looking after their own health needs

Some of these are issues with no easy, short-term solution. Chapter 11 addresses the need for child care practitioners to advocate on their own behalf, in order to increase public awareness and help gain access to necessary resources.

In *Improving the quality of work life* (1986), Jorde Bloom identifies a number of factors affecting the quality of the work environment and ultimately the quality of care. These factors include the amount of support received from the supervisor, opportunities for professional development, clarity of job expectations, an equitable reward system, and the physical work environment.

Over the past decade, considerable energy has been devoted to the improvement of wages and working conditions in early childhood settings. Many early childhood educators are underpaid and feel they are undervalued by society. But even recognizing this underlying dissatisfaction, they can still feel that their own program's policies are equitable and just. It is essential for administrators to have systems in place to ensure that pay, job security, and promotion policies are fairly administered and communicated to all staff.

The Role of Unions

As early childhood educators experience the frustration of fighting individually for improved wages and working conditions, questions often emerge about representation of the field by unions, federations, or professional associations. Who should perform this function for early childhood educators is emerging as a key question.

While wages, benefits, and hours are the items most frequently associated with collective agreements, they also cover many other important issues such as: personnel policies, grievance and hiring procedures, performance review and promotion systems, provision for in-service training, breaks, and input into program decision making.

These non-salary benefits are frequently as important to job satisfaction as the salary benefits are. They can be critical in helping staff provide better services. For example, input into a centre's decision-making process can be an important guarantee in a contract. Members of

Services Employees International Union (SEIU) Local 299, in Moose Jaw, Saskatchewan, negotiated a provision guaranteeing that their employer would meet with them once a month to evaluate concerns affecting the quality of care in the centre. Examples of other innovative contract provisions include a staff room "for the use and enjoyment of employees," and reimbursement for the cost of cleaning and shampoo occasioned by an outbreak of lice at the centre.

Many staff recognize the union or professional association as a long-term political ally that can assist early childhood educators in advocating for better funding and expanded services. The strength and unity of representation can be used to influence government funding for child care.

For staff who are employed by corporate child care chains, unions have been quick to point out organizations operating with huge profit margins and thus well able to increase staff wages without raising parent fees.

Only a small percentage of the child care workforce is unionized. The study *Caring for a living* found that 20% of staff across Canada were unionized. The province with the highest rate of unionization was Quebec, with 30%. There were no unionized staff in New Brunswick, Yukon, or Northwest Territories at the time of data collection. The diverse and isolated nature of the child care delivery system, coupled with an unusually high turnover rate, has worked against the development of successful organizing campaigns. *Taking matters into our own hands*, by the Child Care Employee Project (1990), provides some insightful information on the role of unions.

IN CONCLUSION

Administrators need knowledgeable, skillful, and caring staff to provide responsive care to young children and families. This chapter details the director's roles and responsibilities in facilitating each staff person's growth as a professional. This requires fair and effective opportunities for professional growth, supervision, and evaluation. Employers must accommodate the individual characteristics and developmental stages of each employee. Professionals in early childhood programs believe in and support a code of ethics as well as the importance of keeping current. Early childhood professionals share the responsibility to identify ways to continually improve their practice with children and families.

ACTIVITIES

1. Consider any negative responses you have had from others about your decision to become an early childhood educator. How do you feel about these attitudes? Identify strategies to respond to these opinions.

2. Invite a male caregiver in your community to the class to discuss his experiences and any prejudice he has encountered.

3. Write a job description to be placed in a newspaper for one of the following positions:
   * toddler teacher for centre-based care
   * staff for school-age program
   * home care provider

   Review to assess whether the aspects listed in the sample job description (Appendix A) have been adequately covered.

4. Obtain a copy of the Directory of Canadian Child Care Contacts published by the Canadian Child Care Federation through the Web site **www.cfc-efc.ca/cccf**. Review the list of groups in your

area, and identify which ones you want to learn more about. Contact them and arrange to attend a meeting and/or subscribe to their newsletter.

5. Talk to some early childhood educators about the aspects of their job that are the most satisfying. What is the least satisfying, and what can they do about it? Compare their responses to your own goals and expectations.

6. Develop three questions that could be used when interviewing an applicant.

7. What are the advantages of belonging to a professional early childhood organization? Review several issues of *Interaction* to gain a sense of what organizations such as the Canadian Child Care Federation have to offer.

REVIEW QUESTIONS

1. Describe two methods of staff development.

2. Identify the four stages of development as labeled by Katz and others.

3. What is a grievance process?

4. Name three components that should be included in an orientation process.

5. Who should be included in the hiring process?

FURTHER READING

Jorde Bloom, P., M. Sheerer, and J. Britz (1991). *Blueprint for action: Achieving center-based change through staff development*. Minnesota: New Horizons.

Caruso, J. and M. Fawcett (1986). *Supervision in early childhood education: A developmental perspective*. New York: Teacher's College Press.

Doherty, G., D. Lero, H. Goelman, A. LaGrange, and J. Tougas (2000). *You Bet I Care*. A Canada-wide study on wages, working conditions and practices in child care centres, University of Guelph.

Spodek, B., O. Saracho and D. Peters (eds.) (1988). *Professionalism and the early childhood practitioner*. Columbia University: Teacher's College Press.

APPENDIX A: SAMPLE JOB DESCRIPTION

Title: Early Childhood Educator
Reports to: Supervisor
Responsible for: a group of 16 three-year-olds in cooperation with one other early childhood educator

Major Responsibilities

Cooperate and take an active role in planning and carrying out an education program for children from three to four years of age. Communication with other staff and the parents of the children is a major area of responsibility.

Representative Responsibilities

1. Provides a warm, nurturing environment where children are valued and respected with emphasis on self-esteem, security, choice making, acceptance of the individual, independence, and trust.

2. Plans, prepares, and implements a curriculum based on developmentally appropriate and anti-bias practices that includes fine and gross motor activities, cognitive, receptive and expressive language, social-emotional and self-help skills, both indoors and outdoors.

3. Supervises and educates children in nourishment routines.

4. Observes and assesses the development of individual children.

5. Supervises children in rest periods.

6. Arranges and supervises all transition periods.

7. Reports unusual situations, such as allergies, accidents, parental requests and concerns, or behavioural irregularities to the supervisor.

8. Provides or arranges for first aid in case of emergencies.

9. Attends, shares information, and participates in staff meetings in order to discuss the implementation of the overall program, and works with individual children and their families.

10. Completes intake interviews, initiates the sharing of information with parents on a regular basis, plans and attends parent interviews and parent evenings, and acts as a resource to parents in problem-solving situations.

11. Actively takes responsibility for personal and professional growth and development.

APPENDIX B: SAMPLE EARLY CHILDHOOD STAFF PERFORMANCE APPRAISAL

Employee: _____ Date: _____

Classification: _____

Supervisor: _____

Type of Review: Three month   Six month   Annual

The purpose of the appraisal is to provide employees with some measure of how well they are performing in their current job, and to identify any training/development requirements. Comments should include whether they meet or exceed expectations, or need improvement. Please give specific examples to support your ratings.

Review position description form and revise if necessary. Identify status.

KEY JOB AREAS	PERFORMANCE INDICATORS	COMMENTS
Demonstrates positive human qualities with children	• provides warm, nurturing environment • values and respects children • fosters child's self-esteem, sense of security, and trust • encourages choice making and independence	
Plans, prepares, and implements a developmentally appropriate curriculum	• plans and posts curriculum for specific ages of the children • has resources readily available • carries out planned curriculum for fine and gross motor, receptive and expressive language, social, emotional, cognitive, and self-help skills, both indoors and outdoors • supervises and educates children in nourishment routines, rest periods, and all transitions	
Reports unusual situations to team leader	• reports unusual situations, such as allergies, accidents, parent requests or concerns, and behavioural irregularities to team leader • provides or arranges for first aid in case of emergencies	

KEY JOB AREAS	PERFORMANCE INDICATORS	COMMENTS
Functions as team member	• respects colleagues • resolves conflicts with children, parents, and coworkers • shares resources, skills, and materials	
Supports parental involvement	• initiates the sharing of information with parents on a regular basis • acts as a resource to parents in problem-solving situations • supports and maintains rights of parents as able • completes intake interview and attends parent evening	
Performs professionally	• is punctual • ensures confidentiality • fulfills responsibility • seeks and obtains directions and assistance when needed • acts on previously established objectives • maintains requirements of legislation	

APPENDIX C: CANADIAN CHILD CARE FEDERATION DRAFT CODE OF ETHICS

The Principles of the Code

• Child care practitioners promote the health and well-being of all children.

• Child care practitioners enable children to participate to their full potential in environments carefully planned to serve individual needs and to facilitate the child's progress in social, emotional, physical and cognitive areas of development.

• Child care practitioners demonstrate their caring for all children in all aspects of their practice.

• Child care practitioners work in partnership with parents, recognizing that parents have primary responsibility for the care of their children, valuing their commitment to the children and supporting them in meeting their responsibilities to their children.

• Child care practitioners work in partnership with colleagues and other service providers in the community to support the well-being of children and their families.

• Child care practitioners work in ways that enhance human dignity in trusting, caring and cooperative relationships that respect the worth and uniqueness of the individual.

• Child care practitioners pursue, on an ongoing basis, the knowledge, skills and self-awareness needed to be professionally competent.

• Child care practitioners demonstrate integrity in all of their professional relationships.

LEADERSHIP STYLES AND CHALLENGES

Leadership skills are fundamental to the supervisor's success and the quality of the environment for both children and staff, and need to be included in the study of the administration of early childhood settings. This chapter will discuss:

- *What is leadership?*
- *Leadership styles*
- *Shared leadership*
- *Decision making in a collaborative environment*

Earlier chapters have sketched the varied responsibilities of the supervisor, and pointed to some of the roles she or he fills in an early childhood setting. Among those roles, leadership is central. In this role, the supervisor:

- functions as the point of contact between the board of directors and the staff, interpreting the board's directions to the staff and the staff's concerns to the board
- provides advice to the board or the owner, helps to focus their decisions when necessary, and makes sure they are kept informed of anything of note that occurs at the setting
- works with board and staff to develop a philosophy statement that reflects the collective wisdom and values of those involved in its development
- works with board and staff to ensure that policies and procedures for the centre are developed and adhered to

- guides the relationship between the centre and the external community
- is responsible for ensuring the development and implementation of a high quality program, with a developmentally appropriate curriculum reflecting the cultural diversity of children and their families
- enlists others to develop a shared vision for the future that guides the work of the staff
- encourages staff to experiment, to try new activities, and to learn from subsequent successes and mistakes.

Each of these responsibilities represents a different aspect of a supervisor's position. A supervisor's success in each area depends on his or her ability to bring individuals together and motivate them to work toward common goals in the effective operation of the setting.

WHAT IS LEADERSHIP?

According to Johnson and Johnson (1991), leadership is "the art of ensuring that group members work together with the least friction and most cooperation." This definition implies that leadership is a skill that people can learn, through experience and practice. It is a skill that involves interacting effectively with other people, influencing how they interact with one another, and helping them work together toward common goals. Leadership is the art of influencing the common work of a group so that it performs most productively. It depends on sharing ideas and information in an atmosphere of mutual respect.

In this definition, leadership means moving forward. Viewed in this way, leaders are catalysts for change.

Such a discussion of leadership in the abstract becomes useful when it is placed into the context of our own personal experience. Think of people you have encountered who were leaders—what qualities did they share, and how did they differ? How did they come to be in positions of leadership? Do you think some of them were "born leaders," or is leadership a skill people can learn?

Several theories provide useful frameworks for thinking about leadership. We will look briefly at three general theories of leadership, and then we will consider different leadership styles.

Trait Theories

Is leadership an inherited skill? Are leaders people who are born with a natural ability to lead others? Throughout history, this has been a common belief—kings and queens, for example, were seen as people divinely endowed with an ability to lead.

In the last few years, a number of people have undertaken studies designed to identify personal attributes and abilities that make people stand out as natural leaders. The belief that there are such identifiable qualities or character traits is known as trait theory. Trait theory tends to be static—if some people are born leaders and some are not, then you either have it, or you don't. According to this theory, if you weren't born a leader, there's not much you can do about it.

The findings of these recent studies have not supported the belief that leadership is based on inherent traits. There seems to be no definitive set of personality characteristics or unique behaviours that makes someone a leader. Some leaders are charismatic, outgoing individuals who inspire others to follow them; others are relatively quiet types, who set goals and methodically set out to accomplish them. Leadership seems to depend on situation more than it does on personality.

Influence Theory

Another set of theories defines leadership as the balance of "influence" in a group. The leader is the one who holds this balance of influence, the one to whom others look for comment or direction.

Unlike trait theory, this is a dynamic theory—it considers how you can work to develop leadership abilities. It also has the advantage of considering leaders in the context of the group they lead. It understands leadership as a reciprocal relationship—the leader influences the group because the group is prepared to be influenced by her or him. However, this theory is limited in how far it can be used to analyze a given situation, or in the guidance it gives someone in a leadership position who wants to know how best to act.

Situational Theories

The most useful way of looking at the question is through theories that relate leadership skills to the particular situation they are used in. Not only is it generally agreed that there is no such thing as inherent leadership skill, it appears that no one set of leadership skills will work in every situation. Different situations require different leadership skills.

One of the best known leadership studies, by Hersey and Blanchard (1977), focused on the dynamics of situational leadership—that is, what it takes to be a leader in different situations. Two dimensions of leadership were studied: the extent to which the leader initiated task behaviour and gave the group direction; and relationship behaviour, the ways in which the leader provided support and guidance to individual members of the group.

The study found that different leaders tended to stress one of these elements of leadership over the other. Some focused on accomplishing tasks, while others paid more attention to providing emotional support to their staff. The study went on to find that the maturity of the group was the determining factor in deciding which particular combination of leadership skills was most effective. Generally speaking, groups who demonstrate a high level of individual maturity are more able to assume responsibility for their work, and respond well enough to a leadership style with a low emphasis on task accomplishment and a high level of emphasis on relationship. Groups with less maturity are less able to set their own goals or assume responsibility for their own behaviours, and in this case a combination of high task emphasis combined with low relationship emphasis results in the most effective leadership. The primary lesson to be drawn from this is that leadership style should be varied to fit the group.

Traditional Leadership Theories and Early Childhood Settings

For the most part, traditional theories of leadership originated in the business world and are of somewhat limited application to early childhood settings. Most of these theories are based on the premise that the leader is one individual in an organization, such as the president or CEO of a company. These theoretical frameworks do not include the concept of shared leadership as is presently practised or developing in many early childhood settings.

Another major difference is that corporations function primarily in a competitive rather than a collaborative mode, and survive by being better than their competitors. In this environment, cooperation is relatively unusual (although there are contemporary examples of collaboration within relatively new or reengineered organizations). Collaboration and cooperation are, however, the primary ethos of most early childhood settings. For the most part, supervisors and staff work as a team and promote cooperation, not competition, between children and one another.

Finally, theories of traditional leadership primarily apply to settings where employees work in a hierarchical organization and the goals of the organization are product-oriented. Early childhood settings, by contrast, are people- and process-oriented. Their goals are dynamic and much less rigidly defined, since they need to respond to both the diversity and the individual needs of the young children in the setting. The nature of an early childhood setting dictates a leadership paradigm that is fundamentally different from that of a business environment.

LEADERSHIP STYLES

Just as there are a number of theories about leadership, there are several ways of thinking about differences in leadership styles. You may have worked with someone in a leadership position who consistently focused on tasks. You may also have worked with someone who focused on the needs of the people they worked with. The distinction between styles that emphasize results and styles that emphasize relationship is a useful one in work situations. The appropriate style for a given situation depends on the group. Jorde Bloom et al. (1991) keep these distinctions, and add a third possibility halfway between, to give us three major leadership styles to consider:

- task-oriented
- people-oriented
- transactional

It is unlikely that any supervisor would fit entirely into one of these categories, but the three classes do provide a useful tool to examine how different leadership styles would work in an early childhood setting.

Task-oriented Style

A task-oriented supervisor focuses on achieving the stated goals and objectives of the program. Carrying out the centre's philosophy statement is central to her or his interactions with both staff and parents. This supervisor stresses the need to follow procedures regardless of the situation, and provides detailed expectations to staff through their job descriptions, the policy and procedures manual, and the philosophy statement.

Many supervisors are likely to display some of these behaviours some of the time. A supervisor who is at the extreme of being task-oriented will typically make decisions with little input from others. As the "control centre" for the program, she or he will provide considerable direction in the development of the program, and in its day-to-day operation.

A supervisor who is primarily task-oriented has little opportunity for involvement with the children at the centre, and wants to deal personally with all enquiries from parents and staff. When there is little or no collaboration with staff, the supervisor is likely to be seen as the "boss" rather than as a member of the team. This can alienate staff members, particularly those who are mature and experienced.

When staff are not part of the decision-making process, they cannot share responsibility for the success or failure of the program—this responsibility rests on the shoulders of the supervisor. The tighter the supervisor's control and the greater her or his individual responsibility, the greater the personal stress and the danger of eventual burnout.

People-oriented Style

A people-oriented supervisor focuses on the needs of staff, children, and parents, and pays less attention to giving specific direction for accomplishing specific tasks. While policies and procedures are always important, this supervisor is more likely to consider individual needs in his or her decisions. The majority of this supervisor's time involves attending to the relationships of people within the setting; enhancing the quality of these relationships is the primary goal.

Where an extreme task-oriented supervisor makes most of the decisions, an extreme people-oriented supervisor encourages staff to work autonomously. This supervisor is more likely to be viewed as a colleague, another member of the team. He or she is likely to be involved in the program, working directly with the children, who view her as another teacher. This supervisor has close involvement with parents, and is viewed by staff as a source of emotional support.

The potential negative consequence is that as the supervisor attends more to people and less to tasks, the program will tend to reflect the style and preferences of the individual teachers. This can result in a program that varies in the extent to which it reflects the centre's philosophy. An extreme people-oriented style may provide too little direction, and the program can become uneven or stagnate. Another possible outcome is that a strong-minded staff member will set the program direction, with many potential negative consequences.

Transactional Style

Both task- and people-oriented styles have strengths, and both show weaknesses when taken to extremes or applied in the wrong situation. In many ways, the transactional style represents a point midway between the two.

A transactional supervisor tends to balance the needs of the centre with the needs of staff and others. This is the most situational style—one where the supervisor can shift the balance according to the particular needs of the situation. In the words of Jorde Bloom et al. (1991), "Achieving both centre goals and maintaining high morale is important in this leadership style. This director is flexible and fair, recognizing that different situations may require a different emphasis on centre-wide needs or individual needs."

A transactional supervisor will adapt her or his style to fit each staff member's level of professional development, as outlined in the schema by Lillian Katz described in Chapter 6. She will provide different levels of support to teachers, according to their maturity and experience. For example, a staff member in Katz's first stage, "Survival," will require concrete strategies and ongoing support. The supervisor may ask a more experienced staff member to work with the "survivor" as a mentor, focusing on specific skill areas. On the other hand, a staff member at Stage 3, "Renewal," may require new challenges. Here a transactional supervisor could provide a new area of responsibility—perhaps asking the staff member to design a new parent involvement program, or to assume an administrative task.

For a transactional supervisor, staff morale and program goals are viewed as equally important, and each receives attention. Interactions with staff occur within the context of program needs. This supervisor views her or his role as meeting the staff's professional needs in order to empower them to be effective in their work with children and families. She or he shares control, but does not abdicate it. Neither boss nor team member, this supervisor can be thought of as team leader. A transactional supervisor works in a consultative manner with staff, sharing decision making so that staff share ownership of the program's success. She or he provides a clear framework for those decisions that need to be made, giving clear feedback to staff so they know what is expected of them and feel supported.

In the daily work of an early childhood setting, it is sometimes difficult for staff to know whether or not they have made a difference. When this is combined with a situation where staff have little control, job satisfaction suffers. On the other hand, when staff are empowered and have more control within clear parameters, job satisfaction increases, to the overall betterment of the program. In general, research indicates that job satisfaction is associated with a democratic style of leadership; satisfaction is highest in small interaction-oriented staff groups. A collaborative team approach, where the supervisor is team leader, is usually best.

Women and Leadership: An Additional Consideration

Most of the literature dealing with leadership could not be considered gender-neutral. Traditionally, the leader in most work environments has been male, and the research dealing with leadership reflects this bias.

Early childhood education is a profession dominated by women—fully 98% of the staff in Canadian early childhood settings are female. Publications such as Baines et al. (1991), Gilligan (1982), and Helgesen (1990) have examined the unique qualities of women in leadership roles, and provide interesting insights in a discussion of leadership styles.

Women more typically than men display a capacity for caring and emotional contact. This is a particular strength they bring to their work with others. In a leadership role, women tend not to focus exclusively on task or person, but rather on the relationships between people and their work. Women leaders tend to view their staff in a more holistic manner, and this shapes the kind of decisions they make and how they make them. The transactional style is particularly suited to the typical capacities of women.

SHARED LEADERSHIP

In most cases, early childhood settings are closely aligned with the constructs of systems theory as described in Peter Senge's book *The fifth discipline* (1990). Senge notes that in the new learning organization, the success of any one person is linked to the success of others, and leadership is shared.

The concept of shared leadership is not new. In settings that practise "total quality management" (TQM), problem solving is the shared responsibility of managers and employees, not any one individual. TQM is based on the premise that employees have the experience and skills needed to solve problems as they are encountered, and should be empowered to do so.

Margaret Wheatley relates the learnings from the new science, specifically quantum physics, to the importance of relationships in organizations, noting that "the more that [we] feel part of the organization, the more work gets done" (Wheatley 1992, 144). She goes on to note that as leaders are encouraged to focus on the importance of relationships with other staff, they face new challenges. Leaders need to include stakeholders and empower their colleagues. In settings where more traditional supervisory roles have been established, supervisors need to create more "leaderful" environments. In this context, leadership is not the sole domain of the supervisor but is a role that any staff may assume. Supervisors can encourage this by providing choices, developing competence, and offering concrete support to staff as they learn to assume this role.

There are numerous examples of shared leadership in early childhood settings. While the supervisor is responsible for the overall operation of the setting, staff are viewed as members of a team and work collaboratively to implement the philosophy of the setting. Success is not based in competition, but rather in cooperation. The quality of the care and education provided is directly related to the degree to which the supervisor and staff work collaboratively, sharing decision making.

Working toward Shared Leadership

Shared leadership is not easily established. It requires both shared commitment and shared vision. The supervisor must work together with staff to set the stage and develop skills that are required to effect this environment.

This model of leadership requires more resources than settings in which leadership is assumed by one individual. Consultation and collaboration require skill and time. For this model to work, members of the early childhood team need to learn how to communicate effectively, and how to negotiate and resolve conflict. Opportunities for in-service leadership training that focuses on these skills, as well as on problem solving and consensus building, must be provided.

As discussed in Chapter 10, early childhood settings are most effective when parents are viewed as partners in nurturing the growth and development of young children. This perspective is not new; the ethos of consultation and collaboration characterizes most early childhood settings. Staff and parents share knowledge and responsibility based on the common goal of providing high quality early childhood education. With this end in mind, collaboration is essential.

DECISION MAKING IN A COLLABORATIVE ENVIRONMENT

Even within a collaborative setting, there are different ways of arriving at decisions:

- by consensus
- by majority vote
- by authority, on the basis of position and status
- by expert opinion, on the basis of specific knowledge

Group decision making that involves reaching consensus is preferable in most instances, but each method has its use depending on the particular circumstances. A good supervisor adapts leadership style to fit the staff members and their varying stages of development. She or he will work with the staff and board of directors to find the approach that best fits the needs of the group.

Sharing the responsibility for decision making with staff is essential in building a work environment characterized by trust and respect. The supervisor needs to ensure that staff are involved in decisions regarding resource allocation, program planning, parent involvement, policies and procedures, development of a philosophy statement, etc. The supervisor will need to structure time for the staff to meet and work as a group. In group decision making, meetings may not always involve the entire staff. Some tasks may be assumed by ad hoc groups who then bring recommendations back to the larger group.

In addition, staff will need to be provided with the opportunity to assume leadership roles. As they begin to assume responsibility for tasks, the supervisor should support them in this new role, encouraging them to experiment and to view mistakes as an opportunity to learn and grow.

Working collaboratively is not without its challenges—in many ways, it is easier for a supervisor to make decisions without consultation. It is important therefore to examine the advantages and disadvantages of group decision making.

Common Benefits of Collaborative Decision Making

Collaborative decision making can:

- motivate
- reduce the risk of relying on the skill of one person
- increase the numbers of options available for a decision
- generate greater levels of creativity
- enable people to learn more about each other's roles and to be more empathetic, cooperative, and effective when dealing with colleagues in the future
- generate commitment to successful implementation

Potential Risks of Collaborative Decision Making

Unless carried out effectively, collaborative leadership can:

- result in unclear lines of responsibility
- unnecessarily slow down decision making
- result in compromise
- produce less focused decisions

Collaborative decision making requires maturity. Members need to get outside their own individual needs and consider one another's perspectives. At the same time, a supervisor has to be aware of barriers that limit collaboration or make it impossible. Collaboration requires time, effort, creative thinking, and open-mindedness. The facilitator who leads the decision needs to establish a process that participants can trust. Excellent communication skills, specifically listening, summarizing, and conflict resolution skills, are fundamental to the success of the process. Differences in power among group members, whether real or perceived, may prevent the group from functioning effectively. In a unionized setting, there may be difficulties when the supervisor is not a member of the bargaining unit. Some individuals may feel that their loyalties conflict.

Building genuine consensus does not require unanimity. It does require people with a common objective, willing to find common ground and practical solutions that all members can live with.

SHARED VISION

"When people truly share a vision, they are connected, bound together by a common aspiration" (Senge 1990, 206).

A shared vision creates a common identity. It is especially important given the complexity of the world we live in, the amount of information, and the rapid pace of change. Rather than generating rules or policies for every new situation, a shared vision provides a reference point for decision making. It needs to be simply stated so that everyone can use the vision to guide their behaviour and decisions. Shared vision generates commitment, not compliance.

Developing a shared vision takes time. It emerges through a process of ongoing dialogue. Individuals need to be free to express their visions and listen to those of others. As individuals engage in this dialogue, new insights emerge. The synergy of sharing dreams shapes the group's vision.

The supervisor needs to first work with staff and the board of directors to develop a shared vision for the centre. He or she may help the board focus its vision of a successful centre.

The vision should represent a set of mission statements or guiding principles that form the foundation for the development of a philosophy statement. As discussed in Chapter 3, the philosophy statement is the blueprint for the work of early childhood educators. Commitment to a shared vision connects each individual to the centre. While it takes time, achieving consensus is the best method for producing a sound philosophy statement.

Some early childhood supervisors find it difficult to work collaboratively, because they feel it restricts their autonomy. But effective leadership should not require a choice between autonomy and collaboration. It is important to provide leadership by facilitating group work. This will require administrative support, such as ensuring that staff has time made available. In-service for the team may be needed.

The results of working collaboratively are not always immediate, and everyone will at times experience frustration with the process, but the long-term benefits are worth the investment of time and resources.

Leadership Needs Leadership

A supervisor's job can be lonely. The supervisor has unique responsibilities in the program—she or he is always meeting the needs of others, but the amount of support she can receive back from staff is limited.

However, supervisors can get the support they need from their own network of peers. This network can be built through personal friendships, and by involvement in professional development sessions and professional and advocacy groups that meet regularly. These groups can provide professional support through discussions and workshops, and by providing a place to make informal contacts. In addition, the journal *Child Care Information Exchange* is a good resource and contains a number of articles designed to address the specific needs of supervisors of early childhood settings. The board of directors also can be a great source of support, providing the supervisor with both allies and resources in the work toward a common goal.

A good supervisor needs such a wide range of skills that she or he must learn to accept her or his own shortcomings—no one has equal skills in all areas. The supervisor's own professional development needs must be adequately looked after. Even so, time is limited and she or he can't do everything—a supervisor needs to be familiar with every aspect of the program, but doesn't need to take part equally in everything. Ultimately, supervisors need to be able to trust the skills of each member of the early childhood team and know how to create time for themselves.

IN CONCLUSION

A supervisor has varied responsibilities and roles within an early childhood setting. Among these roles, leadership is central. The effective operation of the centre reflects her or his ability to bring individuals together and motivate them toward common goals.

There are a number of different theories of leadership. Traditional theories of leadership have somewhat limited application to early childhood settings, given the collaborative, consultative culture within most settings.

Similarly, there are different leadership styles: some groups profit most from a style that emphasizes results, others from a style that focuses on relationships. No one set of leadership skills works well in every situation—different situations require different skills.

Shared leadership is a common practice in many early childhood settings. While the supervisor assumes overall responsibility for the setting, staff work collaboratively as a team to implement the philosophy of the setting, often assuming responsibility for specific tasks and projects.

Decision making by consensus has both advantages and disadvantages. While it enables staff to shape decisions and share ownership for the outcomes, consultation and collaboration require skill and time.

ACTIVITIES

1. Write a paragraph describing a director interacting with his or her staff, and try to depict one of the leadership styles in the text. Exchange your description with a classmate's, and see if she or he can work out which leadership style you intended.

2. Consider your own personal style and write a paragraph about the kind of leader you think you are, with another on the kind you would like to become. The Appendix to this chapter is a good resource for this activity.

3. Following the suggestions given in this chapter, think of three people in leadership roles who you have encountered: how were they similar, and how did they differ? How did they come to be leaders? Write a brief description of each person (you don't need to use their real names), and decide which leadership style they most closely follow. Which of them was effective, which was not, and why?

4. What style of decision making do you prefer and feel most comfortable with? Why?

5. Assess the leadership style needed by various staff in your centre.

6. Using the assessment tools in the Appendix, taken from Paula Jorde Bloom's *Blueprint for action,* review the leadership style of the supervisor at your centre.

REVIEW QUESTIONS

1. Define leadership.

2. Identify and describe three theories of leadership.

3. Compare and contrast two of these theories of leadership.

4. Identify and describe three different leadership styles.

5. When is a task-oriented leadership style most effective? Provide an example.

6. In what situations is a people-oriented leadership style most effective? Provide a rationale for your response.

7. Describe shared leadership. What are the benefits of this approach in an early childhood setting?

8. Identify three different methods of decision making.

9. Describe the advantages and disadvantages of decision making by consensus.

FURTHER READING

Baines, Carol, Patricia Evans, and Sheila Neysmith (1991). *Women's caring: Feminist perspectives on social welfare.* Toronto: McClelland & Stewart.

Bennis, W. (1989). *On becoming a leader.* New York: Addison-Wesley.

Caruso, J.J. and M.T. Fawcett (1986). *Supervision in early childhood education: A developmental perspective.* New York: Teacher's College Press.

Covey, S. (1992). *Principle-centred leadership.* New York: Fireside.

Gilligan, Carol (1982). *In a different voice.* Boston: Harvard University Press.

Helgesen, S. (1990). *Female advantage: Women's ways of leadership.* New York: Doubleday.

Johnson, D.W. and F.P. Johnson (1991). *Joining together: Group theory and group skills.* Boston: Allyn and Bacon.

Jorde Bloom, P., M. Sheerer, and J. Britz (1991). *Blueprint for action: Achieving center-based change through staff development.* Mt. Rainier, MD: Gryphon House.

Jorde Bloom, P. (1995, May). "Shared decision-making: the centerpiece of participatory management." *Young Children,* 55–60.

Kagan, S. (1994, July). "Leadership: Rethinking it—making it happen." *Young Children,* 50–54.

Kotter, J.P. (1990). *A force for change: How leadership differs from management.* New York: Free Press.

Morgan, G. (1997). *Imaginization: New mindsets for seeing, organizing and managing.* San Francisco, CA: Berret-Koehler.

Neugebauer, R. (1985). "Are you an effective leader?" *Child Care Information Exchange,* 45–50.

Senge, P.M. (1990). *The fifth discipline: The art and practice of learning organizations.* New York: Doubleday.

Senge, P.M. et al. (1999). *The dance of change: The challenges of sustaining momentum in learning organizations.* New York: Doubleday.

APPENDIX: LEADERSHIP STYLE QUESTIONNAIRE

This questionnaire is taken from Jorde Bloom, Sheerer, and Britz's *Blueprint for action: Achieving center-based change through staff development.*

Rationale

The leadership style of the director of a child care centre is perhaps the most potent factor influencing organizational effectiveness. The director must create an environment based on mutual respect in which individuals work together to accomplish collective goals. The success of this endeavour rests in large part on the director's ability to balance organizational needs with individual needs. The research in this area suggests that leaders who head the most effective organizations tend to be those who apply a transactional leadership style—an ability to adjust their style to the demands of each situation so that both organizational needs and individual needs are met.

Part I of this assessment tool was adapted from the work of Blake and Mouton (1969), Getzels and Guba (1957), Giammatteo (1975), Hersey and Blanchard (1982), and Reddin

(1970). It assesses three different leadership styles: the task-oriented style emphasizing organizational needs; the people-oriented style focusing on people and their individual needs; and the transactional style stressing an appropriate emphasis on both the centre's needs and the individual worker's needs depending on the situation. Part II of Assessment Tool #4 was developed by Exchange Press (Neugebauer 1990). It provides staff with an opportunity to evaluate the director's overall administrative/management style.

Directions

Distribute the five-page "My Director ..." questionnaire and a blank envelope to each individual who works at the centre more than 10 hours per week. (If the director is male, some of the questions will need to be changed first to reflect masculine pronouns.) For more accurate results, it is advisable to distribute questionnaires to both teaching staff and support staff. Place a box labeled "Questionnaire Return Box" in your centre's office or staff room and ask respondents to deposit their completed surveys in this box. Assure staff of the confidentiality of their responses. It is suggested that the director also complete a survey of his/her perceived style. The results of this self-assessment may then be compared to the collective perceptions of the staff.

Scoring

The composite results of Part I summarize the staff's perceptions of the director's dominant leadership style. The following scoring sheet includes a brief description of the three leadership styles assessed by this questionnaire.

Scoring—Part I

To score Part I, tally the responses by noting with a mark each time staff checked a particular response:

1. _____	9. _____	17. _____
2. _____	10. _____	18. _____
3. _____	11. _____	19. _____
4. _____	12. _____	20. _____
5. _____	13. _____	21. _____
6. _____	14. _____	22. _____
7. _____	15. _____	23. _____
8. _____	16. _____	24. _____

Now total the marks for the following responses:

Task-oriented: 1, 6, 8, 10, 14, 17, 19, 22   Total _____

Achieving centre goals is most important in this leadership style. Strong concern for high performance and accomplishing tasks. Emphasis is on planning, directing, following procedures, and applying uniform standards and expectations for all. This director may be viewed as too structured, bureaucratic, and inflexible.

People-oriented: 2, 4, 7, 11, 15, 18, 20, 24   Total _____

Achieving harmonious group relations is foremost in this leadership style. Strong emphasis on maintaining comfortable, friendly, and satisfying working conditions. Allows staff to exercise control and be self-directed with minimal intrusion of centre-wide policies and procedures. Staff working in centres with this style of leadership may complain about the lack of order and coordination.

Transactional: 3, 5, 9, 12, 13, 16, 21, 23   Total _____

Achieving both centre goals and maintaining high morale is important in this leadership style. This director is flexible and fair, recognizing that different situations may require a different emphasis on centre-wide needs or individual needs.

Scoring—Part II

For Part II, add up the total score for each respondent. (Scores will range from 25 to 125.) Add together all respondents' scores and divide by the number of individuals returning questionnaires. This will yield an average score regarding the staff's evaluation of the director's performance in a wide range of administrative and supervisory behaviours.

On any assessment such as this where perceptions may vary considerably, it is important to note the range of scores (the lowest score and the highest score). Also, it is helpful to do an item analysis to discern those two or three items that staff rated the director lowest on, and those two or three items where the director consistently scored highest. This will provide the director specific feedback about those perceived areas where staff may feel he or she has the greatest skill and those areas in need of improvement.

QUESTIONNAIRE

"MY DIRECTOR ..."

Dear Staff:

One of the hallmarks of an early childhood professional is the ability to reflect on one's performance. Your feedback about my leadership style is important in helping me improve and grow professionally. Please take a few minutes to complete this questionnaire. When you are finished, insert it in the attached plain envelope and put it in the "Questionnaire Return Box" in the office. There is no need for you to put your name on the questionnaire.

Thank you.

PART I

Place a check in front of the statement that most nearly reflects your director's leadership style in different situations. (Check only one response in each group.)

WITH RESPECT TO PLANNING, MY DIRECTOR ...

1. _____ does most of the planning herself by setting goals, objectives, and work schedules for staff to follow. She then works out procedures and responsibilities for staff to follow.

2. _____ does very little planning, either by herself or with the staff. She tells the staff she has confidence in them to carry out their jobs in a responsible way.

3. _____ gets staff members together to assess centre-wide problems and discuss ideas and strategies for improvement. Together they set up goals and objectives and establish individual responsibilities.

WITH RESPECT TO WORK ASSIGNMENTS AND THE DAY-TO-DAY OPERATION OF THE CENTRE, MY DIRECTOR ...

4. _____ checks with staff regularly to see if they are content and if they have the things they need. She does not see the necessity of precise job descriptions, preferring instead to let the staff determine the scope and nature of their jobs.

5. _____ is flexible in adapting job descriptions and changing work assignments as needed. Updates centre policies and procedures depending on the needs of the staff, parents, children, and board.

6. _____ tends to go by the book. Expects staff to adhere to written job descriptions. Follows policies and procedures precisely.

WITH RESPECT TO LEADERSHIP PHILOSOPHY, MY DIRECTOR ...

7. _____ tends to emphasize people's well-being, believing that happy workers will be productive workers.

8. _____ tends to emphasize hard work and a job well done. We are a results-oriented program.

9. _____ tends to emphasize both what we do and what we need as people.

DURING MEETINGS, MY DIRECTOR ...

10. _____ keeps focused on the agenda and the topics that need to be covered.

11. _____ focuses on each individual's feelings and helps people express their emotional reactions to an issue.

12. _____ focuses on differing positions people take and how they deal with each other.

THE PRIMARY GOAL OF MY DIRECTOR IS ...

13. _____ to meet the needs of parents and children while providing a healthy work climate for staff.

14. _____ to keep the centre running efficiently.

15. _____ to help staff find fulfillment.

IN EVALUATING THE STAFF'S PERFORMANCE, MY DIRECTOR ...

16. _____ attempts to assess how each individual's performance has contributed to centre-wide achievement of goals.

17. _____ makes an assessment of each person's performance and effectiveness according to predetermined established criteria that are applied equally to all staff.

18. _____ allows people to set their own goals and determine performance standards.

MY DIRECTOR BELIEVES THE BEST WAY TO MOTIVATE SOMEONE WHO IS NOT PERFORMING UP TO HIS/HER ABILITY IS TO ...

19. _____ point out to the individual the importance of the job to be done.

20. _____ try to get to know the individual better in an attempt to understand why the person is not realizing his/her potential.

21. _____ work with the individual to redefine job responsibilities to more effectively contribute to centre-wide goals.

MY DIRECTOR BELIEVES IT IS HER ROLE TO ...

22. _____ make sure that staff members have a solid foundation of knowledge and skill that will help them accomplish centre goals.

23. _____ help people learn to work effectively in groups to accomplish group goals.

24. _____ help individuals become responsible for their own education and effectiveness, and take the first step toward realizing their potential.

WHAT THREE WORDS OR PHRASES MOST ACCURATELY DESCRIBE THE LEADERSHIP STYLE OF YOUR DIRECTOR:

PART II					
Circle the numeral that most nearly represents your assessment of your director in each of the areas described.					

MY DIRECTOR IS …	strongly disagree				strongly agree
… *knowledgeable.* She knows what is going on in the program for staff, children, parents, board, and administrators.	1	2	3	4	5
… *in control.* She has a handle on things and is actively and effectively in charge of the centre's programs and operations.	1	2	3	4	5
… *dedicated.* She demonstrates interest in learning more about her job from peers, professional groups, and reading material.	1	2	3	4	5
… *confident.* She has a sense of mission and a clear vision for the centre.	1	2	3	4	5
… *enthusiastic.* She has the energy to cope with the daily demands of her job.	1	2	3	4	5
… *an effective communicator.* She keeps us well informed about policies, procedures, activities, and schedules.	1	2	3	4	5
… *responsive.* When adults or children need her attention, she is able to focus on their needs.	1	2	3	4	5
… *available to parents.* She knows the families and encourages them to participate in the program.	1	2	3	4	5
… *open.* She encourages employees to participate in decision making and welcomes their suggestions.	1	2	3	4	5
… *fair.* She investigates all sides of an issue and distributes criticism and praise with grace and equity.	1	2	3	4	5
… *predictable.* Expectations are clearly defined, and policies are routinely followed.	1	2	3	4	5
… *a trainer.* She encourages my professional growth by providing opportunities for ongoing training and development.	1	2	3	4	5
… *a delegator.* She uses authority with fairness and according to the staff's talents and time.	1	2	3	4	5
… *prepared.* She has a sense of priority about the centre and the requirements of her role.	1	2	3	4	5
… *respectful.* She understands people as individuals and shapes her expectations of them accordingly.	1	2	3	4	5
… *understanding.* She realizes that each of us has different interests, abilities, attitudes, and personalities.	1	2	3	4	5

MY DIRECTOR IS ...	strongly disagree			strongly agree	
... *available.* I am comfortable bringing my concerns, criticisms, problems, and successes to her.	1	2	3	4	5
... *efficient.* She handles the day-to-day routines of the centre promptly and skillfully.	1	2	3	4	5
... *supportive.* She looks for opportunities to give feedback and offer praise.	1	2	3	4	5
... *a motivator.* She encourages each of us to give our best effort.	1	2	3	4	5
... *realistic.* She has a sense of humour and is able to keep things in perspective.	1	2	3	4	5
... *an influence in the community.* She is an advocate for children and quality care.	1	2	3	4	5
... *genuine.* She greets me warmly and demonstrates interest and concern. I know where I stand with her.	1	2	3	4	5
... *flexible.* She encourages creative problem solving, facilitates personal growth, and keeps things interesting.	1	2	3	4	5
... *resourceful.* She knows where to go and what to do to get things done. She makes good use of community resources.	1	2	3	4	5

FINANCIAL
MATTERS

This chapter will discuss the central importance of budgeting and financial planning and will cover:

- *The importance of financial planning*
- *Different kinds of budgets*
- *An operating budget item by item—staff costs*
- *A budget item by item—non-staff expenditures*
- *A budget item by item—income*
- *Assessing the potential for outside funding*

THE IMPORTANCE OF FINANCIAL PLANNING

Early childhood education programs in Canada face an ever changing and uncertain financial future. Support from the government is volatile, as funding becomes restrictive and unpredictable. Provincial and municipal cutbacks for operating and one-time funding are often uncertain. As a young profession, we are just beginning to understand how to advocate for affordable, accessible, and quality programs and we often lack history and experience to fall back on. It has never been more important for all players in the child care arena to pull together, in order to set new financial directions for the future.

Students aspiring to work with young children may not see the need to learn about the financial planning and administrative operation of a centre. Similarly, new staff and even some more experienced staff may not fully understand the overall financial picture, and how it can affect their work with children. As you work through this chapter, the importance of financial matters and how they involve staff should become clearer. The success of a program depends not only on whether it meets its objectives and goals, but also on whether it does so in a financially responsible manner.

The statement of philosophy draws the blueprint or framework for a centre's financial planning. The budget reflects such considerations as services to be offered, programs to be included, ages of the children eligible for enrollment, hours of operation, staff salaries and benefits, and the maintenance of the equipment and building.

In Chapter 6 we discussed the importance of developing a collaborative environment encouraging staff involvement. To be useful, this involvement requires a beginning understanding about what is involved in financial planning. Without an appreciation of the financial process, staff may decide this aspect of the operation is not their problem. When financial decisions are made that affect staffing, purchase of equipment, supplies, and other aspects of the program, knowledgeable staff will understand the reasons for these decisions. They are also more able to suggest alternatives and be creative in finding ways of easing budgetary restrictions. Difficult financial times require a team approach and a commitment to common goals, rather than staff feeling alienated by decisions they don't understand that were made in isolation from them.

Financial Organization

In any organization, large or small, it is essential to have one person who has overall responsibility for financial management. This guarantees that the financial operation stays on track. At the same time, a budget should reflect sensitive planning that responds to input from the staff. Supervisors and boards will get more commitment from staff if they understand how the budget was formulated and the ongoing implications for carefully monitoring the implementation of the budget.

The structure of an organization will determine who is responsible for various aspects of financial management, as well as the number of people who will contribute to budget development, implementation, monitoring, and year-end analysis. For example, nonprofit centres have boards of directors that are ultimately responsible for the development and final analysis of the budget. In order to make knowledgeable decisions when drawing up a budget, the directors will consult with the supervisor, who will in turn involve the staff. Once the budget is determined, the supervisor is then responsible for its implementation, monitoring expenditures and income accurately. When all goes smoothly, few problems exist. Should enrollment drop, supplies go over budget, or unusual circumstances develop, the supervisor would inform the board and ask for direction. Ultimately, financial success or failure rests in the hands of the board or owner.

In a for-profit setting, the supervisor may also be the owner, and therefore be ultimately responsible for every aspect of budget development, implementation, and decision making.

Budgets are based on the goals and objectives of the centre. Policies and procedures must be clearly articulated in order to ensure that they are covered by the financial plan. For example: one of a centre's goals is to meet the needs of working parents, and it becomes clear that those needs begin at 6:30 a.m. for many parents, rather than the 7:30 a.m. opening time. If it is decided to extend the hours, extra staff may be required, and this must be reflected in the budget planning.

The budget has to balance: that is, expenditures must not exceed income. A balanced budget is essential, regardless of how creative you may be in meeting your stated goals. Once a budget is established it drives every decision made and is the final determining factor in all aspects of program implementation.

One of the challenges that face the financial aspect of most centres is the need to respond to community and societal changing needs in a proactive manner. More and more frequently centres are faced with such things as changing enrollments due to the inclusion and exclusion of junior and senior kindergartens, children in the neighbourhood getting older and needing less care, and new subdivisions opening close by, swelling the number of requests for spaces.

Chapter 5 addresses the need to stay flexible when designing space and environments. This flexibility is also critical in financial planning when changes in enrollment, numbers and ages impact on the budget of a centre. As staff and benefit cost make up the highest percentage of any child care budget, it is prudent to use staff in a flexible and cost-efficient manner to avoid downsizing. While each area has its unique features, all centres have to be ready to react to all the factors that come together to ensure a balanced budget.

DIFFERENT KINDS OF BUDGETS

For our purposes, there are three kinds of budget to consider:

Start-up budgets cover the human resources required to develop and carry out the plan of action. In some cases the purchase of land and initial capital investment are also included in the start-up costs.

Capital budgets cover the costs incurred for land, physical space, and equipment needed to open the centre. They also generally cover large capital items that are purchased from time to time in the operation of the centre.

Operating budgets cover the projected costs of operating the centre for a period of one year, including staff salaries and all ongoing expenses.

Start-up Budgets

For our purposes, start-up costs refer to the dollars needed to hire someone to do the initial planning for the centre. This would include:

* designing, or consulting with other professionals on the design of, the physical spaces
* identifying and making recommendations on the selection and purchase of equipment, furnishings, materials, and supplies for the entire centre
* developing job descriptions and assisting in the hiring of the initial staff
* developing the beginning philosophy, and program goals and objectives, to be later refined and adapted by the program staff and management
* developing the initial administrative forms and procedures
* cooperating with other professionals to develop marketing strategies for the centre
* reviewing the current child care legislation, applying for the licence, and ensuring that the centre meets all provincial and municipal requirements
* addressing budgetary consideration and providing sample budgets

This initial planning person may be hired by a non-profit organization wanting to provide day care services to the community, or by a for-profit organization or individual that needs the expertise. Whatever the case, the main goal is to hire an expert who knows how to set up a successful quality early childhood environment, and can provide the "leg work."

Some organizations may prefer to hire the supervisor early, on a part- or full-time basis, in order to complete these tasks. Others may wish to contract with one or more consultants to do work and to provide more specialized skills in the different phases of the development. Whatever the decision, these human resource costs must be accounted for.

Too often, the board or management group tries to take on these tasks, but lacks the expertise to do so. The frustration and loss of time incurred may cause tasks to fall between the cracks, resulting in poor decisions and expensive delays. A viable program takes careful planning by professionals who have the knowledge and experience to design and implement a high quality program. Experienced guidance will ensure that the board or management team's time and areas of expertise are utilized effectively and efficiently.

Capital Budgets

Annual operating budgets usually include some capital equipment costs from year to year, in order to maintain and upgrade the quality of equipment. However, major capital items can be considered one-time expenditures, and include the following:

- land costs
- building costs
- additions to existing buildings
- renovation or alterations to existing buildings

Budget preparation requires careful planning.

- equipment and furnishings
- outdoor creative playgrounds
- fencing
- playground landscaping

Land, building, and renovation costs are very high. Financial assistance is available for nonprofit organizations in some provinces to assist in this area.

Operating Budgets

The operating budget sets out anticipated costs over a period of a single year, referred to as a *fiscal year*. These costs are projected from the best information collected from other centres' experiences, ministry guidelines, the advice of consultants, and the centre's goals and objectives. Nevertheless, it is important to remember that these are projected costs for a new operation. Once the centre is established, a more realistic picture appears, as experience dictates more accurate costs. However, a budget has to start somewhere.

Once the data has been collected from as many sources as possible, the first year budget is struck.

The budget becomes the centre's financial blueprint. Individual line item amounts may change somewhat as the year proceeds, but the final monthly income and expenditure totals cannot get off track. In other words, if income goes down, expenditures must also be cut back to ensure the continued financial viability of the centre. The balance each month of the expenditure and income columns acts as the financial barometer.

The operating budget must clearly reflect any changes or new directions in the centre, as stated in the philosophy and goals. This usually happens at the beginning of a new fiscal year. For example, if the philosophy supports continued professional development and ongoing in-service training for its staff, two things must happen:

- The philosophy must clearly contain this commitment in its stated goals for the staff. In addition, strategies need to be included to help staff meet these goals. These could include registration fees and replacement staff costs to allow full-time staff to attend workshops and seminars or visit other centres; time to develop new curriculum areas by being replaced on the schedule; reimbursement upon successful completion of approved courses; and so on.
- The budget must include a line item called "professional development" that indicates a clear financial commitment to support staff in their professional development goals. Without a budget, there is no true commitment for staff to reach these goals. The setting should not state goals for staff that are not financially viable.

Setting the operating budget takes planning and consultation. This may involve the board, supervisor, staff, and perhaps parents. Each has expertise to bring to the planning phase, and each has a greater or lesser role to play. Once the budget is prepared, final approval and ultimate responsibility rest with the organizing group, be it an incorporated nonprofit board, a private owner, the executive of a parent cooperative, or a profit-making organization.

Expenditures and Income

Operating expenditures are usually grouped in one of three categories:

Fixed costs occur regardless of the number of children enrolled. They include such things as mortgage or rent, loan payments, utilities, telephone, and the like. They are fixed because there is little the program can do to alter them.

Variable costs are tied to the number of children enrolled. They include food, materials, supplies, etc.

Semi-variable costs are directly related to the child/teacher ratio. For example, if the ratio is 8:1 and you have ten children in your group, you will need two staff members. However, you can add six more children without increasing staff costs.

The other major category in a budget is income.

AN OPERATING BUDGET ITEM BY ITEM—STAFF COSTS

Salary expenditures take up more of the total costs than all other items put together—in some cases, as much as 90%. Salaries for full- and part-time staff should be based on the policies and procedures established by the operation. Quality early childhood programs demand that all teaching staff be qualified, even if this is not a requirement of provincial or territorial regulations. Centres that want to attract and retain qualified staff must present an attractive salary and benefit package.

Historically, salaries in child care have been low and benefits minimal. The result has been high staff turnover, with the accompanying continuous recruitment and new staff orientation stress on existing staff and excessive paperwork. The salaries in most centres strike a delicate balance between the income from fees and the need to attract and keep qualified professionals.

Although full-time staff are the major cost, part-time and supply staff must also be considered. For example, if the centre policy for paid sick days allows twelve days per year per staff member, the budget must include money to bring in supply staff to cover these days. The following formula would apply:

Total number of staff × 12 days × 7.5 hours per day × the cost per hour.

Salary policies must be consistent with budget figures—if your policy on paid sick leave changes, so will your budget allowance.

Other part-time employees include a cook, a janitor, and staff that may be needed to supplement the full-time staff hours. Provincial/territorial legislation will determine the ratios required for the ages of the children and the size of groups. The section "Calculating Staff Costs," below, will show you how to set up the full- and part-time salary items.

Each centre should develop a salary schedule with starting salaries, pay categories for qualification and experience, and proposed increments. This is the basis for hiring staff and finalizing salaries. If the centre is unionized, there will be a negotiated salary scale.

- *Benefits:* Contributions to Unemployment Insurance and the Canada Pension Plan for each staff member are mandatory and must be included in the budget. Contributions to Worker's Compensation are mandatory in most jurisdictions, and highly advisable in the rest. Other benefits such as medical insurance, dental plan, long- and short-term disability, and life insurance are optional but provide additional security for the staff. Overall costs for full-time benefits generally run at about 12% to 18%, while benefits for part-time staff average about 12%.

- *Consultants:* As the need occurs, specialists can supplement staff skills and meet the specific needs of some children. Professionals skills needed might include a speech and language specialist, nutritionist, behavioural consultant, and an accountant. These contract services are similar to salaries, but they are usually not ongoing and don't include benefits.

• *Professional development and in-service training:* An earlier example addressed the importance of having the goals of the centre reflected in the budget. A certain amount of money per staff member is usually the easiest and fairest way to come up with an initial budget amount. This total can then be negotiated among staff as circumstances present themselves, for workshops, conferences and such. A consultant or speaker may be invited to a staff meeting, to provide in-service training for the entire staff at once.

Calculating Staff Costs

Full-time salaries

Supervisor: Determined from the salary schedule.
Teacher Category I: Number of teachers × salary as per schedule.
Teacher Category II: Number of teachers × salary as per schedule.
Teacher Category III: Number of teachers × salary as per schedule (and so on, depending on the categories in the salary schedule).

Full-time benefits

These total between 12% and 18% of total full-time salaries, depending on personnel policies in your centre. There are both mandatory benefits such as Employment Insurance and Canada Pension Plan as well as discretionary benefits such as extended health plans and sick days.

Part-time staff

Supply Staff: Number of sick days allowed per full-time staff member × number of staff × hours per day × amount per hour.
Part-time Staff: Requirements vary—for example, 24 hours per week × number of weeks × amount per hour.
Cook: Number of hours per week × number of weeks per year × amount per hour.
Janitor: Number of hours per week × number of weeks per year × amount per hour.
Secretary: Number of hours per week × number of weeks per year × amount per hour.

Part-time benefits

These total between 8% and 12% of total part-time salaries, depending on personnel policies in your centre.

Consultants

Identify the specialties you may require—e.g., accountant. Then, consultant × number of days × amount per hour or per day, depending on the involvement necessary. As contractors, they do not receive benefits.

A BUDGET ITEM BY ITEM—NON-STAFF EXPENDITURES

- *Mortgage/rental and loan payments:* Many centres make monthly payments for a mortgage or rent. These payments must be included in the operating budget. Some centres also have a monthly payment on a loan they have incurred to cover capital equipment or renovations to an existing building.
- *Property taxes:* These may be payable in some jurisdictions, depending on the auspice under which you operate.
- *Business taxes:* These may be payable in some jurisdictions, depending on the auspice under which you operate.
- *Maintenance and repairs to building:* New centres, and rented buildings where these services are included in the rent, have lower costs in this category. As a centre ages, there is increased wear and tear on the building, and costs go up.
- *Depreciation on building, equipment, and furnishings:* The specific circumstances regarding the category of depreciation will vary from centre to centre. An accountant can assist in determining the amounts to include in this category.
- *Utilities:* These include heat, electricity, and water and sewage service. If the centre rents space, some or all of these costs may be included. More often they are separate costs, which can be estimated on a per-square-metre basis. Estimates from other programs of similar size, plus a call to the public utilities will help in developing the first year's costs.

For an existing program, take last year's charges and add known or projected rate increases, plus a slight allowance for increased use. For example, this winter may be colder than last, and heating costs may rise.

Budget decisions affect the quality of the centre.

- *Telephone:* This is a fixed cost, and advice on the program's needs will be available from the phone company. Long-distance costs can be approximated and spread over the twelve-month operating budget.

- *Insurance:* Insurance coverage becomes a fixed cost once a decision is made about what is included in the insurance package. Each program must decide what is to be insured, and to what extent. Typically, supervisor, board, and staff need to determine the level of insurance for the building, contents, outdoor equipment, and storage buildings. Liability insurance is required for children, employees, and others while they are on the premises. If you transport children to and from the centre, or even on special occasions such as trips to museums or conservation areas, you will need additional insurance to cover it.

You are well advised to call several insurance companies to discuss your needs, and then compare prices and coverage. Costs may rise at intervals as determined by the insurer.

- *Grounds maintenance:* Early childhood programs often overlook the cost for garbage removal, grass cutting, snow removal, and general outdoor maintenance. A variety of creative ways can be found to cover these costs. When budgets are tight, high school students can be hired at reasonable rates to do the work, as opposed to contracting it out to professional services. In unionized situations some restrictions in respect to contracting out must be taken into account.

- *Food:* Not all programs provide meals, but for those that do, the cost of providing a nutritious meal and two snacks per day will vary slightly. When presenting the budget, it is wise to show the formula you used to account for the costs. For example, a figure of $15 912 at the line item "budget for food" might seem high to the board. However, if you clarify this by including the formula, you often get the opposite response from the board—they question how you can feed children for so little a day.

Example: The approximate cost for food for each child per day is between $1.10 and $1.25. In a centre with 45 children and 6 staff, this would work out to: 51 children/staff × 52 weeks × 5 days per week × $1.20 per day = $15 912.00.

Staff is included in food costs because they eat with the children as part of teaching self-help skills. The cost of the cook, of course, will be covered under salaries.

- *Educational equipment:* The capital budget accounts for the initial purchases of educational equipment and toys. The operating budget must allow for additional and replacement items. A rough rule of thumb is to allow approximately $100 per child per year.

- *Teachers' resources and membership in professional organizations:* This part of the budget would include books, subscriptions, and memberships, to keep staff up to date on developments in the field.

- *Educational supplies:* Consumable materials such as paint, paste, paper, and general creative supplies and materials are included in this area. Allow approximately $25 per child per year.

- *First aid:* This would cover the cost of first aid kits and supplies. Always make sure these supplies are up to date—when you need them is not the time to discover that nobody replaced the bandages!

- *Housekeeping supplies:* This would include items like toilet paper, paper towels, cleaning supplies, etc.

- *Kitchen equipment:* Replacement and additional equipment is needed throughout the year to supplement initial kitchen capital purchases. Allow approximately $10 per child per year.

- *Office supplies and equipment:* This category includes stationery, pens, computer paper and software, ribbons, and general office supplies. In a fairly new centre, major pieces of equipment such as an adding machine and a word processor are included in the initial capital costs, and should function for some time without problems. As time goes on, replacement and repairs must be budgeted for.

  Photocopying may need to be a separate budget item.

- *Special programs:* The cost of any special programs, such as dance or music, would be included here.

- *Field trips and travel:* If the curriculum is developed to include visits to various places of interest, then the budget must include the cost of bus trips or whatever means of transport is used. Costs can easily be worked out, once you have established the destination and number of trips.

- *Advertising, postage, courier:* An established program may have few advertising costs or marketing expenses. These expenditures will vary from area to area depending on how well a needs analysis was carried out before setting the centre's location. Ongoing postage and occasional courier services are a common but not high expense item. The budget amount can be established based on the program's estimates of mailings, while the marketing costs can be obtained from professionals in that area.

- *Bank charges:* As banks keep raising their service charges, this is an item to consider. Try to keep operating funds in an interest-bearing account to offset these costs.

- *Audit and bookkeeping fees:* You will need to budget for an annual audit, and perhaps for bookkeeping throughout the year.

- *Legal expenses:* Some early childhood programs will budget for legal costs, although one hopes the need will not arise.

- *Bad debts and low enrollment:* Careful income management should eliminate or minimize unpaid accounts. Nevertheless, it is wise to include one to two per cent of the yearly income in this column, to act as the necessary cushion and assist in case of a drop in enrollment.

- *Miscellaneous:* Licence fees, petty cash, and other small items can be included in this column. This should be a small amount, because you want to know where your costs occur so that you can move them into specific categories. For example, petty cash expenditures should be just that—petty. Otherwise, they should be posted to the line item they fit under.

A BUDGET ITEM BY ITEM—INCOME

The income side balances the line expenditures in a budget. Once expenditures have been determined, the sources of income are evaluated and the fees established. Fees from parents are commonly referred to as "fees for service"; income from subsidizing agencies or social services constitutes the main sources of income for some centres. More recently, some provinces have instituted direct operating grants to centres. Donations make up a very small part of the income for the majority of centres. Whatever the case, total expenses incurred throughout the operating year cannot exceed the projected income from all available sources.

Let's suppose that the total income required for a centre is $290 000. The centre is licensed for 45 children. The means of income is fees paid by the parents. We will allow three weeks for parents to withdraw their children from the centre during the holiday months of July and August without paying the fee. The formula to work out the income needed is as follows, assuming that all places can be filled:

$290 000 ÷ 45 children ÷ 11.25 months = $572.84 per month per child.

The actual fee charged should be higher than the exact formula amount, to allow some income over expenditures as a buffer or contingency fund. Accordingly, the fee charged in this centre would be a minimum of $580. Any money left at the end of the fiscal year is brought forward as income in the next budget year.

The registration fee charged should also be taken into account in the income column.

Calculating Income

Registration Fee: A set fee × number of children in centre.
Parent Fees: Number of children × number of months × the established monthly fee.
Donations: Guaranteed commitments.
Direct Grants: Amount based on the particular government formula.
Total: Total of the above, plus any other categories applicable to your particular centre.

Balancing the Budget

The total of the Income column and the Expenditure column should be expressed in terms of Income over Expenditures. A monthly flow chart can be established to record and monitor monthly costs and income to ensure that the budget stays on track. An accountant or bookkeeper can assist with this process.

ASSESSING THE POTENTIAL FOR OUTSIDE FUNDING

Additional funding for early childhood services may be available through government and/or private sources. The first step in fundraising is to identify available sources of potential support. The following list identifies private sources of funding and fundraising information:

- Your local library may have the annual reports of the larger foundations and their funding patterns. These foundations have clear criteria for applying and it is important to get all your information together and make a professional presentation to be successful.

- Provincial and territorial ministries can provide information on current funding criteria. There is a list of such offices in Chapter 2.

- Service clubs such as Kiwanis, Rotary, and Lions are located in most communities. They sometimes make one-time donations for items such as equipment or improvements to playgrounds.

- The Canadian Centre for Philanthropy distributes helpful publications and will make computer searches for a list of foundations that donate to child care services. See Chapter 11, Appendix A.

- Businesses can be approached to provide assistance. Some types of support include start-up funds, subsidies to employees to offset the cost of child care, salary enhancement grants, and the provision of space either free or at low cost.

You will need to submit a formal, written proposal to request money from government sources, foundations, and businesses. Preliminary personal contacts by telephone or letter or in person will let you know whether you should submit a detailed proposal. Some funders have a preferred format for a proposal. The following describes a general format:

- Cover sheet or title page: A brief descriptive title for the proposed project, the name of the organization or individual submitting the proposal, and the submission date.

- Executive summary: A brief description of the need for the project based on data obtained from your needs assessment, your objectives and procedures, and the amount of money or type of assistance required. The information in this section should be concise, accurate, and complete, because those reviewing the proposal may read only this section.

- Table of contents: Lists the sections of the proposal with corresponding page numbers.

- Introduction: Includes background information about the submitting organization and the target user group, and illustrates the unique qualities of the proposed service.

- Purpose: Outlines why the project is being embarked upon, highlighting the need for and importance of the proposed service.

- Objectives: They are the substance of the proposal, because they must stem from the stated purpose and be reflected in the procedures. Your objectives must be stated clearly and in measurable terms, so they can be subjected to evaluation.

- Procedure: Describes the specific service(s) to be provided to the user group. A description of staff may be included here.

- Evaluation: Indicates how the service will be evaluated, to determine its success in carrying out its objectives.

- Budgets: An accurate, itemized list of start-up and ongoing costs. Include contributions (space, equipment, volunteer help, etc.) and monetary commitments from other agencies.

Minor adjustments may have to be made to the proposal format. Some tips for successful fundraising include making public acknowledgment of contributors and sending them frequent progress reports. If possible, show how the service is seeking additional funding sources and hopes to become self-sufficient.

IN CONCLUSION

Understanding, planning, and monitoring the financial matters of an early childhood setting is the primary responsibility of the board or owner, administrator, or supervisor. Nonetheless, staff needs to understand how budgets are developed and the implications that they have for the quality of the centre's overall operation.

This chapter covered start-up budgets, capital budgets, and operating budgets. You have also had an opportunity to work your way through the development of an operating budget, which should increase your overall awareness of the way budgets are formulated.

Many settings need to look beyond the income they receive from fees, and search for opportunities to generate revenue from outside agencies or by fundraising. This chapter helps you to develop a proposal to reach that goal.

ACTIVITIES

1. Make an appointment to visit a centre that is licensed for 45 children. Find out exactly what line items the centre has included in its budget and why.

2. Name and describe any categories that need further explanation, to justify their inclusion and amount in the budget.

3. Design your own complete budget for a centre for 45 children.

4. You are operating a home child care program for four children. Develop a budget.

REVIEW QUESTIONS

1. Why, today more than ever, is it important to understand the need for sound financial planning in order to operate a quality early childhood education program?

2. Define what is meant by start-up, capital, and operating budgets.

3. List the line items in an operating budget.

4. Describe the need for, and the process you might use to find, alternative sources of income.

FURTHER READING

Cherry, C., B. Harkness, and K. Kuzma (1987). *Nursery school and day care centre management guide.* Belmont, CA: Fearon.

Click, P. and D. Click (1990). *Administration of schools for young children.* Albany, NY: Delmar Publishers.

Morgan, G. (1982). *Managing the day care dollar.* Cambridge, MA: Steam Press.

Sciarra, D. and A. Dorsey (1996). *Developing and administering a child care centre.* Albany, NY: Delmar Publishers.

THE ORGANIZATIONAL FRAMEWORK

In this chapter we examine how early childhood education programs are organized, along with administrative procedures to maintain, control, and monitor up-to-date information. Samples of various forms and policies can be found at the end. We will cover:

- *The organization of early childhood settings*
- *Administrative policies and procedures*
- *Organizing the flow of information*

THE ORGANIZATION OF EARLY CHILDHOOD SETTINGS

The quality of the program along with the knowledge, skill, and personal and professional beliefs of the staff are the determining factors in a program achieving high standards. The next important element in achieving excellence is the way the centre is organized and administered. The organizational framework will also determine the level of parent involvement, the ability to achieve government funding, community input, and the overall professional image of the centre.

Government involvement and support for early childhood programs depends on the party in power, the state of the budget, and the social conscience and commitment of the government to families and children. The swing from high involvement, both financially and legislatively, to the present day trend of non-involvement and privatization makes it important for programs to have sound financial planning in order to survive.

In the present political climate, government support and intervention in early childhood programs continues to decline, and the movement toward self-sufficient group care operations is on the increase. In addition, the alternatives to group care for young children—such as home child care, and extended family and neighbourhood arrangements—have gained political support. For some families alternative, unlicensed, and informal care provide more flexibility in the hours of operation, while others choose these options because of financial considerations. At this point in history, child care remains the primary responsibility of parents to find, fund, and monitor.

The following categories, broadly speaking, identify the types of formal early childhood programs found across Canada. Each has its own characteristics. Group care operations continue to house a significantly smaller population than the informal arrangements parents consider when choosing alternative care for their children.

Non-profit Centres

Also referred to as not-for-profit, these centres may be operated by a church, a parent or community group, an agency such as the YWCA/YMCA, an institution such as a university or college, or some other non-profit group that wishes to make child care available in the com-

A well-organized setting is important to parents.

munity. In some provinces and communities, early childhood education services are offered by the municipality and incorporated as non-profit.

A non-profit or not-for-profit organization must depend on the fees from parents as their main source of income. While some funds may be obtained from local or provincial governments, the board of directors is responsible for the overall income in order to balance their budget. Often fund-raising events occur throughout the year, which helps to buy equipment and add to the income as needed. Boards often struggle to balance their budgets. When balanced budgets are not achieved, additional fund-raising events or income from other sources must be found. In the event that there is an excess of income over expenditures, the balance is moved into the next year's budget income line or used for capital equipment. The agency or group sponsoring will nominate a board of directors to manage its operations in conjunction with the supervisor hired by the board.

Forming a Non-profit Corporation

A non-profit corporation may be established by a group of people committed to an identified goal. In order to arrange financing and seek a suitable location for an early childhood setting, the group may become incorporated in order to ensure recognition as a legal entity, continuity over time, and limited liability for its members.

Incorporation requires selecting a board of directors from among the members, and following other established legal procedures. A lawyer's help will be necessary. Once incorporated, the non-profit corporation is well on its way to accomplishing the goals for which it was founded.

As the centre develops, the board's ongoing responsibilities include:

- administration of the centre
- management of finances
- program development
- human resource matters/personnel/staffing
- community relationships

While the board determines a centre's overall direction, the supervisor is responsible for its day-to-day operation. The supervisor's responsibility must be clearly defined from the outset—it must be clear what kinds of issues she or he will address, and what issues belong to the board. A good communication and working relationship is critical.

The board that develops policies for the centre's operation is ultimately responsible for implementation of the policies and procedures, however, the supervisor, and when possible the staff, should also be included in the process. Studies have linked staff involvement in decision making to job satisfaction and ultimately to the quality of program offered in the centre. For example, the supervisor and staff should be involved in the policies relating to curriculum and documentation of daily activities, in order to make sure that these policies are useful for planning, meet regulations, are helpful for parents, and are consistent with the centre philosophy.

Commercial or For-profit Centres/Agencies

The free enterprise system is also involved in the operation of child care centres. Sole owners, partnerships, or corporations can provide child care services as a profit-making business.

The organization and its operations will be structured in such a way as to generate a profit for the owners. The director will be responsible to the owner, who will determine the organizational structure. From time to time governments have been more or less supportive to the for-profit sector of child care. Some provinces have encouraged and financially supported centres that are "for-profit" changing their status to "not-for-profit." This would require a board of directors to be established in order to follow all the guidelines required under the not-for-profit status. This move was a government incentive in the past, but seems to have lost emphasis as do many child care incentives linked to the politics of the government in power.

Proprietary Agencies

In some cases a local business or government may provide a child care centre for its employees, or may purchase space from a community centre, or else enter into a partnership with another business or local college on a collaborative basis. The organizational structure of the centre will be determined by the circumstances. For example, a business might decide to purchase child care spaces for its employees in either a non-profit or a for-profit centre. Or it might operate its own centre as part of its larger organization, in either for-profit or non-profit fashion.

As the political, social, and financial structures of the provincial and federal governments shift and change, so do the standards, policies, and procedures related to government involvement. While some governments support and sponsor the non-profit concept for early childhood education programs, others believe that free enterprise should play a significant role in the provision of early childhood services.

Home Child Care

Home day care programs operate within both the informal and formal systems. In some provinces formal home day care programs are operated under a licensed agency or municipality, while in others individual homes are licensed. The agency arranges child care in private home settings and monitors the program to ensure minimal standards are met.

Informal child care, which accounts for the majority of children being cared for outside of their home, includes extended family, neighbours, and any individuals who choose to take children into their homes while parents work.

Resources and Supports for Parents

Child care remains the responsibility of parents to locate and evaluate, fund, and monitor while their child is in attendance. However, some communities are developing resource or information centres to help parents achieve quality care for their children. This service provides assistance in locating centres or formal or informal home care settings. Methods to evaluate the standards used in these settings and ongoing monitoring systems are also available in many communities. Educating parents to enable them to make informed decisions about child care is an attempt to raise the standards of care for children of working parents.

ADMINISTRATIVE POLICIES AND PROCEDURES

Developing, organizing, and monitoring a program's policies and procedures is one of the important tasks performed by the staff and supervisor in a well-run centre. They form the framework within which the daily life of the program takes place. They have an impact on numerous variables, including the level of involvement of parents, availability of resources and supports for staff, assignment of finances, and the leadership style of the supervisor.

The philosophy of the centre is at the heart of how policies and procedures are developed. For example, a philosophy that reflects cultural diversity would have policies that integrate this belief—in staffing, nutrition, diversified books and materials, and language considerations for children and parents. Cultural diversity will be interwoven throughout the entire program and organization of the centre and not in just one activity or area of the centre. For examples of a policy considered in more detail see Chapter 6, where the development of a centre's personnel policy is outlined.

Guidelines

Centres may also develop guidelines, in addition to policies and procedures. Guidelines help explain the policies with some examples, suggestions, and alternatives that apply to various situations. For example, a guideline for student teachers first entering a field placement may suggest that they not be intrusive, since children need time to become familiar with new people in the room.

Regulations

A program's policies must incorporate provincial/territorial and municipal regulations. For example, your centre may want to develop a policy that parents park in a certain area for easy access in the morning. Then you discover that the fire department doesn't allow parking in that area, because it is on the fire route.

Once the regulations and their implications are clearly understood, policies to support and extend them need to be established. A regulation on guiding children's behaviour might state that staff may not use corporal punishment, degrade a child, or in any way lower a child's self-esteem. The centre would incorporate that regulation into its policy, extending it by adding how and why children's behaviour should be guided and directed, as well as the consequences for not following the policy.

Programs must adhere to laws such as employment standards acts, freedom of information legislation, and others that are dictated by the province or territory.

ORGANIZING THE FLOW OF INFORMATION

All written information we collect on children and their families should be collected and handled with sensitivity, consideration, and confidentiality. The centre's forms, policies, and procedures should reflect the philosophy and objectives of the centre. Since the brochure and other forms often give people their first impression of the centre, it is important to think carefully about what we want this impression to be.

Confidentiality

We early childhood educators are party to a lot of personal information about the children in our care and their families. We must always be sure to respect the confidential nature of this information. It is the responsibility of the program and each staff member to become familiar with the freedom of information guidelines.

Caution must be exercised in this area, as there are greater legal complications than ever before. This topic should be reviewed as a regular agenda item for staff meetings, to ensure that each person has a clear understanding of the implications, professionally and legally, surrounding confidentiality. For example, it can happen that a staff member or student-teacher may share information with a parent about a child their child is playing with, intending to be helpful, but it is essential to examine the appropriateness and even the legality of this action.

The need for confidentiality cannot be overstated. Written permission to disclose information must always be obtained from parents, and information should never be disclosed without such consent. Files and information must be housed in a safe and secure manner, with access allowed only to approved personnel.

Information about the Children

Application Form

The initial application contains the information needed by the supervisor and staff in order to enrol the child. However, many parents do not fill out more than the simplest questions on the application. There are several possible reasons for this. First, this may not be the only centre they are applying to. Second, they do not know who is going to read the information and how it may be used. Lastly, they may prefer to discuss the information directly with staff, rather than writing it on a form. Therefore it is best to ask only for information you must know in order to continue the enrollment process, rather than complicate the application with questions that are not likely to be answered.

Provinces and territories generally specify the information that must be filed on each child enrolled in the centre. That requirement should be the basis of forms to be completed by parents or guardians, but you will need further information in order to obtain the data you will need to understand and plan for each child registered in the centre.

A moment for a hug and to say goodbye.

Consider the following when developing an application form:

- Review the human rights code, so you are clear on what you may and may not ask.
- Make the form easy to follow and simple to complete. Parents do not enjoy filling out long complicated forms, especially on the initial application.
- Be clear about why you are asking certain questions, and be prepared to explain the reason for them if asked by the parent. It is not good enough to say you didn't design the form and so you don't know why the question was asked.
- Make sure the application reflects the belief that parents are important partners in your setting, and understand and know their child best.

Medical Form

Whether legislated or not, the completion of a medical form is essential. Local health departments can provide programs with the forms a doctor needs to complete prior to the child's enrollment. Some programs send the medical form in the same mailing as the brochure and application form, in order to avoid a second mailing and to red flag to the parents the need to fill it out. It often takes parents time to arrange an appointment with their family doctor, and having the form in hand helps speed up the process.

Developmental Information Form

The use of this form varies from centre to centre. It can provide a good starting point for teacher and parents to begin a dialogue about the child. Parents know their children best, and the form is a good way to reinforce this. Helping teachers and parents work together is the blueprint for success for both child and centre, and what better way to begin this than to share information about the child's strengths, interests, activities, and needs? The information also provides staff with the basis for delivering a program based on the child's individual needs.

This form should be completed just prior to the child's admission into the centre. This timing is particularly important for infants and toddlers, since their development is so rapid.

Special Instructions for Individual Children

Whether required by legislation or not, it is good centre policy to have parents provide written instructions for feeding and caring for young children. This should be done when children enter the program, or when any major changes in diet or procedure occur. For example, a common allergy for young children is peanut butter or peanut by-products. When this occurs it is sometimes best to remove that food totally from the centre if at all possible. Cultural considerations should also be considered and incorporated into your program's policies.

Daily Information Sheets

The daily information sheet is particularly important with infants. The first part of the page should include information provided by parents regarding details of sleeping and eating during the last twelve hours. The second part allows staff to record similar information, so that parents know how their child's day has gone. In addition, activities and developmental milestones are recorded, since children change and grow at such a quick pace at that age. The form can also help ease the discomfort parents can experience when first using group care for their infant.

Information for Parents

The Centre Brochure

The centre brochure gives parents a strong first impression about the setting's philosophy, objectives, program, and services. It is crucial that this impression be a positive one. The brochure should be uncluttered, and contain only the information parents need to know in order to understand the philosophy and objectives of the centre. More detailed information takes away from the initial presentation and can follow later.

The brochure should contain:

- the program's name, address, and phone number
- its licensing body
- a summary of the philosophy and main objectives
- staff qualifications
- the age range of children accepted
- an overview of the program
- a brief description of the facilities
- fees (you may want to include the fees on an insert, since they will probably change more frequently than your printed brochure)
- the process for enrollment
- a statement or two about what makes this program special or unique

Pictures with captions that reflect the centre's philosophy enhance the appearance of the brochure and often capture the essence of the program. After you design your brochure, field test it with parents and with other early childhood educators. This will help you make sure it is clear, attractive, and includes all necessary information.

Financial Policy

The program should have a clear financial policy. This should include the registration fee, schedule of payments, notice necessary for withdrawal, and any other policies outlining the financial responsibility of parents. For example, some programs allow parents to take several holiday weeks, while their place remains reserved and no fee is payable. Others require a portion of the fee to be paid to hold the place. It is important for parents to understand that fees may be due regardless of inclement weather, statutory holidays, or the number of days the child attends. Whatever the centre's policy about fees, a clear explanation is necessary so parents understand the commitments they are making when they enroll their child.

Health and Safety Policies

The health and safety policies of the program are designed to protect the safety of all the children and adults. Parents need to plan for alternative care in the case of their child's illness.

It is important that parents understand the reasons for this policy. In addition, accidents may happen in the centre that necessitate parental decisions and medical care. Each centre should spell out the procedure so that everyone concerned is fully aware of the process to be followed should an accident occur. Local and area evacuations may also occur, and a plan of action should be available for both parents and staff to follow. In areas where heavy snow is a frequent occurrence, plans for morning or early closing may also be important.

In addition, the program needs to have very specific procedures to ensure the health and safety of the children in its care. Chapter 5 contains a discussion of specific steps to take, with a suggested checklist.

Return after Serious Illness Form

This form is to be completed by the family doctor after a child has had a serious illness, childhood disease, or accident. It is important that the child not return to the centre until well enough to join the other children safely. In some cases it may be possible for the child to return, but with activity limitations. The doctor should explain these limitations. Several copies of this form should be given to the parents upon enrollment, and the purpose for it explained.

Administration of Medication at School

Each centre must develop policies and procedures for the administration of prescription and non-prescription medications. The licensing authority in each province or territory will outline its own requirements here, and some prohibit the administration of non-prescribed medication. More and more children are requiring the administration of medication such as insulin, asthma medication, and antibiotics. This puts increased responsibility on staff, requiring a clear procedure to ensure safety and proper record keeping. The Canadian Pediatric Society's publication *Well Beings* (1997) is an excellent resource to have in every early childhood education program.

Supervisors who feel their program is unable to handle these needs must make their position clear to all parents and prospective parents at the time of the admission interview, so that children needing regular medication are not accepted into care.

Permission for Field Trips

The aim here is to guarantee that parents are informed about any activity that occurs off the property, and to ensure they are fully apprised of where their child will be at any time. This process can be handled in several ways. One form can be used to grant permission to go on any field trip arranged by the program. Another way is to give parents the option of which field trips they would like their child to participate in.

Additional Forms Required

Some settings are involved in research that requires permission from parents, while other centres may be engaged in videotaping for special events, or for study by student teachers in college lab situations. Parents are generally cooperative and want to have their children involved in such interesting ventures, but it is critical to gain permission first.

Other Information for Parents

Once parents have decided to enrol their child, they will need other information about the operation of the program. A handbook for parents may be designed that includes the following specifics:

- recommended clothing
- how children's behaviour is guided
- specific information about the staff in the centre
- information on when and how to reach their child's teacher
- specific information about their child's program
- parking—describing location and safety considerations
- policy on bringing toys from home
- arrival and departure procedures
- parental involvement
- newsletters
- information on nutrition
- carpooling
- special visitors
- special procedures for various age groups
- transitional objects from home

This information will vary depending on the setting. The main goal is to help parents understand as much as possible about the program and its overall operation, and the reason why the information is being asked for. Although personal one-to-one communication is essential, some information can more readily be communicated in the parent handbook.

Information Provided by Staff

Staff must review the application form, medical information, and other forms completed by parents. The forms discussed in this next category are completed by staff.

Intake Interview Form

This form provides a guideline for staff to follow when meeting with the child for the first time. The information gathered in this first meeting helps the teacher plan to make the child's initial experience a success. In addition, general information about the child's interests, abilities, and overall developmental level may be assessed.

Generally, information recorded includes:

- response to visiting centre
- response to interviewer
- activities preferred during visit
- special information from parents about play habits

- mastery of language
- coordination
- parents' reaction to centre

Checklist for Initial Interviews

This checklist provides a guide for staff in the initial interview. Ensure all necessary information is covered with each family.

The checklist could include:

- description of the program for parents
- completion of all forms
- information on the child's beginning days in the centre
- arrival and departure procedures
- information boards, newsletters, parental involvement
- discussions on behaviour management
- question time for parents

Guide for Subsequent Parent Interviews

Based on the stated goals of the program, this interview guide is completed by staff prior to a parent interview. It includes categories where staff can list specific information they need from parents in order to better understand and plan for the child. In addition, it provides areas for staff to record information about the child that they want to share with the parents. It assists the teacher in outlining each developmental area and identifying the child's

Well-designed forms are clear and easy to follow.

strengths in each of these areas. This planning enables the teacher to enter an interview with the confidence that the important aspects of the child's development and involvement in the program are included.

Accident Form

Careful consideration given to safety eliminates many unnecessary accidents. However, children move quickly and often unsteadily, with the result that some mishaps do occur. The accident form records such incidents when they happen, and describes the situation to the parents. After going over the information on the form with the parent, it is wise to have them sign it so the information is not misunderstood.

Child Guidance Policy

Each centre should have a procedure outlining the guidance policy to be followed by every staff member. In this procedure, the process of guiding children's behaviour should be outlined in very specific detail, including general principles accepted by all staff and parents. The policy should also spell out any behaviour that is clearly unacceptable and that may result in disciplinary action.

Child Abuse Policy and Procedures

It is important to know and understand the legal requirements for staff in cases of suspected child abuse. The centre should provide the staff with as much information on this subject as possible. This information should be updated frequently and the implication for not following the legal and centre regulation understood. A detailed format to record information in the case of alleged abuse should also be in place.

Serious Occurrence

Depending on your province or territory licensing agency, a serious occurrence may be defined as a child breaking a bone, an incident serious enough to require hospitalization, an alleged case of child abuse by a staff member, and so on. A serious occurrence policy describing how to report and record such an incident must be in place in every centre. This will ensure that each staff member understands and follows prescribed practices and procedures. Whether this policy is required by the licensing body or not, it is important to clearly record such incidents for parents, medical personnel that might become involved, insurance purposes, and so on. In some provinces it is mandatory to telephone the government licensing agency to report a serious occurrence.

Emergency Information

A current list of emergency telephone numbers should be posted in several obvious locations and at the telephones. This list should include the fire department, nearest hospital, ambulance service, poison control centre, police department, and taxi service. Some centres may have specific services that they use regularly, and need to be included on this list.

Allergy Lists and Information

The kitchen and playrooms should contain lists of the children with allergies and medical conditions, and these lists should be referred to frequently. Every precaution should be taken to ensure that children are protected from foods or materials that cause reactions. Staff should be provided with detailed information on any condition of a child in their care and what to do in case of a reaction or emergency.

Severe allergies to many common foods are widespread, and child care staff need to be rigorous and sensitive in their commitment to keeping children safe.

Filing and Use of Forms

The information contained in the child's file is good only if it is used by and useful to the staff. Continue to review the need for the information you collect, and make sure it is useful and up to date. Each centre should develop some means of ensuring that all the information on each child is correctly filed. Whatever administrative system is used, it should be easy for staff to use, protected for confidentiality, and well organized.

Computers are commonly used to generate many of the policies, procedures, and forms. There are a wide variety of software packages available to suit the varying needs of different centres.

IN CONCLUSION

Quality early childhood programs do not just happen. It takes careful planning, good organization, and teamwork on the part of all those involved in the centre. This chapter is an introduction to the important administrative elements necessary to manage a centre efficiently and effectively.

As a beginning professional, you need to understand all aspects of the centre's operation that impact on the quality of the program for the children, parents, staff, and other professionals you will come into contact with. The information in this chapter will assist you in understanding the administrative aspects that are a necessary part of the holistic quality operation of all settings.

ACTIVITIES

1. Visit two different child care centres and ask if you can have copies of several policies and procedures prepared for the use of parents. Compare the two sets of information and make a list of the strengths and weaknesses of each form and each set of policies and procedures.

2. Design a brochure for a centre for children aged four months to five years. Describe why you included the information you did, and how you feel it makes your centre appealing to parents.

3. Outline in detail the financial policy for a centre.

4. Make a list of ways that you could make parents feel an integral part of your centre. Now take that list and incorporate your ideas into the centre's policies and procedures.

5. Encourage students to collect copies of key policies for each of their field placement experiences. Use these to compare with the ideas developed in this chapter.

REVIEW QUESTIONS

1. Why is it important to understand the administrative aspects of operating a child care centre?
2. What are the responsibilities of the board in the operation of a child care centre?
3. List the forms necessary to effectively manage the centre's operation.
4. Why is confidentiality such an important issue for early childhood educators?

FURTHER READING

Andre, T. and C. Neave (1992). *The complete day care guide.* Toronto: McGraw-Hill Ryerson.

Bertrand, J. (1990). *Childcare management guide: A comprehensive resource for boards of directors.* Toronto: OCBCC.

Chapman, E. (1990). *Supervisors' survival kit.* New York: Macmillan.

Decker, C. and J. Decker (1992). *Planning and administering early childhood programs.* New York: Maxwell Macmillan.

Hildebrand, V. (1993). *Management of child care development centers.* New York: Maxwell Macmillan.

Seefeldt, C. (1990). *Continuing issues in early childhood education.* New York: Morrow.

APPENDIX A: EXAMPLE OF AN APPLICATION FORM

APPLICATION FORM

1. Child's name _____

   F _____ M _____ Date of birth _____ Telephone no. _____

   Address _____

   City_____ Postal Code _____

2. Mother's name _____

   Place of business _____ Telephone no. _____

   Address _____

3. Father's name _____

   Place of business _____ Telephone no. _____

   Address _____

4. Family doctor_____

   Address _____

   Telephone no. _____ Child's health card number _____

5. Please name two people who could be called in an emergency if you cannot be reached

   1st name _____ Relationship _____

   Address _____ Telephone no. _____

   2nd name _____ Relationship _____

   Address _____ Telephone no. _____

6. Commencement data _____ Centre _____

   Period preferred: Full days _____ Half days   am   pm

   1/2 Day Kindergarten Program   am_____   pm_____

   School age: Before school_____ Hot lunch?_____ After school_____

   Arrival time _____ With whom?_____

   Departure time _____ With whom?_____

7. Describe previous/present child care arrangements: _____

   _____

   _____

   _____

8. Would you tell us a little about your child? (use n/a if appropriate)

   a) Physical abilities, health (any allergies, toilet abilities, and method of letting you know s/he needs to use toilet): _____

   _____

   _____

   b) Personality characteristics (shy, outgoing, any fears): _____

   _____

   _____

c) Eating habits (strong likes and dislikes): _____
_____
_____

d) Sleeping habits (special toys, blanket, etc.) _____
_____
_____

e) Is there anything else you can think of that would help us to know and understand your child better? _____
_____
_____

9. Other children in the family:

Name _____ Age_____ Sex_____

Name _____ Age_____ Sex_____

Name _____ Age_____ Sex_____

Other people living in household: _____
_____
_____

PLEASE NOTE

• Children will be released to the parent(s) who register their children in the Centre.

• CHILDREN WILL NOT BE RELEASED TO ANYONE NOT LISTED ON THE FORM UNLESS THE CENTRE IS ADVISED OF THE CHANGE OF PERSON (INCLUDING TAXI SERVICE).

• Fees (see Fee Schedule).

• A registration fee of _____ is required with this application. This fee is not refunded.

• If for some reason it becomes necessary to withdraw your child, a minimum notice of ONE MONTH is required or one month's fee in lieu of notice.

• It is important that parents read and understand the Health and Emergency Policy, and the Financial Policy.

Date_____ Signed _____

(Parent or Guardian)

APPENDIX B: PERMISSION FOR GIVING MEDICINE

PERMISSION FOR GIVING MEDICINE

Date:_____

I hereby give my permission for_____
"name of child"

to be given _____ of _____ at_____
"amount of medicine"   "type"   "time(s) of day"

_____
"date (or dates) medicine to be given"

_____
Parent's signature

For school use only   Administered by _____

APPENDIX C: SAMPLE RETURN TO CHILD DAY CARE CENTRE FORM

RETURN TO CHILD DAY CARE CENTRE FORM

Parents:
This form is to be completed by a family physician after your child has a serious illness, childhood disease, or accident.

To: Early Childhood Education Centre

Date:_____

I have examined_____, and find him/her recovered
"child's name"

well enough to return to the Early Childhood Education Centre, taking part in all activities

with these limitations: _____

_____

Signed: _____
(Physician's signature)

APPENDIX D: ACCIDENT FORM

ACCIDENT FORM

Date: _____   Name: _____

Time: _____

Type of injury (please describe result of accident)

_____

_____

First aid administered (please describe)

_____

_____

Administered by: _____

Were the parents informed? _____   _____
                                                    Parent's signature

How did the accident occur? (please describe in detail)

_____

_____

_____

_____

_____

_____

_____

_____

Your name: _____

Note: This form is to be completed as soon as possible after any accident. Parents to be informed by the teachers only.

APPENDIX E: INFANT/TODDLER PROGRAM DAILY INFORMATION SHEET

DAILY INFORMATION SHEET

Name: _____ Arrival Time: _____

Date: _____ Departure Time: _____

1. When did your child eat or drink last? Time: _____

   Type and amount of food: _____

2. Did your child sleep well last night? _____ If not, please describe: _____

   What time did your child get up this morning? _____

   How is your child feeling this morning? _____

3. If your child has had a bowel movement this morning, please describe:_____

4. Is there any other information that will help us take better care of your child?

   _____

THE FOLLOWING TO BE COMPLETED BY STAFF

FOOD	AM	NOON	PM
Refused Ate Little Ate Moderately Ate Well			
Comments:			

BOTTLES	AM	NOON	PM
Formula Milk Juice Water			
Comments:			

BOWEL MOVEMENTS	AM	PM
Normal/Formed Soft/Loose Diarrhea		
Comments:		

SLEEP	ASLEEP BY:	AWAKE BY:
AM PM		

ACTIVITIES AND DEVELOPMENTAL MILESTONES:

APPENDIX F: SAMPLE MEDICAL RECORD

MEDICAL RECORD

Name_____   Nickname _____   Birth Date _____

Parent or Guardian _____   Phone (Home) _____

Mother's Phone (Work) _____   Father's Phone (Work) _____

Doctor_____   Telephone _____

Immunization Record (Approx. Dates)	Childhood Diseases	Medical Examination
Quad (Primary Series)	Chickenpox _____	General Appearance _____
Dose 1 _____	Measles (Rubella) _____	Height_____ Weight_____
Dose 2 _____	Mumps _____	Hearing _____ Vision_____
Dose 3 _____	Measles _____	Chest_____ Abdomen_____
1. Quad Booster _____	Others _____	Skin_____ Extremities ____
2. Quad Booster _____	Allergies _____	
Mumps_____	_____	
Measles _____	_____	
TB Skin Test _____		
Haemophilus Influenzae Type B (HIB) _____		

Please add any other information that would help us meet this child's needs.

Child's Health Card Number	M.D. _____
	Date _____

APPENDIX G: SAMPLE INTERVIEW FORM

GUIDE FOR PARENT INTERVIEWS

Based upon the stated goals of our centre, this guide is based upon the observed characteristics of each child.

Name of Child: _____ D.O.B.: _____

Date of Completion of Form: _____

Date of Interview: _____

Interview: _____

Parent (s):_____

Specific Information to be Requested From Parents:

_____

_____

_____

_____

Additional Information Resulting From Interview:

_____

_____

_____

_____

_____

_____

_____

_____

_____

SELF-CONCEPT	
Assertion of needs	
Pride in accomplishments	
Need/Response to approval	
Persistence in achievements	

Reaction to limits: _____

General Comments: _____

_____

EMOTIONAL	
Demonstration of awareness of emotions	
Emotions freely expressed	
Acceptance of assistance	

Expression of emotions _____

Most commonly expressed emotions _____

Response to conflict _____

General Comments: _____

_____

COMMUNICATION	
Understands and responds to teacher's direction	
Understands and responds to peer direction	
Comprehension of spoken words	
Clear verbal expression	
Uses language to share information or ideas	
Age-appropriate sentence structure	

Enjoys literary experiences	
Interest in written language	

General Comments: _____

_____

SOCIAL	
Awareness of others	
Enjoys interacting with peers	
Plays with variety of children	
Relationship with adults	
Relationship with peers	
Problem-solving skills	

Quality of play with peers _____

General Comments: _____

_____

CHOICE MAKING	
Makes choices	
Follows through on choices made	
Direction needed	
Chooses a range of activities	

General Comments: _____

_____

CREATIVE EXPRESSION	
Interest in creative art activities	
Interest in dramatic play	

Interest in musical activities	
Interest in creative movement	
Chooses own materials	

Preference of activities: _____

General Comments: _____

_____

GROSS MOTOR

Outdoors: Skilled use of equipment Enjoyable time	

Favourite activity _____

_____

Indoors: Skilled use of equipment Enjoyable time	

Favourite activity _____

Activities not attempted_____

General Comments: _____

_____

FINE MOTOR

General competence Eye-hand coordination and manual dexterity	

Favourite activity _____

General Comments: _____

_____

SELF-HELP	
Independent dressing Independent toileting	

General Comments: _____

_____

EATING HABITS	
Enjoys snack/lunch Self-help skills	

General likes and dislikes_____

General Comments: _____

_____

SLEEPING HABITS	
Able to relax Awareness of others	

Length of sleep_____

General Comments: _____

_____

APPENDIX H: INITIAL INTERVIEW FORM

INITIAL INTERVIEW FORM

Your Name _____

Child's Name _____ Nickname _____

Parent (Guardians) Who Come in With Child _____

_____

---

1. Child's response to visiting centre:

   a) undisturbed ( )   d) extremely active ( )

   b) anxious to stay close to parent ( )   e) whining ( )

   c) cried ( )   f) other (please specify) _____

2. General appearance: a) well-groomed ( )

   b) healthy ( )

3. Relationship to interviewer:

   a) cooperative ( )   e) aggressive ( )

   b) hostile ( )   f) dependent ( )

   c) fearful ( )   g) demands full attention ( )

   d) shy ( )   h) friendly ( )

4. Activity preference throughout interview: _____

5. Relationship with parent during interview:

   a) warm ( )   d) understanding ( )

   b) hostile ( )   e) hanging on to ( )

   c) demanding ( )

6. Special information from parents:

   a) play with other children _____

   b) relationship with siblings _____

   c) allergies _____

   d) physical problems (e.g., sight, hearing, etc.) _____

   e) parent's special request or concern _____

   f) physical markings or characteristics _____

7. How do you feel child will manage at the preschool centre?

   Initially shy but soon feel comfortable ( ) Other (please specify) _____

   Frightened ( )

   Ready to enter immediately ( )

8. General Description:

   a) active ( )

   b) sedentary ( )

   c) very quiet ( )

   d) quick ( )

   e) other _____

9. Coordinations: large muscle — good ( ) fair ( ) poor ( )

   small muscle — good ( ) fair ( ) poor ( )

10. Language mastery: vocabulary above average ( ) average ( ) poor ( )

11. Expresses self in: a) words ( )

   b) phrases ( )

   c) short sentences ( )

   d) longer sentences ( )

12. Enunciation: a) clear ( ) d) impediment ( )

   b) baby talk ( ) e) other (please specify) _____

   c) mumbles ( ) _____

   _____

13. Parent's reaction to school: a) cooperative ( ) d) somewhat hostile ( )

   b) eager ( ) e) other (please specify)

   c) apprehensive ( ) _____

   _____

Starting date agreed upon: _____

Teacher responsible for child: _____

Any additional comments you wish to make: _____

_____

_____

_____

APPENDIX I: INTAKE INTERVIEW CHECKLIST

INTAKE INTERVIEW CHECKLIST

---

1. Description of the Program
   - developmentally appropriate
   - based upon the needs and interests of children
   - themes used as a point of departure and focus for all developmental areas
   - staff and student teachers
   - schedule established but flexible—describe child's day

I/T—sensorimotor

---

2. Forms
   - explain and sign—video
     - —permission to leave premises
   - check for signature—application
     - —2 policies
     - —registration fee paid
   - give to parents—medical form—tell parents a doctor's signature is required
   - explain drug administration
     - —original container
     - —medicine form
     - —medicine cabinet and fridge
     - —permission-to-return forms
     - —general information form—highlights
   - complete initial interview form—ask relevant questions
   - confirm start date

I/T—daily info sheet   I—feeding schedule

---

3. Arrival and Departure
   - rooms open—early morning arrivals
   - separation anxiety—say goodbye—use of observation booth
   - remind parents to sign children in and out —daily forms
     - —clipboards

4. General Information

   I/T   Preschool

   - daily info box   - sign-in/out clipboards

   - drawer/security items   - curriculum charts

   - diaper storage   - high-low cubbie

   - sanitary procedure   - security items

   - parent information boards

5. Tour

   - orange room, infant room, toddler room, muscle room, green room, blue room, creative room, observation booths, playgrounds, kitchen, parent bulletin board, menu posted, office-slot for cheque, (preschool) medicine forms/cabinet, resource centre

6. Discipline

   - children helped to take responsibility for their own actions

   - problem solving/child's active role

   - positive approach

   - stop undesired behaviour

   - biting

7. Summary

   - ask parents if they have any questions

   - clear on first-day procedure

   - arrangements made for—name on cubbies, lunch plan, bed plan

                           —post necessary allergy information

   - complete file and return to team leader

APPENDIX J: GUIDE FOR INFANT/TODDLER PARENT INTERVIEWS

GUIDE FOR INFANT/TODDLER PARENT INTERVIEWS

Based upon the stated goals of our centre, this guide is based upon the observed characteristics of each child.

Name of Child: _____ D.O.B.: _____

Date of Completion of Form: _____

Date of Interview: _____

Interviewer: _____

Parent(s): _____

Specific Information to be Requested From Parents:

_____

_____

_____

_____

Additional Information Resulting From Interview:

_____

_____

_____

_____

(use back if more space needed)

OVERALL RESPONSE TO PROGRAM

Level of Enjoyment, Approach, Comfort

_____

_____

_____

_____

GOAL & GUIDELINE CONSIDERATIONS
HABITS AND ROUTINES

Sleeping patterns_____

_____

Eating patterns _____

_____

Toileting patterns_____

_____

ACTIVITY TIME

Favourite activities_____

Gross motor_____

Fine motor _____

Response to sensory/creative stimuli_____

_____

Cognitive _____

Response to outdoors _____

_____

SOCIAL

Awareness of others/recognition of familiar people _____

_____

Method of communication/interaction _____

_____

Interactions with adults of particular enjoyment (i.e., songs; body games; peek-a-boo)

_____

Attachment to particular children

_____

Response to group activities_____

_____

Method of play _____

_____

EMOTIONAL

Emotions expressed/method of expression _____

_____

Ability to make needs known/method of making needs known _____

_____

Stressful situations _____

_____

Reaction to change _____

_____

Acceptance of comfort _____

_____

Attachment relationships with adults _____

_____

SELF-CONCEPT

Demonstrates awareness of self (i.e., recognition of: name; self in mirror; possessions; etc.)

_____

Awareness of body parts _____

_____

Self-help motivation/abilities (i.e., feedings; dressing) _____

_____

Response to positive reinforcement/approval _____

_____

Response to limits _____

_____

Level of persistence _____

_____

APPENDIX K: HEALTH AND EMERGENCY PROCEDURES

HEALTH AND EMERGENCY PROCEDURES

1. If your child should become ill while at school, the staff will call you at the numbers listed on the application to come and pick him/her up. The staff will make the decision to call you based on the best interest of both your child and the health of the other children in the centre. For this reason it is important that your business numbers and the people listed on the application as alternative emergency numbers be kept up to date.

2. If your child should have a minor accident while at school, the staff will call you to come and decide on medical treatment. If the centre nurse and/or doctor deem the injury serious, an ambulance will be called and we will meet you at the hospital.

   We will use _____ Hospital if you are from the area or

   _____ if you are from _____.

3. Should it become necessary to evacuate the Early Childhood Education Centre, children would be

   safely moved to _____.

   Arrangements have been made for us to use the_____

   on a twelve-month basis. Parents would be notified should it become necessary to use the alternative

   facility. The phone number at _____ is _____.

4. Should a major area accident occur and we were required to immediately evacuate the entire

   _____ area, the children would be safely transported by the

   centre to the _____ telephone _____.

   Facilities are available to accommodate the children until they can be picked up by parents.

   The above procedures are designed to keep parents informed and reduce concerns should unusual incidents occur.

   I have read and understood the Health and Emergency Procedures.

   Date: _____ Signed: _____

   (Parent or Guardian)

APPENDIX L: FINANCIAL POLICY

FINANCIAL POLICY

---

1. A registration fee of $10 is required with an application for enrollment. This fee is not refunded.

2. Fees are due at the beginning of each month. The Early Childhood Education Centre is operated on a non-profit basis and fees are our main source of income. Therefore it is important that fees are paid at the beginning of each month.

3. The monthly fee is due regardless of the number of days in the month, absenteeism due to illness or inclement weather, plus school and statutory holidays. The centre closes for two professional development days a year, one day in November and Easter Monday. In addition the Half-Day Nursery School Program is closed during Winter Break Week,

   usually _____ . The centre closes the week between Christmas and New Year's Day.

4. Parents withdrawing their child(ren) for summer holidays will not be required to pay the fee for up to two weeks during the months of July and August only. A minimum of two weeks' notice for holiday time is required. Beyond the two-week period fees are charged in order to reserve your child's space.

5. If, for some reason, it becomes necessary to withdraw your child, a minimum notice of one month is required, or one month's fee in lieu of that notice.

6. Parents may apply to the _____
   child care office to seek assistance with all or part of the fee to send their child to the Early Childhood Education Centre.

   Date: _____ Signed: _____

                                                                (Parent or Guardian)

FAMILIES AND EARLY CHILDHOOD PROGRAMS— A VITAL PARTNERSHIP

What place do early childhood settings have in the lives of families? Although work-ing with parents is an integral part of what we do, we often find our role in this area needs definition. This chapter addresses the partnership between families and early childhood settings. Areas covered include:

- *Why involve parents?*
- *The benefits of partnerships with parents*
- *Obstacles to parental participation*
- *Ways for parents to get involved*
- *Communicating with parents*

WHY INVOLVE PARENTS?

In order to think about the relationship between parents and early childhood educators, it is useful to look at the early childhood setting as a *service,* a *support,* a *resource,* and a *partner.*

A Service

The last two decades have seen a dramatic increase in the number of mothers who work outside the home. Now, two out of every five Canadian workers are women. The service pro-vided by early childhood settings responds to the resulting need for child care. The nature of families has also changed, and more single parents are requiring care for their children while they work outside the home.

A Support

Early childhood settings provide an important support for young families. This is a relatively new role for early childhood educators. While some may caution that it potentially diminishes the rights and responsibilities of parents, such involvement can enhance family life, reduce the strain of everyday parenting, and support parents in their roles of raising young children.

The Canadian family is in a process of transition. Significant social pressures are profoundly affecting the lives of young children and their families. At the same time, the world of work is changing. As private companies and public institutions "downsize," "out-source," and privatize in response to fiscal pressures, finding and keeping a job for life is becoming increasingly less common. This has created additional stress for families. Parents are now spending more of their time looking for work, retraining, furthering their education on a full-time or part-time basis, and/or creating their own employment.

Higher divorce rates and increasing economic pressures have resulted in more single-parent families and families in which both parents work outside of the home. These changing family structures have led to greater demands being placed on early childhood educators, who may be asked to support families in ways that were once the responsibility of the extended family. Caregivers may find themselves in the position of discussing personal issues, and must be mindful of issues related to confidentiality as they provide the family with nonjudgmental support.

Early childhood settings provide an essential service for working parents.

A Resource

Alice Honig (1979) talks about parents' rights to have access to tools that can help them fulfill their roles as parents. The early childhood setting is in a unique position to provide these tools. Through parent education programs, such as behaviour management workshops, caregivers can play a significant role in providing information to enable parents to be more effective.

Informal discussions, surveys, and brainstorming sessions can help parents identify their specific needs and interests. Parent education programs can then be organized in response. These programs can take many forms, including workshops, parent meetings, and self-help groups.

This sounds like a straightforward proposition—but it isn't. First, the needs of families are as diverse as the needs of individual children, representing a range of values, beliefs, and customs. Second, training programs focus on preparing students to work with children, so early childhood educators may lack experience related to working with parents. Additional opportunities for professional development in this area must be provided.

There is no one way to parent. Early childhood educators must adopt a nonjudgmental approach, selecting strategies that best meet the unique needs of each family and respect their values and background.

A Partner

Parents and early childhood educators need to see each other as partners in the care and education of children. Parents have the final responsibility, but the centre where a child spends many hours a day for five days a week has a great effect on that child's development.

Children's experiences of child care are enhanced by parents' involvement.

Each partner must collaborate with the other in order to maximize the growth and development of each young child.

THE BENEFITS OF PARTNERSHIPS WITH PARENTS

When parents are involved in the education and care of their young child, everyone wins. An examination of some of the potential outcomes indicates that parental involvement is indeed powerful.

Parents and children come as a package: "As children enter the classroom, their families also come with them," says Lightfoot (1978). By working together, parents and early childhood educators can ensure that settings provide the best possible care for young children. A collaborative effort utilizes the skills and knowledge of both partners, enhancing the program and standards for care.

As Doherty (1995) shows, there is a correlation between parent involvement and quality care. This finding is corroborated by the research of Endsley, Minish, and Zhou (1993). In particular, their work indicates that early childhood programs are higher quality when the supervisor promotes formal parental involvement and facilitates informal daily communication between parents and staff. At present, early childhood educators primarily define their roles in terms of their work with young children. But if we work with the child alone, we fail to acknowledge the depth of influence and involvement of parents with their children. We must implement strategies that respect and complement the role that parents play in the care and education of their young children. Parent involvement is fundamental to ensuring that children's needs are met.

There is increasing evidence that parental involvement is the key to sustaining the gains achieved in early intervention programs for children believed to be at risk. It follows that parental participation enhances children's experiences in all early childhood settings.

Some parents experience a sense of guilt when they place their child in an early childhood setting. By empowering parents and affirming the central role they play in the care and education of their children, early childhood educators can relieve some of the anxiety parents feel here. At the same time, involvement enables parents to exert some influence over the setting to which they entrust the care of their child.

For the child, parental involvement helps form a bridge between home and child care. Transition from one to the other is often not easy, and the presence of parents in the setting helps to reassure the child of the connections. In addition, there is substantial evidence that parental involvement affects children's cognitive development.

Participation gives parents opportunities to interact with and observe early childhood educators working with their children as well as other children in the same age range. They have the opportunity to meet other parents and share ideas, resources, and child-rearing dilemmas. These interactions can enhance their understanding of child development, methods of guiding behaviour, and knowledge of appropriate toys and materials. They are also able to see children playing with other children and to increase their overall knowledge of early childhood settings. Some parents will develop new skills from this participation, thus contributing to their self-confidence and sense of competence.

Educators benefit when interactions with parents provide some new understanding about a child, enabling them to meet the child's needs more effectively. Parent participation can also result in a greater variety of activities at the centre, reflecting the talents and skills of individual parents.

Finally, it is the parents' right and perhaps even a responsibility to be involved in the education of their child. They did not abdicate their rights to influence their child's development when they enrolled him or her in the early childhood setting. On the contrary, they expressed their nurturing role through their choice of a setting that provides quality care, and this role can be further enhanced by their involvement in that setting.

OBSTACLES TO PARENTAL PARTICIPATION

Philosophical commitment to working with families is not enough to ensure parents' participation. If parental involvement is so powerful, why is it so difficult to establish?

Early childhood educators may interpret lack of parental participation as lack of interest. Is this true? Closer examination reveals a number of obstacles on the way to meeting a commitment to work with families.

Parents are busy people with many demands on their time and energy—work, family commitments, continued studies, and the like. However, time is not the only obstacle to involvement. Parents may not realize they have something to offer to the early childhood setting, or they may hesitate because they don't know what to do. This hesitation may result in their feeling uncomfortable and unable to contribute.

Barriers to staff working in partnership with parents may also originate within the setting:

- Staff may not fully understand the value of parent participation. Often staff are not parents themselves, and they may have difficulty fully comprehending the importance—or the difficulties—of parent involvement.

- Some educators may believe that mothers should not work and leave their children in the care of others. In her work, Galinsky (1990) found it not uncommon for early child-

Parent involvement helps form a bridge between home and the early childhood setting.

hood educators to hold this view. Such a belief could create a barrier interfering with educators' readiness to work with parents.

- Staff may lack the skills needed to work effectively in partnership with parents. It is also difficult for students to see, at first glance, the importance of working closely with parents. In some cases, students have little opportunity to interact in a meaningful way with parents as they complete their practicums.

- The educator may feel threatened when parents perform some of the tasks she or he usually does in the early childhood setting.

- Some may view the parent's presence as an intrusion and may choose to work in isolation.

- Parent participation requires additional work on the part of staff, who may already feel overburdened by existing demands on their time.

While working in partnership with any parents requires shared commitment and effort, there are a number of additional considerations when working with families representing diverse cultural, racial, and linguistic populations. Depending on the specific background of each family, there may be a number of differences, including customs, holiday celebrations, language, child-rearing practices, family values, and expectations. While most staff will appreciate that such diversity enriches the experiences of young children, they also acknowledge that early childhood educators require additional training if they are to work in partnership within a diverse multicultural environment. During the last few years more understanding about the need to help students become knowledgeable and insightful in this regard has seen new emphasis on this area in the students' educational program.

WAYS FOR PARENTS TO GET INVOLVED

It is more difficult for today's parents to participate in their children's education, given the competing demands for their time. Traditional parent involvement schemes that invited the participation of parents in the child's early childhood program may no longer work. Supervisors need to provide leadership to ensure that a range of strategies is implemented to foster the partnership between parents and staff.

Participation can take many forms, ranging from informal conversations to parent membership on the board of directors. Different possibilities include:

- parent meetings
- newsletters
- open-house events
- special parent programs, including support groups, self-help groups, and special interest groups
- collecting "beautiful junk" to be contributed to the centre
- volunteering, fundraising, membership on the board of directors or advisory group
- informal visits to the setting
- recording informal observations about their child's growth and development
- sharing parent skills, talents, needs, interests
- parent–teacher conferences

- toy-lending libraries
- coffee hours, muffin mornings, potluck dinners

Parent Meetings

For parent meetings to be successful, it is important for parents to play a central role in planning the event. By connecting with other parents and designing the meeting on the basis of their needs and interests, they will be more likely to feel a sense of ownership and be encouraged to participate.

In planning the event, a questionnaire or suggestion box can be used to collect information about parents' needs and interests. A list of topics can then be compiled and parents can be involved in ranking the topics. They can also select a topic to be the basis for a presentation and/or discussion that responds to their interests.

Attendance at parent meetings will also be enhanced if child care is provided. With the many competing demands for parents' time and energy, the provision of child care during the meeting relieves families of the burden of making individual arrangements.

Parents might find it very helpful to have a "call the centre time" set aside each week. Perhaps a half hour or hour per week could be identified when a parent knows that staff are available by phone to talk about any topic the parent may have wanted to discuss but just couldn't find the time or place to do so. Sometimes answers to a few quick questions are all the parents want to know, or they may find it easier to broach a concern by phone initially that really needs more personal follow-up. This opportunity to know that staff can be readily reached may ward off issues that when left unaddressed may develop into bigger and more unsolvable concerns.

Finally, it is important to evaluate the effectiveness of the methods you have used to make staff and parents partnerships more meaningful. Providing opportunities for parents to provide feedback can do this. A brief checklist with a space for comments will assist in the future planning. Asking for feedback will also demonstrate the centre's commitment to providing meaningful experiences that respect parents' input.

No idea or strategy is too insignificant to consider when brainstorming ideas to involve parents in a centre. Sometimes it's like working with a specific child or a group of children. You know that some things will work in some instances, but you have to try new and innovative ideas to achieve your goal. This is also true when working with parents, who come with a diverse set of needs, background, and experiences.

COMMUNICATING WITH PARENTS

A commitment to working with parents is not usually lacking on the part of staff, but the communication systems to make the partnership work may be underdeveloped. The leadership provided by the supervisor in developing these systems is very important.

Good communication links the child's two worlds, and is critical if staff and parents are to work as partners. Effective communication takes work. Staff may encounter problems in trying to communicate with parents at either end of their workday, when both parties may be tired or pressed for time. This can be mistakenly interpreted as a lack of interest. While parents will confirm that these pressures play a role, they also report that they are uncomfortable in their initial contacts with staff, or that they don't know what to ask. Thus supervisor and staff must take responsibility for initiating contact and sharing information with parents.

First impressions are important. A parent's first contact with an early childhood setting sets the stage for future involvement, or lack of it. For example, when a parent first calls a centre, a staff representative should be prepared to provide whatever information is required to make the parent feel welcome.

The philosophy, organization of the centre, and the physical environment as described in previous chapters tell parents whether they are welcome to fully participate in their child's world at child care or whether they are not encouraged to do so.

The unfamiliar setting, and sometimes guilt about entrusting their child to another's care, may make parents feel uneasy prior to their first visit. The supervisor and staff must help parents feel comfortable. This may include strategies for responding to parents' varied cultural backgrounds and/or their individual needs. By describing the setting and the program, and emphasizing the importance of the parents' role, staff will make the parent more aware of what to expect and how to behave in the setting.

During the first visit by parents, the supervisor should plan for an informal tour, a classroom observation, and an interview. Some programs may wish to provide a checklist or questionnaire to assist parents in focusing their observations and questions. At the end of the visit, it is important to discuss the parents' reactions and impressions, and to answer any questions. Parents should also be encouraged to visit other centres, to make sure the one they've chosen is the right one for their child.

Separating from home is difficult, particularly for young children, but it can be less disturbing when parents and early childhood educators work together. Separation can be difficult for parents too. Supervisors and staff can support them by acknowledging this difficulty, and encouraging them to discuss their responses. One approach may prefer that parents leave shortly after their arrival if the child seems overly upset during the first few days of adjustment. Another will encourage parents to stay until their child is calm. Whatever the preference, the staff need to discuss their expectations with parents beforehand, so that both are consistent in their response.

Early childhood educators play a vital role in helping children make the transition from home to child care.

Communication Strategies

The supervisor needs to provide leadership, by working with staff and board to define the centre's level of commitment to working with families, and articulating policies to reflect this commitment. Such policies could enable parents to visit the setting without an appointment, or to stay with their children during their first days in the centre. Policies like these send a clear "Welcome" message to parents.

The supervisor can work with staff to develop strategies for involving parents, and a plan for assessing these strategies effectiveness. Part of this approach is to work with staff to explore their attitudes about working with parents, and provide related staff training needs. Parental involvement will meet with resistance if staff does not have attitudes and skills that facilitate parent integration.

An orientation program for parents should be developed for the centre. This program might include a review of centre philosophy and goals, an informational tour or video, an opportunity to meet the teachers, a discussion of the fee schedule, and an overview of policies and procedures. This is also a good opportunity for the administrator to learn about the child and to discuss any special requirements, needs, or concerns.

Parents should be involved in decision making. A parent advisory committee can provide feedback and recommendations to the centre, and advocate for parents and their involvement in the setting. Parents can also serve as advocates in the community at large.

Specific communication strategies might include some of the following:

- Surveys could be used to gather information about parents' skills, needs, and interests. This can be used to create a card or computer file with information about tasks that parents can be involved in. Information gained in the survey can help ensure the program is responsive to the cultural needs of each family. An example of such a survey is given in the Appendix.

- A notice board could be reserved for parents. Brochures displayed could include guidelines for interacting with children, or articles and news of centre and community interest. Parents could be asked to post their own information. Daily information can also be shared using message centres, mailboxes, journals, or conversations, and by using parent–teacher conferences to discuss a child's progress.

- Newsletters could feature children's work, parent contributions, anecdotes, plans for future activities, and other information related to the operation of the centre. It is important to keep a positive tone in these communications.

- A parents' space could be set aside, with comfortable seating, coffee, reading materials and resources, pictures of children, posters, etc. As an adjunct, coffee hours could be arranged for parents to chat informally with one another, staff, and even children.

- An open house with slides or a video could illustrate the centre's program or philosophy.

- The family could be visited in their home, or phoned to share their child's accomplishment.

- Technology could be used to support effective communication between staff and parents. Answering machines, voice mail systems, faxes, videos, and e-mail can be useful in supplementing the exchange of information. At present, some parents are communicating with teachers via e-mail on a regular basis.

As early childhood educators, we need to move beyond a verbal commitment to designing mechanisms to involve parents in the education of their young children. Once the role of families in early childhood settings has been defined, we need action plans to give life to our definitions. Good intentions are not enough.

IN CONCLUSION

Early childhood settings are an important resource and support for families facing increased stress and pressure. By working together, parents and early childhood educators can ensure that settings provide the best possible care for young children. A collaborative approach that views parents as partners is most effective.

Parent involvement is central to ensuring that children's needs are met. The results of research confirm the importance of the parents' role.

While collaboration between early childhood educators and parents benefits all involved, it is not easily attained. Settings need to implement a number of strategies to strengthen their relationships with families, and to recognize that there are a number of obstacles to parent involvement.

Participation takes many forms. Parent meetings can be an effective mechanism for communication if parents are involved in planning and evaluating the event.

A number of communication strategies can be implemented to connect with parents. Staff and supervisors need to establish policies that reflect their commitment to their partnership with parents and the value of parent involvement.

ACTIVITIES

1. Design a parent survey that will identify needs, interests, and talents. Such a questionnaire could also solicit feedback about the effectiveness of the early childhood setting. Once completed, what will you do with the information to encourage parental involvement in an early childhood setting?

2. Draw a diagram of an early childhood setting, and modify the space to incorporate an area for parents. The design should take into account traffic patterns and noise levels, and should be situated in such a way that it invites parents to make use of it.

3. Survey your community and identify potential resources and support systems for families with young children.

4. How could you evaluate the effectiveness of different strategies designed to encourage parent participation in the early childhood program? Identify several mechanisms.

5. Design a questionnaire or activity that will help staff assess their values and beliefs about parenting and/or their attitudes to parent involvement at their centre.

REVIEW QUESTIONS

1. In what ways can early childhood settings support families?

2. Identify several strategies for involving parents in early childhood settings.

3. Identify the benefits of parent involvement for children, parents, and staff.

4. Describe some of the barriers to parental involvement.

5. Describe some of the different ways in which parents can be involved.

6. Describe a process for planning an effective parent evening.

7. How can staff ensure that a parent's first impression of an early childhood setting is positive?

8. Identify strategies that help to maintain effective communications between parents and early childhood staff.

FURTHER READING

Bjorklund, G. and C. Burger (1987, January). "Making conferences work for parents, teachers and children." *Young Children*, 26–31.

Denholm, C., R. Ferguson, and A. Pence (1987). *Professional child and youth care: The Canadian perspective*. Vancouver: University of British Columbia Press.

Galinsky, E. (1988). "Parents and teacher-caregivers: Sources of tension, sources of support." *Young Children*, 4–12.

Galinsky, E. (1978). *Easing parents through beginnings and endings*. Child Care Information Exchange.

Honig, A. *Parental involvement in early childhood education*. (Rev. ed.). Washington, DC: National Association for the Education of Young Children.

Joffe, C. (1979). *Friendly intruders: Childcare professionals and family life*. Berkeley: University of California Press.

Lightfoot, S. (1978). *Worlds apart: Relationships between families and schools*. New York: Basic Books.

Manburg, A. (1985). "Parent involvement: A look at practices that work." *Child Care Information Exchange*, 9–11.

Wilson, L. (1997). *Partnerships: Families and Communities in Canadian Early Childhood Education*, ITP Nelson.

APPENDIX: SAMPLE PARENT INVOLVEMENT QUESTIONNAIRE

Hi. My name is _____ and I am doing a survey for _____. We are interested in using parents as resource people to broaden the learning of the children. I was just wondering if you could give me three or four minutes of your time.

---

1. a) Would your workplace or place of study be willing to have a small group of approximately

   10–12 children of _____ ages for a brief tour or visit?

   Yes   (   )   Go to 1(b)   Maybe   (   )   Go to 1(b)
   No   (   )   Go to 2   Don't go to work or school (   )   Go to 2

   b) How interesting do you think this would be for children of this age group?
   Very interesting (   )   Fairly interesting (   )   Not very interesting (   )

2. Do you have any hobbies or interests you could share with the children in a classroom visit?

   Sports   (   )   Presentations   (   )
   Arts/crafts   (   )   Cultural activities   (   )
   Music/dance   (   )   No   (   )
   Collections   (   )   Other _____

3. a) If you are willing to say, which ethnic or cultural groups did your ancestors belong to?

   _____

   b) Is there an aspect of your heritage you might share with the children in the way of food, dance, music, or costumes?

   Yes   (   )   No   (   )

   c) Are other languages besides English spoken in your home?

   None   (   )   Other languages _____

4. Would you be able to contribute in other ways?

   Donating materials   (   )   Sewing cushions   (   )
   Donating storybooks/toys   (   )   Making story tapes (   )
   Baking/buying snack ingredients (   )   No   (   )
   Making games/toys   (   )   Other _____

5. Would you be interesting in getting involved in fundraising for our early childhood program?
   Yes (   )   No (   )   Maybe (   )

6. Do you have any other ideas or suggestions for a way in which you could participate in the child care centre?

   No   (   )

7. When might you have extra time available to participate further in the child care centre?

   Mornings   (   )   No time   (   )

   Afternoons   (   )   Other _____

   Evenings   (   )

8. a) Is there another parent or guardian in your household who would be available to answer our questions?

   Yes   (   )   Go to 8 (b)

   No   (   )   Go to next question

   b) What would be the best time to contact them by telephone?

   Mornings   (   )

   Afternoons   (   )

   Evenings   (   )

CLASSIFYING SECTION

9. [DO NOT ASK] The respondent is

   Male   (   )

   Female   (   )

10. Can I have your name, for the centre's reference?

    Respondent's name _____ Phone_____

    Parent/Guardian of _____

    Name refused   (   )

    Interviewer's name_____ Date _____

SOURCE: This questionnaire was developed by, and is used with the permission of, Sarah Allan and Adrienne McRuvie, of Ryerson Polytechnic University.

COMMUNITY, RESOURCES, AND ADVOCACY

As early childhood educators, we have a wide public responsibility: to work to provide necessary services; to speak out to gain the critical mass of support needed for accessible, quality early childhood environments; and to identify community partners and outside funding possibilities. Key areas of this chapter will examine this public responsibility and discuss the following points:

- *Developing new programs within the community*
- *Ensuring a variety of programs*
- *Community partners and outside funding*
- *Marketing new and existing programs*
- *Public education and advocacy*

Many Canadians have experienced confusion, frustration, and disappointment in their efforts to find quality settings for their children that provide the reassurance and confidence level they need to rest easy while they work. Regulated care continues to be unavailable, unaffordable, or unsatisfactory, and in some cases all three problems exist. We have heard the phrase "child care crisis in Canada" bandied around for years, but still parents struggle to find satisfactory settings for their babies, toddlers, preschoolers, and school-age children. When a quality setting is located for one child in the family, the service provided in that environment does not provide care for the older or younger child in the family. This often requires one, two, or in some cases three child care settings to meet the needs of the range of ages of children in one family. Quality is sometimes poor; existing services are often unresponsive to differing needs. There are legitimate concerns that children will suffer from broken federal government promises (see Chapter 2). While some parents prefer informal arrangements, a number of studies, such as Lero (1994), have shown that many parents who would prefer regulated care cannot find or afford it.

Mothers still bear the primary responsibility for child care arrangements. Most employers have not responded adequately to the changing needs of families. In parts of the country, regulated services are almost nonexistent for parents working shifts and irregular hours, or for those needing part-time, seasonal, or emergency care. Regulated services for infants and school-age children are even less available than those for children of other ages—less than 15% of early child care needs are met by the licensed care sector. Special needs services for children who are physically or mentally challenged, aboriginal children, and other children from diverse backgrounds are often lacking. In some places, long waiting lists for subsidized spaces exist alongside full-fee vacancies in established programs.

This is a long list full of challenges. Most Canadians have little understanding of the crucial issues, and it is up to us in the early childhood community to increase public awareness. As a student working to become a professional early childhood educator, little energy from yourself and from your educational institution is directed toward advocating for a comprehensive child care policy. Your energy as you study and practise to enter the early childhood field is focused on the knowledge, skills, and personal characteristics needed to work successfully with children and their families. One challenge for you as you complete your studies and enter the workforce is to learn how to work as a professional early childhood educator. Another challenge is work on behalf of the children and families whose needs you know and understand. Provide leadership and join with parents and other professionals to help the public and the various levels of governments to fully comprehend the need for quality, accessible, diversified, and affordable care for young children.

The results will be:

- happier, healthier, and more competent children,

- parents who can concentrate on their jobs or studies knowing that their children are well cared for

- decreased number of settings needed by one family

- reduction in unnecessary travelling time

- siblings who are able to see each other for parts of the day

- reduction in the stress many families are experiencing with both parents working or as a single parent

What can you do?

Understand and articulate the issues clearly in your own mind so that you know the facts and can speak confidently and capably about the issues surrounding the needs of families and their children in a changing and demanding society.

Join with other professionals by joining local associations, study groups, advisory councils, and active government agencies that are addressing child care issues. Look at your community and find out how the government structure will allow you to have input into municipal, regional, provincial, and federal concerns surrounding child care issues. You can help by offering to speak to groups about early childhood education or, as you increase your knowledge and understanding about early childhood settings, some of you might even decide to run for public office in the future. Remember that we have a continuous responsibility to be advocates for children and their families.

DEVELOPING NEW PROGRAMS WITHIN THE COMMUNITY

There is a strong unmet need for early childhood services. A doubling of total spaces would not meet the needs of parents who prefer regulated child care spaces. An increase in the number of licensed subsidized spaces requires planning and money. Existing programs may choose to expand their capacity, or broaden the types of services they offer, or both. Practitioners, parents, and interested community representatives will need to work together to realize this expanded system. The current trend is definitely away from reliance upon government support, assistance, and funding.

Creating new programs in a community is an exciting challenge requiring abundant creativity and energy. Changes in today's Canadian economy dictate that community groups must work, more than ever, in partnership to coordinate local programs for children, making sure that individual, cultural, and regional needs are met. Services to consider include licensed programs such as family home child care, group settings in parent cooperatives, community-sponsored environments, workplaces, franchises, and small professionals' business settings. One example is Doctor's Doolittle Daycare Centre in Kingston, which was begun by three female doctors who could not find affordable, accessible care for the hours they required. They met their needs by hiring an early childhood educator and assistant to look after their children, and later expanded this service to include other children. The centre is in the same building as their offices.

Given that less than 15% of child care is in licensed settings, other services must be considered, and these include care for children in their own home or care in a home setting other than the child's home. An early childhood educator, home care provider, nanny or baby-sitter may staff these environments. Other support services for parents and caregivers include toy libraries, drop-in centres, parenting workshops, and information and referral services. For example, a very clear need was determined in the Regional Municipality of Waterloo to address parents' inability to locate child care settings for their children and to know what to look for to ensure that their child was in a high quality and safe situation. This need was met by a not-for-profit organization that added this new service to their already existing resource centre and provided an easy-to-use system for parents to find and monitor child care environments. Visit their Web site at **www.cccndsa.on.ca** to see the range of services they offer to parents and to get an idea of the kinds of support services that need to be developed to assist working parents.

The need continues for the development of flexible and innovative models for all parents and with particular emphasis on rural and isolated communities, and for parent relief and emergency care.

Steps in Establishing a New Program

When embarking on a new venture, time spent planning is always worthwhile in the long run. It is important to do your homework, researching funding priorities and assessing existing services. If you feel the project has potential for outside funding, then you need to talk with funders to determine their priorities before you develop your proposals. Potential funders may be able to provide you with helpful information about service design and the development of a realistic time frame. Visiting other early childhood programs is also highly beneficial to provide you with opportunities to explore a variety of models and approaches. Above all, your motivation and enthusiasm for developing a relevant, high quality service is essential and infectious. When you believe in what you are doing, others will too.

These are the steps in developing the plan for a new program:

- Create the vision.
- Assess community needs.
- Review the legal requirements.
- Ensure a variety of programs.
- Identify potential partners in your community.
- Assess the potential for funding.
- Develop a marketing plan

Create the Vision

A new program must meet a need in the community, and the community's needs must now be the driving force to realize the vision. This driving force may come from an individual, often an early childhood educator with a strong desire to develop a child care service. It may alter-

Determine the number of families and children who will use your planned service, and the type of service they want.

natively be a group of parents or community professionals who have an interest in responding to needs for child care in their neighbourhood or workplace. Or it could be a community agency whose members wish to expand their current services to include some form of child care.

Whoever the original motivators are, they must be prepared to carry out all the preliminary tasks for the new program until a supervisor/leader or manager is hired. Some groups find it beneficial to work with a consultant experienced in developing early childhood settings. There will be no revenue until children are actually attending, so there is usually no reimbursement for the time and energy invested in the planning stages.

This is the creative stage of planning, a time to envision the full potential of the program. The dream will be refined by what families want and, it must be stressed, the available resources. Additional services can be phased in over time when funds become available.

Assess Community Needs

The first step in realizing your vision is to assess the need for early childhood services in the community. What programs currently exist, and what services do families require? Obtain information, feedback on your ideas, and support from other programs that are similar to your idea that are already functioning in your community:

- what services are available
- age groups served, and hours of operation
- current enrollment
- waiting lists
- utilization patterns
- plans for expansion
- fees, including subsidy allowances
- staff salary range
- development plans and growth potential in the area
- demographics

The answers will help you determine the current availability of early childhood services, while information about local fees and subsidy allocations (if any) and salaries will serve as reference points for determining a preliminary financial plan.

You will need to determine the number of families and children who will use your planned service, and the type of service they want. It is important to gather your information directly from potential users, and to do it before you seek a location or do any financial forecasting or program planning.

Some planning information may be available through local municipal offices, or the community may have recently conducted similar surveys. Before beginning your own survey, you need to define your objectives, to determine what kind of information you need. The development and use of a survey to determine community need involves six basic steps.

1. Define the Objectives

Be clear about why you are doing a survey. You want to ensure that your planned program meets real community needs.

Determine who will be surveyed: for example, parents of children attending the local elementary schools. Determine how many parents will be surveyed—this is called the sample size. After the target group has been chosen, research must be done on how to effectively approach the group. Have other recent surveys been completed? If they have, they may be helpful in fine-tuning your survey questions. Determine how you are going to collect information.

2. Prepare the Questions

Construct questions to fit your objectives, making sure each question solicits useful responses that can be compared and tabulated. If you gather information you don't need just because it seems interesting, the survey will take longer to complete and you run the risk of reducing participation. Always remember to ask yourself:

- Why am I asking this?
- What will it tell me?
- What will I do with the information?

Arrange the questions in a logical order, each leading to the next. Test out the completed survey on a small sample group, to make sure instructions are clear and the questions are being interpreted the way you intended them. You may need to revise the survey after the test.

Here is what is usually considered in a survey:

- number of families and children
- socioeconomic status or family income
- ages of children to be served
- location of program
- types of service families require and prefer

A sample questionnaire is provided in Appendix C.

3. Gather the Information

You will need to determine how you will collect the data. Possible methods include questionnaires, telephone surveys, use of key informants, and small group meetings. Personal interviews are the most costly and time-consuming of the suggested methods, but they often provide the best results. Telephone interviews are also useful for asking in-depth questions, although they too can be time-consuming. Phone to arrange appointments with individuals who have been difficult to contact. Train the individuals conducting the interviews so that questions are asked and recorded in a standardized manner—you will need to be able to compare the results.

Mailed questionnaires are less expensive, but usually have a lower rate of return. To assist participants in returning their completed questionnaires, provide a stamped, self-addressed envelope. A reminder phone call should follow up the mailing. Despite these measures, you may still have to call and make an appointment to collect the questionnaire.

Sending out letters to prospective users also serves as an effective way to promote the program.

4. Canvass the Community

Inform local community and service organizations of plans for the child care service. This helps market the service to professionals who work with potential users. Home and school associations, early childhood resource centres, and public health and social services departments may also be able to assist with the selection of neighbourhoods and workplaces for distributing questionnaires.

5. Evaluate the Findings

You will need to analyze the information you collect, and put it into a suitable format for presentation. Elaborate statistics are often not necessary; reporting total numbers and percentages may suffice. Keep in mind who will be reviewing the results when the findings are completed. Sharing the information with a committee, or a corporate or government body, may determine the method of presentation: for example, graphic illustrations or detailed statistics may be required.

6. Take Action

The information gathered and analyzed will hopefully confirm that the proposed service will be a welcome addition to the community. On occasion, a survey will show that the original plan needs to be substantially revised, or even that it is not a viable project.

Remember, though, that the thought, time, and energy spent making a thorough needs assessment will pay dividends—whether it is to create a new early childhood environment, to expand spaces in existing situations, or to strengthen or maintain subsidized spaces.

Reviewing the Legal Requirements

Across Canada, the care of groups of children is subject to regulatory control, in the jurisdiction of each province and territory. Standards vary greatly across the country and are difficult to compare, since each province employs different criteria to define categories of care. Changes in the political, economic, and social climate are also being reflected in child care regulations throughout Canada at present. Therefore it is crucial that anyone planning to open a child care program be in touch with his or her provincial/territorial consultant, who will provide the current, appropriate licensing requirements. In addition, municipalities usually have building, zoning, and health requirements. Chapter 2, "Changing Roles of Government," provides an overview of Canadian legislation and a list of provincial licensing offices.

ENSURING A VARIETY OF PROGRAMS

Facilities may offer a combination of full-, half-, and part-time programs. Some programs, usually half-day programs, provide services to children with special needs. The type of program being developed should relate to the assessed need identified by representatives of the community. Other factors that may affect program design are the philosophy, goals, and objectives of the group initiating the program, and the sources of funds available.

Infant-toddler Care

Quality group programs for infants and toddlers are costly. Small ratios and group sizes demand high fees in order to cover staff costs and special program costs. Providing proper care for infants and toddlers is physically hard work and requires special equipment, a highly child-proofed environment, and a meticulous approach to health and caregiving practices. While some parents continue to prefer home-based settings for this age group, there is an increasing demand for infant care settings that provide consistent, quality care that is easier for parents to monitor. The availability spaces for infants and toddlers also assist parents in meeting their child care needs for all their children to be located in one centre.

Preschoolers

Preschoolers, children aged three to six, are the best-served sector. This group uses the majority of licensed group spaces, and family caregivers tend to prefer caring for children of this age range. However, as school boards increase the number of junior kindergartens available in communities, centres may need to re-think the age span that their centre can accommodate. Centres need to respond to the changing needs of parents as the ages of children eligible for public school continue to fluctuate within boards of education.

School-age Children

Kindergarten-age children attend school for part of a day or part of a week. The availability of public kindergarten programs is changing and varies across Canada. In some areas,

The type of program you develop should relate to the needs identified by representatives of the community.

junior kindergartens offered through the school system are meeting the needs traditionally served by nursery schools

Part-time care for school-age children is offered in some communities at the local school, community centres, or the "Y." Some of these programs adhere to standards set by provincial and territorial governments. Combinations of child care arrangements can be shaped to meet parents' overall needs.

Some caregivers are reluctant to provide care for school-age children, because of the part-day nature of the care, and complicated scheduling around the school calendar. Parents are often forced to leave their children in before- and after-school "self care"—so-called "latch key" children. Another problem for school-age children arises because of the need for coordination among the different parties responsible for their care: parents, school, and child care provider.

Exceptional Care

Children with special needs, including physical and mental disabilities and exceptional health care needs, usually benefit from attending an inclusive or integrated quality child care program. Inclusion or integration with "typical" peers provides such children with irreplaceable opportunities to develop and enhance their social and adaptive behaviours.

An early childhood environment requires additional resources to accommodate the needs of such children. Inclusive programs would provide consultative and health-related supports, as well as environments that facilitate both physical and social integration. A family focus and meaningful parent involvement are critical. All the challenges that face parents seeking care are increased for the parents of children with special needs. The framework for the development of an accessible, affordable, quality continuum of child care options should include the "fundamental principles of access, equity, opportunity, and inclusion" (Guralnick 1990).

Aboriginal Children

Cultural integrity is a major consideration for aboriginal families, whether early childhood programs are provided on or off reserves. Child care models must be consistent with aboriginal cultural values. Native families will feel more inclined to enrol their children in programs that clearly value their involvement. The most effective way of ensuring cultural integration is to increase the number of aboriginal staff.

Inclusive Programs

As Beach (1992) states, all children should be welcomed as individuals regardless of ability or disability, cultural background, family income, or where their parents work. Children require caring adults who not only meet their physical needs, but are concerned for their intellectual, social, and emotional growth as well. Inclusive programs welcome cultural, racial, and linguistic diversity. Such programs are not targeted to a particular segment of the population, because programs that are targeted create inequalities in service provision. Consideration should be given to hiring, training, and educating caregivers who will foster appreciation of different child-rearing and nurturing styles, as well as attitudes and values from diverse cultures.

Group Care Programs

Group care refers to centre-based care for children ranging from newborn to twelve years, including nursery school and school-age care. The child care centre is generally the first image that comes to mind. Most group centres tend to serve children aged three to five years. Many parents choose group care because of location, increased opportunities for socialization with children of a similar age, the child-centred environment, and the reliability that comes from having backups when a staff member is ill or moves.

Group facilities vary in terms of resources, toys, and outside areas, but all must meet minimum standards defined by each province or territory. Care is usually offered on weekdays, typically from 7 a.m. to 6 p.m. Some centres provide part-time programs, although these are in short supply in Canada.

Some centres have an arrangement whereby the government subsidizes fees to low-income families. Each province and territory licenses child care centres. As most provinces and territories require some level of training for teachers in group care, the caregivers in these programs are more likely to have some training in child care and child development. In many cases, these required qualifications only apply to the lead caregiver.

The costs for centre care are generally higher than for home child care. It can be difficult to obtain a space, particularly for an infant or a toddler. The location is not always convenient, and transportation can present a problem for some families. The quality of care and programming will depend very much on the particular staff involved, the leadership of the supervisor in the centre, and the resources available to the program.

Part-time programs are geared to provide a half-day educational experience for children from $2\frac{1}{2}$ to 5 years of age. The options include nursery schools, preschools, Montessori programs, kindergartens, play groups, and some group care programs.

Home Child Care

Parents working or studying either part- or full-time need care for their children. Existing centres are rarely structured to accommodate irregular working hours or to care for children who are sick, and this presents difficulties for many parents. Parents who remain at home often wish for, and sometimes require or could benefit from, child care while they shop, go to a medical appointment, study, perform community or volunteer activities, are involved in recreational activities, recuperate from an illness, or care for another family member. Home child care generally offers more flexible hours than child care centres, and it is also attractive because of the home environment and the small number of children being cared for. Some parents choose home child care because all their children, of varying ages, can be looked after in one location.

Home child care can be licensed or informal. If parents are to be provided with quality options, support must be available to both. Home child care should not be viewed as a smaller version of group care, but rather as a different kind of care provided in a home environment.

Depending on the relevant legislation, in licensed care the provider may care for up to nine children in her or his own home. Though government may still subsidize some fees, this source of funding is diminishing. In some provinces, private homes are supervised by agencies licensed by the government. The agency is responsible for recruiting, screening, training, and monitoring the home care providers. In other jurisdictions, the home child care providers are licensed directly by the provincial or territorial government, and receive occasional inspection visits. Currently no jurisdiction in Canada requires home child care providers to obtain any formal training in child care or child development.

Informal care arrangements are the norm for the majority of Canadian children. This care can be provided in the child or caregiver's home, by a relative, neighbour, friend, or babysitter. According to Cooke et al. (1986), the caregiver is usually not related to the child.

Parents want a variety of options and they are concerned with the quality of care. Cost, location, and availability are often the key reasons parents choose home child care. A number of studies, such as Beach (1992), have shown that more parents would prefer regulated care than currently use it.

As politicians make decisions to cut taxes, balance budgets, and pay off pre-existing debts, savings need to be identified. Unfortunately, child care is all too often a target for these cuts. In the last two years the media has devoted more space than ever before to child care and controversies surrounding it. It is hard to believe that in this new millennium, one still hears people saying, "If women stayed at home." It is heartening to have more space devoted to our profession in the media, but the occasional inappropriate question or comment underscores the reasons for early childhood educators to take greater responsibility for sharing information in a high quality, professional fashion. It is important to keep in mind that the principles described in the section "Developing New Programs within the Community" above are the same principles that apply to "Marketing New and Existing Programs" discussed further on in this chapter. In times of economic cutbacks, marketing of services becomes an especially important skill for the early childhood educator.

Community Partners and Outside Funding

Quality early childhood environments require strong partnerships among representatives of the child care community, parents, schools, employers, and all levels of government. These partnerships can help make early childhood services more available, accessible, affordable, and generally better. Cooperative efforts between employers and child care experts, or with the school system, already exist and serve as models.

Potential partners for a new centre in your community include:

- non-profit child care programs sponsored by community organizations such as churches, businesses, societies, colleges, or charities

- parent-run cooperatives

- programs operated by a municipality

- employer-sponsored or supported child care programs at or near the workplace

The membership of the board of directors of an early childhood environment should reflect these partnerships. Parent representation is vital—it is essential that parents be at the core of decision making about the program.

When forming a new program, identify what types of skills are needed on the board of directors. You will need someone with financial planning skills, such as an accountant or manager. A faculty member could represent an expert in the developmental needs of children from the local college or university. This individual may also facilitate student placements in the program. A lawyer can be helpful, particularly at the early stages when the program is undergoing the process of incorporation. There should be someone with expertise in health issues, such as a public health nurse or pediatrician. A supervisor/director from another child care program in the community can add firsthand knowledge of the issues faced by the program, such as setting appropriate fees and developing schedules. Someone with expertise in personnel issues is essential.

This is not an exhaustive list. At various times members will be required with particular skills, such as fundraising, public relations, and construction.

Assess the Potential for Funding

With continuing fluctuations in politics, and the desire of all levels of government to pay off backlogged deficits, the acquisition and maintenance of funds for child care is very difficult. Therefore it is important to understand that securing funds to start and maintain an early childhood program is a very challenging task, but not impossible. Administrators may find themselves either carrying the full responsibility for fundraising, or developing ways to meet the budget. In some situations board members or prospective parents may be willing to help find funding sources. Obtaining start-up capital is more difficult than funding an operating program. When parent fees are the only source of income, initial capital must be obtained through loans, donations, or grants. Though very limited funding for child care services may be available through government and/or private sources, it is difficult to obtain. Private sources include service clubs such as Kiwanis, foundations, and businesses.

A few early childhood programs are subsidized by local charities, church groups, or United Way funds. Groups such as community organizations, school boards, and workplaces sometimes provide in-kind contributions such as free rent, janitorial services, and coverage of utility bills, or administrative help. Many of these sources are becoming more difficult to locate as organizations address their own financial cutbacks.

The first step in fundraising is to identify available sources of potential support. See the section "Assessing the Potential for Outside Funding" in Chapter 8 for a list of funding sources and fundraising information.

MARKETING NEW AND EXISTING PROGRAMS

Marketing is more than just an advertisement in the local paper announcing the opening of your centre. Marketing strategies and advertising techniques need to focus on the fact that a service is being made available. The service is child care, and the customers are the parents and guardians.

Marketing includes not only advertising, but also

- selling your program through public relations initiatives in your community such as coordinating your services with other organizations
- having board members and staff involved in organizations in the community for child care and related professions
- ensuring that your staff, board members, and all levels of the Ministry have sufficient information to promote the service through word of mouth and with printed materials
- actively responding to local, provincial/territorial and federal government, union and lobby group direction and initiatives
- creating unique fund-raising events that highlight your program objectives and needs

- writing articles about child care in general as well as your services specifically, and finding newspapers, magazines, periodicals, etc., to publish them
- approaching other businesses to secure in-kind donations such as paper materials, and thanking them through public announcements with flyers, in advertising, and so on
- announce your service with an open house, and provide fun, educational, and interesting activities for children to experience when they come, in order to attract them to the event
- introduce yourself to your local politicians and invite them to an open house, for lunch at the centre, to answer controversial questions, and to address election concerns

Every time someone asks questions, makes an inquiry about the service, or discusses the operation, a marketing opportunity is available. Marketing is crucial in order to develop, maintain, and save programs and spaces.

Child care, for the most part, must be thought of as a service that is run like all other services or businesses. Any business that is to survive has to be presented in a professional, competent manner, highlighting the centre's mission statement and identifying its unique strengths and services. We have seen wonderful services developed and available in the community that have had difficulty meeting their objective. Often the energy exerted in developing the service has excelled, but the marketing plan to promote the program was not given the necessary consideration to make the project successful.

To market child care services successfully, a comprehensive marketing plan should be developed. This plan includes:

- Develop a marketing budget. While money may be tight, as it seems to be in all child care ventures, a budget is essential in order to carry out your marketing plan.

- Identify the potential users of the services. Re-visit your needs assessment in order to target the group that identified the need for the service, and the information they provided such as fees they were willing to pay, hours of service needed, and so on.

- Communicate with the original respondents from your needs analysis study. It is important to let these people know that you have gone ahead with your project and that they were an important factor in the development of your project. Hopefully they will become your first clients in your venture.

- Integrate all of the ideas discussed above and use them as a springboard to develop new and innovative marketing strategies. Involve everyone associated with your program when brainstorming ideas to get your program front and centre.

Some Advertising Strategies

Effective advertising depends on knowing the community well, and knowing where to focus advertising. Some advertising techniques are more appropriate for small communities, while others work better in larger metropolitan areas. In both cases, cultural sensitivity, good taste, and a good understanding of development needs of children needs to be considered in any form of advertising.

Bright, bold colours and a unique, simple, eye-catching logo that people will recognize and associate with your early childhood setting are assets. It is worth investing in a colour or two and using distinctive professional graphics to create a quality image. When your image has been chosen, it should be reflected throughout your advertising materials and throughout your entire marketing plan.

Marketing venues can range from brochures and community events to business cards and Web pages. See Appendices D and E for additional details.

PUBLIC EDUCATION AND ADVOCACY

There are many misconceptions about child care and the needs of Canadian families. Some continue to believe that the "traditional family" of two parents, two children, and a mother at home is typical. A few continue to think a mother's working will harm her children. Some Canadians question why their tax dollars should be spent on child care, and why these services are so expensive. Some people believe that children do not learn much when they are young, so the education of caregivers is unnecessary.

A concerted public and government education effort will continue to be needed to meet the never-ending challenge to achieve comprehensive, high quality early childhood environments in Canada. This effort is hampered by non-standardized nomenclature in the field. For example, there is no consensus on what we should call ourselves: early childhood educators, child care workers, caregivers, to mention a few. Some groups have evolved a glossary of terms, but no one term has been universally adopted.

The public's image of child care needs clarification and improvement. The report *Caring for a living* (Canadian Day Care Advocacy Association and the Canadian Child (Day) Care Federation (1993)) found that only 16% of child care staff surveyed felt they were respected by the general public. It identified promoting more respect for child care workers as a priority second only to providing better salaries. As discussed in Chapter 1, education in child development is linked to higher quality care. Caregivers with appropriate education deserve to receive adequate wages. Early childhood educators have been caught up in increasing layoffs and loss of employment opportunity due to labour force cutbacks. These cutbacks often intensify problems such as already inadequate salaries, the resulting effect on the quality of care, and the cost of care, which continues to be poorly understood.

Businesses can be approached for assistance.

Some early childhood educators are reluctant to take an active role in public education and advocacy, and others feel powerless to do anything. But there are a number of ways to be involved. Caldwell (1987) identifies three types of advocacy—personal, professional, and informational.

Personal advocacy can be as straightforward as helping your neighbours understand what you do at your job. When they refer to an early childhood educator as a "baby-sitter," gently but firmly correct them. Encourage friends to think about why child care costs as much as it does, and how it helps them in their own jobs. Enlighten them on the critical importance of the early years for learning. Correct the assumptions that child care is a custodial service for the poor by making clear that child care is a service used by families of all income groups.

Personal advocacy is generally carried out on one's own time. Some employers, such as public institutions, do not allow advocacy efforts by employees. In such situations, make it clear that you are speaking as a citizen, not as a public employee.

Professional advocacy is more appropriately labelled *lobbying*. Like personal advocacy, its aim is to benefit your profession and the children and parents it serves. There are many groups that advocate for quality early childhood programs. It is important to work toward greater public understanding and support for high quality child care, by broadening the base of support to include other groups such as pediatricians and the business community.

Caldwell entitles her third category *informational advocacy*. This refers to attempts to raise public awareness about the importance of the period of early childhood, and the capacity of high quality programs to strengthen families and provide opportunities for optimal growth and development. To be an effective advocate, all one requires is first-hand knowledge of the issues facing children, families, and staff.

Some effective messages to communicate include:

- Child care is not just an issue for women. Both men and women feel the stress of work and family responsibilities.

- Child care services need to be maintained as well as expanded. The gap between supply and demand is significant. Local agencies report long waiting lists for many child care programs. Parents have great difficulty finding care for their infants, toddlers, and school-age children.

- The training of teacher-caregivers is a major determinant of how well children do in early childhood settings. Research studies have found that one of the most important components of high quality programs is the ongoing training of the staff. In programs where the caregivers had training in early childhood education, the children behaved more positively, were more cooperative, and were more involved in the program.

- Child care is not only a concern of the individual family. It affects business and society as a whole. Employers are becoming increasingly aware and in some cases attempting to respond to the problems that arise when families are unable to make adequate child care arrangements.

There are a number of ways in which early childhood educators can convey these messages. It is essential to get more accurate images of the field of child care to the public and government. This requires personal efforts using professional supports.

Membership in a professional organization provides an effective channel for communication with the public and to government. Local, provincial, and national groups are usually involved in public education and advocacy efforts, and it is beneficial to be aware of the objectives of these groups and to work with them. Some organizations have local branches. National organizations are listed at the end of this chapter in Appendix B. The Canadian Child Care Federation (CCCF) publishes a comprehensive directory of provincial and local child care organizations. This publication is a useful tool for contacting others who are concerned with quality child care. See Child and Family Canada at cfc-efc.ca/cccf

Each practitioner can participate in a number of public education strategies, either through membership in a professional organization or through their work at an individual centre. While these strategies may be similar to those used as marketing tools for new and existing programs, they are worth re-visiting from this perspective as well. You can:

- share information and anecdotes with others about your experiences in the program and its significance in the community
- speak to service clubs and the local media
- arrange visits to your program from decision makers
- write letters to the editor of your local newspaper
- write for professional newsletters or journals
- write for popular magazines
- speak on radio programs
- get involved with interactive conferences on the Internet
- make television appearances
- provide leadership at workshops or conferences
- prepare a deputation to policy makers on an issue affecting children, families, or staff in your program
- participate in lobbies
- run for public office

Some individuals you might talk with about your program could include legislators, members of the business community, politicians, media representatives, parents, and other professionals. They are often interested in knowing the number of children you serve and their ages. Describe your program, explaining the service it provides children and families. Take the opportunity to explain the support you require in order to improve the service for children and their families. It is useful to have photographs of the children engaged in positive activities. Encourage prearranged visits to the program. Include parents and staff in presentations.

Starting Points

The following points will assist your thinking about the kinds of information you could provide through public education endeavours:

- Think about the availability of child care in your community. Are there waiting lists for infant care? Is part-time care available for school-age children?
- Is funding available to assist families with the cost of child care? What percentage of a family's total income is needed for child care?
- What are the average salaries of early childhood educators in your community?

- Are there enough training opportunities for child care staff in your community?
- Are salary levels affecting staff retention and the quality of programs? Are salary levels attracting appropriate candidates to the field?
- Do parents have access to information about early childhood services?
- Are provincial/territorial licensing standards adequate?
- Is there support for child care from your business community?
- Is there a need for care for the children of parents who work shifts? Is there care for children who are sick?

It is important to recognize that we early childhood educators can and do make a difference in improving the quality of programs for young children and their families. Some early childhood educators need to consider running for local, provincial/territorial, or national office. Only by working diligently together can we hope to change public attitudes toward child care and early education. This change is required to get the critical mass of support needed to provide a comprehensive, high quality child care system that responds to the diverse needs of Canadian families. As you become more aware of the need to take a stand in improving the field, you will continue to add effective strategies to your list to promote public education and advocacy.

IN CONCLUSION

This final chapter focuses on issues and dilemmas such as the affordability, availability, and quality of early childhood programs, and the need for programs that match the needs of a specific population. The steps have been outlined to initiate new programs in a community. Emphasis on the development of a comprehensive marketing plan is included.

Advocacy and professional empowerment are two ways to address the future of the field. Early childhood educators need to take a stand to improve the field so that current and future generations will benefit. Communication is crucial to understanding the many possibilities that could be made available for child care environments. Marketing may assist in gaining the critical mass of support needed to build a quality child care system.

This chapter may be summarized as follows:

- Child care is not only a women's issue. Both men and women feel the stress of work and family responsibilities.
- The gap between the supply and demand for child care is great. Local agencies report that there are long waiting lists for many programs.
- The training of teacher-caregivers is a major determinant of how well children do in child care.
- Teacher-caregivers deserve to receive adequate salaries.
- Child care is an issue that affects society and business—it is not only a concern of the individual family.
- The development of new programs requires a close assessment of community needs, potential partners, and legal requirements.
- Services must have a comprehensive marketing plan.
- Public education and advocacy are needed to combat misconceptions about child care.

- Advocacy can be personal, professional, or informational.
- Advocacy activities include active membership in child care organizations, writing letters to influence policy makers, speaking to the media, and writing informational articles.

ACTIVITIES

1. Identify an organization in your community that is working for better child care. Make arrangements to attend a meeting or interview staff about the goals of the organization, or subscribe to their newsletter.
2. Develop a marketing plan for a child care service in your community.
3. Take out a membership in a professional organization.
4. Attend a conference of a child care organization.
5. Identify three potential funders of a pilot child care service in your community.
6. In small groups, develop a brief presentation on why child care is important for children, parents, and employers.
7. Approach a new early childhood service and find out the details of how they were able to get started. Compare their experiences with the suggestions in this chapter on steps to follow for new programs.

REVIEW QUESTIONS

1. What are the steps to follow in establishing a new program?
2. How does child care affect society and business?
3. Why is it important to ensure a variety of programs? What are some examples?
4. Why is marketing important to caregivers?
5. What would you include in a marketing plan?
6. List some basic marketing ideas.
7. Why are community partners important?

FURTHER READING

Hendrick, J. and K. Chandler (1996). *The whole child*, Sixth Canadian Edition. Scarborough, ON: Prentice Hall Canada.

Pruissen, C.M. (1993). *Start and run a profitable home day care: Your step-by-step business plan.* North Vancouver, BC: Self-Counsel Press.

APPENDIX A: SOURCE OF FUNDING INFORMATION

The Canadian Centre for Philanthropy
1329 Bay Street, 2nd floor
Toronto, Ontario
M5R 2C4
Phone: (416) 515-0764

APPENDIX B: NATIONAL CHILD CARE ORGANIZATIONS

Canadian Child Care Federation
383 Parkdale Avenue, Suite 201
Ottawa, Ontario
K1Y 4R4

Canadian Day Care Advocacy Association
323 Chapel Street
Ottawa, Ontario
K1N 7Z2

Canadian Association for Young Children
5417 Chemin-Rannock Avenue
Winnipeg, Manitoba
R3R 0N3

APPENDIX C: SAMPLE CHILD CARE SURVEY QUESTIONNAIRE

> The establishment of a child care facility in this community is being explored. Your help is needed in this crucial developmental stage. Please complete this survey. The information you provide will remain confidential.

1. My current family status is

   _____ single   _____ one parent   _____ two parent

2. _____ I have children under 6 years of age living with me.

   _____ I do not have any children 6 years of age living with me, but am expecting children within 3 years.

   _____ I do not have children under 6 years of age living with me and am not expecting within 3 years.

3. Please indicate the age category of your children:

   _____ Newborn to less than 6 months   _____ 18 months to less than 36 months

   _____ 6 months to less than 18 months   _____ 36 months to six years

4. How satisfied are you with your present child care arrangements?

   _____ Very satisfied   _____ Somewhat dissatisfied

   _____ Somewhat satisfied   _____ Very dissatisfied

5. If you could have your choice of child care arrangements, what would you prefer? Circle one only.

   _____ Child care in my own home   _____ Group child care centre

   _____ Out-of-home caregiver   _____ Other (please describe)

6. What are your usual child care hour needs?

   From _____ to _____

7. When would you require child care

   _____ Weekends, evenings and/or nights   _____ Occasionally

   _____ Regularly   _____ Never

> Your response to this survey is appreciated. Please take a few minutes to share any comments or suggestions you might have regarding child care services.
>
> Further comments

APPENDIX D: MARKETING STRATEGIES FOR CHILD CARE SETTINGS

Brochures/Posters

Brochures are an inexpensive means of making available information about your child care services. They can be designed, incorporating your marketing colour scheme and logo, quite professionally on your computer and copied at the local print shop.

A well-designed poster that reinforces your marketing colour scheme can assist in name and service recognition. The message on a poster needs to be clear and concise, and a line of tear-off phone numbers makes it easier for potential customers to contact you.

Bulletin Boards

Bulletin boards are everywhere: the workplace, apartment buildings, community colleges, employment centres, grocery stores, health clubs, laundromats, libraries, places of worship, and shopping centres, to name a few. While the use of them is often free, it is important to ask permission to post information. It is also important to find out the criteria for announcement size and the duration allowed for postings.

Business Cards

Business cards are a basic low-cost marketing tool. They make a statement about your philosophy and management style, and they identify you as a professional.

Business cards often increase first-time caregivers' confidence and enthusiasm. They also assist parents when they are considering your services, since they readily provide a name, address, and phone number.

Community Events

Organizing a book or garage sale will make more people aware of the services you provide. This creates an opportunity to put up signs or posters telling people that you are sponsoring the event, hand out flyers, and display children's art work or activity photographs about your setting.

Word-of-mouth advertising is the best you can get, and it's free. It is always important to do your best and show a willingness to go that extra mile in service for children and their parents. When you do this, they will usually tell their friends about you.

Internet Technology

New technology is a lifeline of communication for many parents. Even children "surf the Net" to find school-age activities. Learn how and where you can access it. If you do not have your own equipment, find other avenues to access technology. Some coffee houses have Internet services available, and charge a small fee for use. Develop a Web page for your centre and join with other early childhood educators to develop a child care informational Web page.

Multimedia Presentations

Multimedia presentations can be as uncomplicated as posting children's art work or displaying an overhead transparency. Coloured overhead transparencies are impressive, and can be made inexpensively at the local copy shop from coloured photos of the centre. These media tools can be useful in formal situations, such as when making a presentation to a corporation, local service club, etc. Slides, display boards, video, and children's art work provide other means through which to educate your audience about your services. Be sure to explain your goals, and ask parents' permission if you are photographing their children in activities for public presentation.

Your skills in making classroom presentations as an early childhood education student, and in performing for children (reading stories) and with children (songs and finger plays), can be transferred to public speaking. Familiar props (children's art work, overheads, or slides) can help build your confidence and add interest to your presentation. To ensure that you don't "freeze," practise what you might say with friends. If you have a lot of nervous tics such as "ahhs" or "ums," make use of a Toastmasters' Club tip: They fine their speakers five cents each time one of these tics occurs.

Be prepared and offer to speak at events or meetings. Service clubs such as the Lions or Rotary Club have speakers weekly. The chances are good that they will take up your offer to speak.

Newspapers and Newsletters

Advertisements and announcements may be placed in daily, weekly, or community newspapers and buy-and-sell tabloids. Newspaper advertising can be expensive and is most effective for making centre opening announcements or for advertising available spaces. When asking a newspaper for rates, ask for the line rate as well as the display rate. Display rates are mostly used for block ads or announcements, while line rates (for classified ads) are cheaper, and more appropriate when you have spaces available.

Information or announcements are often free when placed in carefully selected, audience-targeted community newspapers. You may also wish to invest in your own newsletter to keep both parents and the community informed about your services.

Letters to the editor can be useful, especially when they include positive comments or praise about the community. Newspapers and their readers often welcome letters commenting on access to clean parks for children, or well-beveled crosswalks for children's strollers or wheelchairs. If your letter gets published, your centre is recognized as a caring environment that is involved with the community.

Press releases may be followed up by newspapers, workplace newsletters, and radio and television stations. When they do this, they are, in effect, providing you with free advertising. It is worthwhile to call the paper or station and ask for a specific editor, reporter, or community announcement program host who would be willing to look at your press release.

A press release should not be more than one or two pages in length, and should contain enough *exciting information* to catch the attention and sound like *potential news*. It is an opportunity to give facts and tell the news media about your services. It should be written in the third person, as though you were the writer of the news story. Use "she," "Jane Doe," or "her" instead of "I," "me," or "my." If you use quotes, be sure to get permission from the person you are quoting.

Remember the importance of the five Ws: *who, what, where, when,* and *why*—and *how to contact you.* These should be covered in the first paragraph or two, which must contain your most important facts. Be prepared for a media representative to contact you to ask for additional information. You may wish to develop an information kit consisting of several marketing tools (brochure, poster, current press release, application form, fee schedule), and have it ready to deliver if someone calls for information.

Phones and Yellow Pages

The way the phone is answered often determines people's perception of the image and quality of service. Do you sound cheerful, exhausted, or bored? Tone is as important as content. Professionalism and quality are strengthened if the phone is answered in a consistent manner. For example, "Oakwood Child Care Centre, this is Kitu, may I help you?" If key information is posted next to the phone (including answers to the most common questions about hours, fees, space availability, staff ratios, public transportation locations or directions, etc.), then the same clear, concise information is given out by all who answer the phone. When a caller is told to call back because you can't answer basic questions, or that someone will call them back (but never does), professionalism and quality may be perceived as lacking.

All staff should be trained to immediately write down the name and phone number of a prospective parent who contacts the program. Their address can also be useful, if they are willing to provide it, as it can be added to your mailing list. Notes should be made of any other information given such as children's ages or names, so that follow-up contacts can be made.

Make a brief call to prospective parents a day or two after their visit or phone call, rather than waiting for them to call you back. Ask if they have any additional questions. Refer to their child or children by name and age, if you can, in the conversation. "Seth seemed to enjoy playing with the large tractor when he was here. He might also enjoy next week's walk to the nearby construction site." If prospective parents have looked at several settings, your personal touch may sway their decision.

If you take a listing or an ad in the Yellow Pages, study the existing ads for your area. Your entry will be surrounded by many others, and this can make for tough competition.

Make use of the competition and learn from it. Competitors will probably list items that make their business unique or special. Identify what special services make your care unique.

Radio and Television

Radio and television announcements can be costly. However, community or public service announcements are often free or affordable. An effective public service announcement can be constructed from a clear, concise, and informative press release. Again, remember to keep it short.

Professional Associations

There are many reasons to join professional child care associations, including marketing reasons. Associations provide up-to-date information about child care, which can be passed on to parents and other members of the community. Moreover, membership assures parents of your commitment to quality child care.

Program Creativity

Sometimes a change in program description fills available spaces. If spaces are available for the two-afternoons-per-week class, a program description about "math enrichment for school-age children" or "enriching music and drama experiences for preschool children" will often fill the spaces and sometimes create waiting lists. If summer causes lower enrollments, the same principle can be applied by offering, for example, a "Summer Science Camp for Children." A change in program focus often provides fresh interests for parents, children, and even caregivers!

Referral Agencies

The number of referral agencies is large. Some offer various forms of membership. Networking with them offers an opportunity to share information and resources. Keep in mind that when parents are looking for child care services, they may call an agency. When they do, you want to be on that list.

APPENDIX E: SAMPLE MARKETING PLAN

ADVERTISING INFORMATION	DATE(S)	COST	EVALUATION NEW CHILDREN

Brochures/posters
  Brochures Written
    Sent to:
      names from survey
      organizations
      public health unit
  Posters Designed
    placed at:
      elementary school
      high school
      library
      public health unit			

Bulletin Boards
  Poster Placements:
    library
    college			

Business Cards
  Designed &
  Ordered			

Community Events Garage Sale			

Multimedia Presentations
  Rotary Club
  Home and School Association			

ADVERTISING INFORMATION	DATE(S)	COST	EVALUATION NEW CHILDREN

Newsletters and Newspapers
Research
   ad (for garage sale)
   ad (for available spaces)
Press Release Written
   Release Sent:
      radio station
      community newspaper			

Yellow Pages Ad
   Contacted Telephone Company
   Ad outlined
   Ad completed			

Radio and Television
   Cable Net Community
   Community Bulletin Board Ad			

Professional Associations
   Information Requested
   Membership Taken			

Referral Agencies/Contacts
   Media Kit Sent:
      New Immigrants
      Association
      Medical Association (local)			

 # Weblinks

Canadian Child Care Web Sites

The Internet's World Wide Web includes useful child care resources. The following is a list of addresses of some national and regional organizations.

    If you are new to the Web, here is a tip. When searching for Web sites, it is recommended that you choose specific key words. For example, if you need information about school-age child care, the search string "child care" may trigger 1 200 entries (which are very time-consuming to check through), whereas "school-age" may produce fewer entries for you to check.

Canadian Child Care Federation:
cfc.cymbiont.ca/home.htm

Canadian Resource & Research Unit:
www.epas.utoronto.ca:8080/~crru/home.html

Child and Family Canada:
cfc-efc.ca/cccf

Child Care Advocacy Association of Canada:
plumadge.com/ccaac/

Childcare Resource & Research Unit:
childcarecanada.org

Connections Nova Scotia:
istar.ca/~cccns.istar/index.html

Federal Government Child and Youth Web Site:
hc-sc.gc.ca/hppb/childhood-youth/index-html

Ontario Coalition for Better Child Care:
worldchat.com/public/tab/ocbcc/ocbcc.htm

Metro (Toronto) Task Force on Services to Young Children and Families:
children.metrotor.on.ca/taskforce.html

Ontario Coalition for Better Child Care:
wordlchat.com/public/tab/chldcr/ocbcc.htm

SpeciaLink:
highlander.cbnet.ns.ca/~specialink/

Bibliography

Abbott-Shim, M. and A. Sibley (1986). *Child care inventory.* Atlanta, GA: Humanics.

AECEO (1993). *Final report for the feasibility study regarding legislative recognition of early childhood educators in Ontario.* Prepared by Levy-Coughlin Partnership. Toronto: Author.

Allen, P. (1994, Fall). "When children speak a different language." *Day Care and Early Education,* 38–39.

Almy, M. (1975). *The early childhood educator at work.* New York: McGraw-Hill.

Andre, T. and C. Neave (1992). *The complete day care guide.* Toronto: McGraw-Hill Ryerson.

Association for Early Childhood Education, Ontario (1988). *High quality child care statement.* Toronto, Ontario.

Ayles, T. and S. Becker-Griffin (1990). *An A–Z handbook for boards of directors of non-profit community-based child care programs.* Toronto: Umbrella Central Day Care Services/Child Care Initiatives Fund, Health and Welfare Canada.

Ayles, T. and S. Becker-Griffin (1990). *Daily operations manual with supplement on finance management.* Toronto: Umbrella Central Day Care Services/Child Care Initiatives Fund, Health and Welfare Canada.

Baines, Carol, Patricia Evans, and Sheila Neysmith (1991). *Women's caring: Feminist perspectives on social welfare.* Toronto: McClelland & Stewart.

Baker, M. (1995). *Canadian family policies: Cross-national comparison.* Toronto: University of Toronto Press.

Baker, M. (1999). "Child care and family policy: cross national examples of integration and inconsistency," presented at Good Child Care Symposium, Toronto.

Beach, J. (1992). *A child care agenda for the 90s: Putting the pieces together—A comprehensive system of child care.* Toronto: Ontario Coalition for Better Child Care/Canadian Advocacy Association.

Beach, J., J. Bertrand, and G. Cleveland. (1998). "Our childcare workforce from recognition to remuneration: a human resources study of child care in Canada," Human Resources, Ottawa.

Belsky, J. (1980). "Future directions for day care research: an ecological analysis." *Child Care Quarterly II,* pp. 82–99.

Bennis, W. (1989). *On becoming a leader.* New York: Addison-Wesley.

Berger, E. H. (1981). *Parents as partners in education.* St. Louis, MO: Mosby.

Berlew, D. (1982). *Effective leaders make others feel stronger.* Child Care Information Exchange.

Bernhard, J., M. Lefebvre, G. Chud, and R. Lange (1995). *Paths to equity: Cultural, linguistic, and racial diversity in Canadian early childhood education.* Toronto: York University.

Bertrand, J. (1990). *Childcare management guide: A comprehensive resource for boards of directors.* Toronto: OCBCC (Ontario Coalition for Better Child Care)/Ottawa: Canadian Advocacy Association.

Bertrand, J. (1991). "George Brown College guide to work place child care." *Health Care Facilities Manual*. Toronto.

Bjorklund, G. and C. Burger (1987). "Making conferences work for parents, teachers and children." *Young Children*, 26–31.

Blenkin, G.M. and A.V. Kelly (eds.) (1988). *Early childhood education: A developmental curriculum*. London, England: Paul Chapman Publishing Ltd.

Boutte, G.S., D. Keepler, V. Tyler, and B. Terry (1992). "Effective techniques for involving 'difficult' parents." *Young Children*, 19–22.

Bredekamp, D. (ed.) (1997). *Developmentally appropriate practice*. Washington, DC: NAEYC.

Bredekamp, S. (ed.) (1987). *Developmentally appropriate practice in early childhood programs serving children from birth through age 8*. Washington, D.C.: National Association for the Education of Young Children.

B.C. Task Force on Child Care (1991). *Showing we care: a child care strategy for the 90s*. British Columbia.

Bronfenbrenner, J. (1979). *The ecology of human development*. Cambridge, MA: Harvard University Press.

Brown, J. (ed.) (1982). *Curriculum planning for young children*. Washington, DC: National Association for the Education of Young Children.

Bryant, B., M. Harris, and D. Newton (1980). *Children and minders*. Ypsilanti, MI: High Scope Press.

Buchanan, T. and D. Burts (1995, Summer). "Getting parents involved in the 1990s." *Day Care and Early Education,* 18–22.

Caldwell, B. (1984). "What is quality care?" *Young Children 39* (3), pp. 3–8.

Caldwell, B. (1987, March). "Advocacy is everybody's business." *Child Care Information Exchange*, 29–32.

Canada, Ministry of Health and Welfare (1987). *Sharing the responsibility—Federal response to the report of the special committee on child care*. Ottawa: Queen's Printer.

Canada Mortgage and Housing Corporation (1978). *Play spaces for preschoolers* (advisory document prepared by P. Hill, S. Esbensen, and W. Rock). Ottawa: CMHC.

Canadian Child Care Federation (1991). *Definition of high quality child care*. Ottawa.

Canadian Child Care Federation (1998). "Draft code of ethics," Ottawa.

Canadian Child Care Federation (1991). *Issues in post-secondary education for quality early childhood education care: a discussion paper*. Ottawa: Canadian Child Care Federation.

Canadian Child Care Federation (1999). "Research connections Canada: supporting children and families," Ottawa.

Canadian Child (Day) Care Federation (1991). *National statement on quality child care*. Ottawa: Canadian Child (Day) Care Federation.

Canadian Child Care Federation (1995). *Towards excellence in early childhood care and education training programs: A self assessment guide*. Ottawa: CCCF.

Canadian Day Care Advocacy Association (1985). *Child care facts*. Ottawa: Canadian Day Care Advocacy Association.

Canadian Day Care Advocacy Association and the Canadian Child (Day) Care Federation (A joint project) (1993). *Caring for a living: A study on wages and working conditions in Canadian child care*. Ottawa: Karto Communications.

Canadian Pediatric Society (1997). *Well beings: A guide to promote the physical health, safety and emotional wellbeing of children in child care centres and family day care homes.* Toronto: Creative Premises Ltd.

Canadian Standards Association (1990). *A guideline on children's playspaces and equipment.* (CAN/CSA–Z614–M90).

Carter, M. and E. Jones (1990, September). "The teacher as observer: The director as role model." *Child Care Information Exchange.*

Caruso, J. and M. Fawcett (1986). *Supervision in early childhood education: A developmental perspective.* New York: Columbia University: Teacher's College Press.

Cassidy, D.J. and C. Lancaster (1993, September). "The grassroots cirriculum: a dialogue between children and teachers." *Young Children*, 47–51.

Chandler, K. (1997). "What do we know about ECE training in Canada?" Paper presented to the Steering Committee of Early Childhood Care and Education Training in Canada. Ottawa: Association of Canadian Community Colleges and Canadian Child Care Federation.

Chandler, K. (1988). "Accreditation: One route to professionalism." Presentation at the annual conference of the Alberta Association for Young Children.

Chandler, K. and P. Hileman (1986). "Professionalism in early childhood education." *Association for Early Childhood Education Newsletter.*

Chandler, K. (1994). *Voluntary accreditation and program evaluation.* Ottawa: Canadian Child Care Federation.

Chapman, E. (1990). *Supervisors' survival kit.* New York: Macmillan.

Cherry, C., B. Harkness, and K. Kuzma (1987). *Nursery school and day care center management guide.* Belmont, CA: Fearon.

Child Care Employee Project (1990). *Taking matters into our own hands: A guide to unionizing in the child care field.* Berkeley, CA.

Child Care Resource and Research Unit (1996). *Child care in Canada: Provinces and territories.* Toronto: Child Care Resource and Research Unit, Centre for Urban and Community Studies, University of Toronto.

Child Care Resource and Research Unit (2000). *Child care in Canada: Provinces and territories 1999,* Toronto: University of Toronto.

Chud, G. and R. Fahlman (1995). *Honouring diversity with child care and early education: An instructor's guide.* Victoria: British Columbia Ministry of Skills, Training and Labour.

Chud, Gyda, et al. (1985) *Early childhood education for a multicultural society: A handbook for educators.* Vancouver: Pacific Educational Press.

Clark, Silvana. "Marketing when your creativity is high and your budget is low." *Child Care Information Exchange,* July 1995.

Cleveland G., and M. Krashinsky (1998). "The benefits and costs of good child care: the economic rationale for public investment in young children," Toronto: University of Toronto.

Click, P. and D. Click (1990). *Administration of schools for young children.* Albany, NY: Delmar.

Coletta, A. (1982). *Working together: A guide to parent involvement.* Atlanta, GA: Humanics.

College Standards and Accreditation Council (1996). *Early childhood education program standards.* Toronto, Ontario: Ministry of Education and Training.

Cooke, K. et al. (1986). *Report of the task force on child care.* Ottawa: Supply and Services.

Covey, S. (1992). *Principle-centered leadership.* New York: Fireside.

Decker, C. and J. Decker (1992). *Planning and administering early childhood programs.* New York: Maxwell Macmillan.

Denholm, C., R. Ferguson, and A. Pence (1987). *Professional child and youth care: The Canadian perspective.* Vancouver: University of British Columbia Press.

Department of Finance Canada (1995). *Budget in brief.* Ottawa: Department of Finance.

Derman-Sparks, L. (1993/94, Winter). "Empowering children to create a caring culture in a world of differences." *Childhood Education*, 66–71.

Derman-Sparks, Louise and the A.B.C. Task Force (1989). *Anti-bias curriculum: Tools for empowering young children.* Washington, D.C.: National Association for the Education of Young Children.

Doherty G., M. Friendly, and M. Oloman (1998). "Women's support, women's work: child care in an era of deficit reduction, devolution downsizing, and deregulation," Status Of Women, Canada.

Doherty G., D. Lero, H. Goelman, A. LaGrange, and J. Tougas (2000). "You bet I care! a Canada-wide study on wages, working conditions and practices in child care centres, University of Guelph.

Doherty G. (1998). "Program standards for early childhood settings," Canadian Child Care Federation, Ottawa.

Doherty, G., R. Rose, M. Friendly, D. Lero, and S. Hope Irwin (1995). *Child care: Canada can't work without it.* Toronto: Child Care Resource and Research Unit, Centre for Urban and Community Studies, University of Toronto.

Doherty-Derkowski, G. (1995). *Quality matters: Excellence in early childhood programs.* Don Mills: Addison-Wesley Publishers.

Early Childhood Educators of British Columbia (1995). *The early childhood educators of British Columbia code of ethics.* Vancouver: ECEBC.

Eiselen, S.S. (1992). *The human side of child care administration—a how-to manual.* Washington, DC: National Association for the Education of Young Children.

Endsley, R., P. Minish and Q. Zhou (1993). "Parent involvement and quality day care in proprietary centers." *Journal of Research in Childhood Education*, 7(2), 53–61.

Esbensen, S.B. (1984). *Hidden hazards on playgrounds for children.* Hull, Quebec: Université du Québec à Hull.

Esbensen, S.B. (1987) *The early childhood education playground: An outdoor classroom.* Ypsilanti, MI: High Scope Press.

Evans, E.D. (1975). *Contemporary influences in early childhood education.* New York: Holt, Rinehart & Winston.

Federal-Provincial-Territorial Council of Ministers on Social Policy Renewal (1999). "A national children's agenda: developing a shared vision," Human Resources Canada, Ottawa.

Feeney, S. (1987). "Ethics case studies: The working mother." *Young Children*, 42 (5), 16–19.

Feeney, S. (1988a). "Ethics case studies: The agressive child." *Young Children*, 43 (2), 48–51.

Feeney, S. (1988b). "Ethics case studies: The divorced parents." *Young Children*, 43 (3), 48–51.

Feeney, S., D. Christensen, and E. Moracvik (1987). *Who am I in the lives of children?* (3rd ed.). Columbus, OH: Merrill.

Feeney, S. and R. Chun (1985). "Research in review: effective teachers of young children." *Young Children*, 41 (1).

Feeney, S. and R. Chun (1987, May). "Ethical case studies for reader response." *Young Children.*

Feeney, S. and K. Kipnis (1985). "Public policy report: Professional ethics in early childhood education." *Young Children*, 40 (3), 54–58.

Feeney, S. and K. Kipnis (1987). "Ethical case studies for NAEYC reader response." *Young Children*, 42 (5) 24–25.

Feeney, S. and K. Kipnis (1989). "Code of ethical conduct and statement of commitment." *Young Children*, 45 (1), 24–29.

Feeney, S. and L. Sysko (1986). "Professional ethics in early childhood education: Survey results." *Young Children*, 42 (1), 15–20.

Friendly, Martha (1994). *Child care policy in Canada: Putting the pieces together.* Don Mills: Addison-Wesley Publishers.

Friesen, B. (1995). *A sociological examination of the child care auspice debate*, Occasional Paper #6. Toronto: Child Care Research and Resource Unity, University of Toronto.

Frost, J.L. (1992). *Play and playscapes.* New York: Delmar.

Galinsky, E. (1978). *Easing parents through beginnings and endings.* Child Care Information Exchange.

Galinsky, E. (1988). "Parents and teacher-caregivers: Sources of tension, sources of support." *Young Children*, 4–12.

Galinsky, E. (1990, July). "Why are some parent/teacher partnerships clouded with difficulties?" *Young Children*, 2–3, 38–39.

Galinsky, E. and D. Friedman (1986). *Investing in quality child care: A report for AT&T.* Short Hill, NJ: Bank Street College of Education.

Gilligan, Carol (1982). *In a different voice.* Boston: Harvard University Press.

Glickman, C.D. (1985). *Supervision of instruction: a developmental approach.* Boston: Allyn & Bacon.

Goelman, H. and A. Pence (1985). "Towards the ecology of day care in Canada: a research agenda for the 1980s." *Canadian Journal of Education.*

Goffin, S. and J. Lombardi (1988). *Speaking out: Early childhood advocacy.* Washington: NAEYC.

Government of Alberta (1987). *Day care regulation 14.* Edmonton: Publication Services.

Government of Alberta (1988). *The social care facilities licensing act.* Edmonton: Publication Services.

Government of Alberta. (1990). *Day care regulation—Alberta regulation 333/90.* Edmonton: Publication Services.

Government of British Columbia (1989). *Community care facility act—child care regulation.* Regulation 319/89. Victoria: Queen's Printer for British Columbia.

Government of British Columbia (1979). *Community care facility act.* Chapter 57. Victoria: Queen's Printer for British Columbia.

Government of British Columbia (1979). *Guaranteed available income for need act.* R. S. Chapter 158. Victoria: Queen's Printer for British Columbia.

Government of Canada (1994a). *Agenda: Jobs and growth—Improving social security in Canada*; A discussion paper. Ottawa: Ministry of Supply and Services Canada.

Government of Canada (1994b). *Improving social security in Canada—Child care and development: A supplementary paper*. A discussion paper. Ottawa: Supply and Services Canada.

Government of Manitoba (1987). *The community child day care standards act—child day care regulation.* Winnipeg: Queen's Printer for Manitoba.

Government of Manitoba (1986). *Manitoba regulation 62/86*. Winnipeg: Queen's Printer.

Government of Manitoba (1987). *The community child day care standards act—Child day care regulation*. Winnipeg: Queen's Printer for Manitoba.

Government of New Brunswick (1983). *Child and family services and family relations act.* Fredericton: Queen's Printer for New Brunswick.

Government of New Brunswick (1983). *Child and family services and family relations act.* *Fredericton*: Queen's Printer for New Brunswick.

Government of New Brunswick (1983). *Family services act.* Chap. C–2.1, Part II Community placement resources. Fredericton: Queen's Printer for New Brunswick.

Government of New Brunswick (1985). *Day care facilities standards*. Fredericton: Queen's Printer for New Brunswick.

Government of New Brunswick (Consolidated to June 30, 1985). *Family services act regulations 8385; under family services act. O. C. 83–457.* Fredericton: Queen's Printer for New Brunswick.

Government of Newfoundland (1982). *Newfoundland regulations 219/82: Day care and home-maker services regulations, 1982.*

Government of Newfoundland (1982). *The day care and homemaker services regulations.* Newfoundland Regulations 219/82, 1982 (under *The day care and homemaker services act, 1975*). St. John's: Queen's Printer for Newfoundland.

Government of Newfoundland (1990). *The day care and homemaker services act.* St. John's: Queen's Printer for Newfoundland.

Government of Nova Scotia (1989). *Day care act and regulations: Chapter 120 of the revised statutes, 1989.* Halifax: Queen's Printer for Nova Scotia.

Government of Ontario (1987). *Initial steps in starting a day nursery in Ontario.* Toronto: Ministry of Community and Social Services.

Government of Ontario (1985). *Day nurseries: Highlights of the legislation.* Toronto: Ministry of Community and Social Services.

Government of Ontario (1987). *New directions.* Toronto: Ministry of Community and Social Services.

Government of Ontario (1988). *Day nurseries manual.* Toronto: Queen's Printer of Ontario.

Government of Ontario (1988). *The Ontario study of relevance of education and the issue of dropouts.* Toronto: Queen's Printer for Ontario.

Government of Ontario (1990). *Day nurseries act* (Revised Statutes of Ontario, 1980. Chapter 11). Toronto: Queen's Printer for Ontario.

Government of Ontario (1990). *Ontario regulation 760/83.* (Under the *day nurseries act.*).

Government of Prince Edward Island (1987). *Guiding principles for the development of child care services.* Charlottetown: Acting Queen's Printer.

Government of Prince Edward Island (1988). *Prince Edward Island's child care facilities act regulations.* R. S. P. E. I. Cap. C–5. (including any amendments to December 31, 1990). Charlottetown: Acting Queen's Printer.

Government of Quebec (1987). *Regulations respecting day care centres.* Quebec City: Editeur Officiel du Québec.

Government of Quebec (1992). *Loi sur les services de garde à l'enfance L. R. Q., chapitre S–4.1* 1979 (incluant les modifications apportées jusqu'au 1er octobre 1992, à jour au 1er décembre 1992). (*An act respecting child care.*) Quebec City: Editeur Officiel du Québec.

Government of Quebec (1993). *Règlements sur les services de garde en garderie, dernière modification:* 17 octobre 1991, à jour au 16 février 1993. (*Regulations respecting child care centres.*) Quebec City: Editeur Officiel du Québec.

Government of Saskatchewan (1990). *An act to promote the growth and development of children and to support the provision of child care services to Saskatchewan families.* Regina: Queen's Printer for Saskatchewan.

Government of Saskatchewan (1989). *The child care act.* Chapter C–7.3. Regina: Saskatchewan Social Services.

Government of Saskatchewan (1990). *The child care regulations* 948/90. Chapter C–7.3 REG. 1 Section 27. Regina: Saskatchewan Social Services.

Government of the Northwest Territories (1987). *Child day care standards regulations.* Yellowknife: Queen's Printer.

Government of the Northwest Territories (1988). *Northwest Territories child day care act.* Yellowknife: Queen's Printer.

Government of the Yukon (1990). *Child care centre program regulations, O.C. 1990/115.* Whitehorse: Commissioner of the Yukon.

Government of the Yukon (1990). *Child care act.* Bill 77. (Statutes of the Yukon.) Whitehorse: Commissioner of the Yukon.

Government of the Yukon (1990). *Child care subsidy regulations.* Order-in-Council, 1990/116. (Pursuant to section 40 of the *Child care act.*) Whitehorse: Commissioner of the Yukon.

Government of the Yukon (1990). *Family day home program regulations.* Order-in-Council, 1990/117. (Pursuant to section 40 of the *Child care act.*) Whitehorse: Commissioner of the Yukon.

Green, Barbara (Chair) (1991). *Canada's children: Investing in our future—Report on the standing committee on health and welfare, social affairs, seniors and the status of women.* Ottawa: Queen's Printer.

Greenberg, P. (1989, May). "Parents as partners in young children's development and education: A new American fad? Why does it matter?" *Young Children,* 61–75.

Greenman, J. and R. Fugua (1984). *Making day care better: Training, evaluation and the process of change.* New York: Teacher's College Press.

Griffen, Sandra (1994). *Professionalism: The link to quality care.* Ottawa: Canadian Child Care Federation.

Guralnick, M. (1990). "Major accomplishments and future directions in early childhood main-streaming," in *Topics in Early Childhood Special Education,* Vol. 10, No. 2: p.1–7.

Halpern, R. (1987, September). "Major social and demographic trends affecting young families: Implications for early childhood care and education." *Young Children*, 34–40.

Harms, T. and R. Clifford (1980). *The early childhood environment rating scale.* New York: Teacher's College Press.

Harms, T. and R.M. Clifford (1989). *Family home day care environment rating scale.* New York: Teacher's College Press.

Harms, T., D. Cryer, and R.M. Clifford (1990). *The infant/toddler environment rating scale.* New York: Teacher's College Press.

Harms, T., E. Jacobs, and D. White (1996). *School-age care environment rating scale.* New York: Teacher's College Press.

Hawkins, Jim (1997). *1001 Fundraising Ideas and Strategies.* Fitzhenry and Whiteside.

Hayden, J. (1996). *Management of early childhood services: An Australian perspective.* Wentworth Falls, N.S.W., Australia: Social Science Press.

Health and Welfare Canada. (1992). *The child benefit—A white paper on Canada's new integrated child tax benefit.* Ottawa: Queen's Printer.

Helgesen, S. (1990). *Female advantage: Women's ways of leadership.* New York: Doubleday.

Hendrick, J. and K. Chandler (1996). *The whole child,* Sixth Canadian Edition. Scarborough, ON: Prentice Hall Canada.

Herr, J. R. D. Johnson, K. Zimmerman (1993, May) "Benefits of accreditation: a study of directors' perceptions," *Young Children*, pp. 32–35.

Hersey, P. K. and Blanchard (1977). *Management of organizational behavior: Utilizing human resources.* Englewood Cliffs, New Jersey: Prentice Hall.

Hildebrand, V. (1993). *Management of child development centers.* New York: Macmillan.

Honig, A. (1979). *Parental involvement in early childhood education.* (rev. ed.). Washington, DC: National Association for the Education of Young Children.

Human Resources Development Canada (1994). *Agenda: Jobs and growth—Improving social security in Canada.* A Discussion Paper. Ottawa: Government of Canada.

Human Resources Development Canada (1996). *Child care: Where we stand.* Ottawa: The Ministry.

Hunsaker, P. and A. Alessandra (1980). *The art of managing people.* New York: Simon and Schuster.

Hurst, Lynda (1992, March 15). *A death blow for day care—How Tories reneged on their promise to set up a national system.* Toronto: *Toronto Star*.

Janmohamed, Zeenat (1992). *Making the connections—Child care in Metropolitan Toronto.* Toronto: Metro Toronto Coalition for Better Child Care.

Joffe, C. (1979). *Friendly intruders: Childcare professionals and family life.* Berkeley: University of California Press.

Johnson, D. W. and F.P. Johnson (1991). *Joining together: Group theory and group skills.* Boston: Allyn and Bacon.

Johnson, D. W. and R. Johnson (1989). *Cooperation and competition: Theory and research.* Edina, MN: Interaction Book Company.

Johnson, J. and J. McCracken (1994). *The early childhood career lattice: Perspectives on professional development.* Washington, D.C.: NAEYC.

Jones, E. and L. Derman-Sparks (1992, January). "Meeting the challenge of diversity." *Young Children.*

Jones, E. and J. Nimmo (1994). *Emergent Curriculum.* Washington, D.C.: National Association for the Education of Young Children.

Jorde Bloom, P. (1986). "The administrator's role in the innovation decision process." *Child Care Quarterly,* 15 (2), 182–197.

Jorde Bloom, P. (1986). *Improving the quality of work life: A guide for enhancing the organizational climate in the early childhood setting.* Evanston, IL: National College of Education.

Jorde Bloom, P. (1988). *A great place to work: Improving conditions for staff in young children's programs.* Washington, DC: National Association for the Education of Young Children.

Jorde Bloom, P. (1995, May). "Shared decision-making: the centerpiece of participatory management." *Young Children,* 55–60.

Jorde Bloom, P., M. Sheerer, and J. Britz (1991). *Blueprint for action: Achieving center-based change through staff development.* Minnesota: New Horizons.

Kagan, S. (1994, July). "Leadership: Rethinking it—making it happen." *Young Children,* 50–54.

Katz, L. (1972). "Developmental stages of preschool teachers." *Elementary School Journal,* 73, 50–55.

Katz, L. and E. Ward (1978). *Ethical behaviour in early childhood education.* Washington, DC: NAEYC.

Kilbride, Kenise (1990). *Multicultural early childhood education: A resource kit.* Toronto: Ryerson Press.

Kipnis, K. (1987). "How to discuss professional ethics." *Young Children,* 42 (4), 26–30.

Kotter, J. P. (1990). *A force for change: how leadership differs from management.* New York: Free Press.

Kritchevsky, S., E. Prescott, and L. Walling (1983). *Planning environments for young children: Physical space.* Washington, D.C.: National Association for the Education of Young Children.

Kuhn, M. (1994). "Quality child care and partnerships with parents," Canadian Child Care Federation, Ottawa.

Kurtz, R. (1991, January–February). *Stabilizer, catalyst, troubleshooter, or visionary—Which are you?* Child Care Information Exchange, 27–31.

Kyle, I. and D. Lero (1985). *Day care quality: Its definition and implementation.* Ottawa: Task Force on Child Care.

Lally, R. (1995, November). "The impact of child care policies and practices on infant/toddler identity formation." *Young Children.*

Lemire, Denise (1993). *Services de garde au Québec.* Ottawa: Federation canadienne des services de garde à l'enfance.

Lero, D. S. and Kyle, I. (1985). *Day care quality: Its definition and implementation.* Paper submitted to the Task Force on Child Care.

Lero, D.S. (1994). "In transition: Changing patterns of work, family life and child care." *Ideas: The Journal of Emotional Well-Being in Child Care,* 1 (3): 11–14.

Lightfoot, S. (1978). *Worlds apart: Relationships between families and schools.* New York: Basic Books.

Lovell, P. and T. Harms (1985). "How can playgrounds be improved? A rating scale." *Young Children,* 40 (3): 3–8

Manburg, A. (1985, January). "Parent involvement: A look at practices that work." Child Care Information Exchange.

Manitoba Community Services Child Day Care (1986). *Competency based assessment: Policy and procedures.* Winnipeg, MB.

Martin, S. (1987). *Sharing the responsibility: Report of the special committee on child care.* Ottawa: Queen's Printer.

Maxwell, Anne (1993). *Child care in Alberta.* Ottawa: Canadian Child Care Federation.

Maxwell, A. and C. Ryerse (1995). *National child care policy in Canada 1966–1995.* Ottawa: Canadian Child Care Federation.

McCain, M. and F. Mustard (1999). "Reversing the real brain drain: early years study final report," The Canadian Institute for Advanced Research, Toronto.

McLean, C. (1994). *Regulations, standards and enforcement.* Ottawa: Canadian Child Care Federation.

Meyerhoff, M. (1994). "Of baseball and babies: are you unconsciously discouraging father involvement in infant care? *Young Children,* May 1994.

Ministry of Culture and Recreation, Ontario. (1982). *A guide to creative playground equipment.* Toronto: Government of Ontario.

Mitchell, M. (1987). *Caring for Canada's children—Special report on the crisis in child care.* Ottawa: Queen's Printer.

Morgan, G. (1982). *Managing the day care dollar.* Cambridge, MA: Steam Press.

Morgan, G. (1997). *Imaginaization: new mindsets for seeing, organizing, and managing.* San Francisco: Berret-Koehler.

Morgan, G. (1984). "Change through regulation," in J. Greenman and R. Fuqua, *Making daycare better: Training, evaluation and the process of change.* New York: Teacher's College Press.

Morris, J. (1995). *Early childhood continuing education certification standards and individual competency-based ECE training and assessment in Newfoundland and Labrador.* Newfoundland: Cabot Institute of Applied Arts and Technology.

Moss, P. (1994). *Quality targets in services for young children: Proposals for a ten year action plan.* European Commission.

NAEYC (1995, November). "How many ways can you think of to use NAEYC's code of ethics?" *Young Children.*

NAEYC (1998). "NAEYC position statement on licensing and public recognition of early childhood programs, Washington.

National Academy of Early Childhood Programs (1985). *Guide to accreditation by the national academy of early childhood programs: Self-study, validation, accreditation.* Washington, DC: National Association for the Education of Young Children.

National Association for the Education of Young Children (1987). *Developmentally appropriate practice in early childhood programs serving children from birth through age 8.* Washington, DC: NAEYC.

National Association for the Education of Young Children. *Position statement on licencing and other forms of regulation of early childhood programs in centres and family day care* (535). Washington, DC: National Association for the Education of Young Children.

National Association for the Education of Young Children (1984). *Accreditation criteria and procedures of the national academy of early childhood programs.* Washington, DC: NAEYC.

National Association for the Education of Young Children (1986). "Position statement on developmentally appropriate practice in early childhood education programs serving children from birth to age 8." *Young Children,* 41(6), 3.

National Association for the Education of Young Children (1987). *NAEYC position statement on licencing and other forms of regulation of early childhood programs in centers and family day care.* Washington, DC: NAEYC.

National Council of Welfare (1988). *Child care: A better alternative.* Ottawa: Minister of Supply and Services Canada.

National Council of Welfare (1992). *The 1992 budget and child benefits.* Ottawa: Minister of Supply and Services, Canada.

National Council of Welfare (1999). *Preschool Children: Promises to Keep.* Ottawa: Minister of Public Works and Government Services Canada.

National Day Care Information Centre (1987). *National strategy on child care.* Ottawa: Health and Welfare Canada.

National Day Care Information Centre (1991). *Status of day care in Canada.* Ottawa: Health and Welfare Canada.

National Day Care Information Centre (1986). *Provincial day care requirements—Nutritional requirements, space requirements, minimum staff/child ratios.* Ottawa: Health and Welfare Canada.

National Day Care Information Centre (1986). *Provincial funding of day care services.* Ottawa: Health and Welfare Canada.

National Day Care Information Centre (1987, December). *National strategy on child care.* Ottawa: Health and Welfare Canada.

National Day Care Information Centre (1988). *Child care initiatives fund.* Ottawa: Health and Welfare Canada.

National Day Care Information Centre (1991). *Status of day care in Canada.* Ottawa: Health and Welfare Canada.

Nedler, S. E. and O.D. McAfee (1979). *Working with parents.* Belmont, CA: Wadsworth.

Neugebauer, B. (1990, September–October). *Are you listening?* Child Care Information Exchange, 62.

Neugebauer, R. (1985, November). *Are you an effective leader?* Child Care Information Exchange, 45–50.

Olenick, M. (1986). *The relationship between quality and cost in child care programs* (7). Los Angeles, CA: Brief reports on current research compiled by the Bush Program in Child and Family Policy.

Oloman, Mab (1992). *A child care agenda for the 90s: Putting the pieces together—child care funding.* Toronto: Ontario Coalition for Better Child Care/Canadian Day Care Advocacy Association.

Ontario Coalition for Better Day Care (1986). *Child care challenge: Organizing in Ontario.* Toronto: Ontario Coalition for Better Day Care.

Parkay, F. and S. Damico (1989, Spring). "Empowering teachers for change through faculty-driven school improvement." *Journal of Staff Development,* 10(2) 8–14.

Pence, A., H. Goelman, and D. Lero (1993). *Where are the children: An analysis of child care arrangements used while parents work and study.* Ottawa: Statistics Canada.

Pence, Alan (1992). *Canadian child care in context: Perspectives from the provinces and territories.* Ottawa: Statistics Canada.

Peters, D. (1988). "The child development associate credential and the educationally disenfranchised," in *Professionalism and the early childhood practitioner.* Columbia University: Teacher's College Press.

Phillips, Deborah (ed.) (1987). *Quality in childcare programs: What does the research tell us?* Washington, DC: NAEYC.

Pruissen, C.M. (1993). *Start and run a profitable home day care: Your step-by-step business plan.* North Vancouver, BC: Self-Counsel Press.

Radomski, M. (1986, July). "Professionalization of early childhood educators: How far have we progressed?" *Young Children.*

Read, K. and J. Patterson (1993). *The nursery school and kindergarten—a human relationships laboratory.* New York: Holt, Rinehart & Winston.

Ruopp, R., H. Travers, F. Glantz, and C. Coelen (1979). *Children at the center: Final report of the national day care study,* Vol. I. Cambridge, MA: Abt Associates.

Saifer, Steffen (1990). *Practical solutions to practically every problem: The early childhood teacher's manual.* St. Paul, MI. Redleaf Press.

Schom-Moffat, Patti (1992). *Caring for a living: National study on wages and working conditions in Canadian child care.* Ottawa: Canadian Child Care Federation and Canadian Day Care Advocacy Association.

Schwartz, S. and H. Robison (1982). *Designing curriculum for early childhood.* Boston, MA: Allyn and Bacon.

Schweinhart, L. and D. Weikart (eds.) (1985). *Quality in early childhood programs: Four perspectives.* Ypsilanti, MI: High Scope Early Childhood Policy Papers.

Sciarra, D.J. and A.G. Dorsey (1996). *Developing and administering a child care center.* Albany, NY: Delmar Publishers.

Seaver, J. and C. Cartwright (1986). *Child care administration.* Belmont, CA: Wadsworth.

Seefeldt, C. (1980). *Teaching young children.* Englewood Cliffs, NJ: Prentice Hall.

Senge, P.M. (1990). *The fifth discipline: The art and practice of learning organizations.* New York: Doubleday.

Senge, P. M. et al. (1999) *The dance of change: the challenges of sustaining momentum in learning organizations.* New York: Doubleday.

Seshagiri, Lynne (1993). *Child care in Canada—Highlights of the 1992/1993 background papers.* Ottawa: Canadian Child Care Federation.

Sissons, Brenda and Heather McDowall Black (1992). *Choosing with care—The Canadian parent's practical guide to quality child care for infants and toddlers.* Toronto: Addison-Wesley Publishers Limited.

Spodek, B. (1970, October). "What are the sources of early childhood curriculum?" *Young Children.*

Spodek, B., O. Saracho, and D. Peters (eds.) (1988). *Professionalism and the early childhood practitioner.* Columbia University: Teacher's College Press.

Spodek, B., O. Saracho, and D. Peters (eds.) (1990). *Early childhood teacher preparation.* Columbia University: Teacher's College Press.

Statistics Canada (1998). "Perspectives on labour and income," Vol. 9, # 4, Ottawa.

Stengel, S. (1982). "The preschool curriculum." In D. Streets (ed.), *Administering day care and preschool programs* (pp. 27–69). Boston, MA: Allyn and Bacon.

Stevens, J.H., Jr., and E.W. King (1976). *Administering early childhood education programs.* Boston: Little, Brown.

Swick, K.J. (1995, Spring). "What parents really want from family involvement programs." *Day Care and Early Education,* 20–23.

Taylor, B.J. (1993). *Early childhood program management—People and procedures.* New York: Merrill.

The Roeher Institute (1992). *Quality child care for all: A guide to integration.* North York, Ontario: The Roeher Institute.

Townson, M. (1986). *The costs and benefits of a national child care system for Canada.* Halifax: DPA Group Inc.

VanderVen, K.D. (1988). "Pathways to professional effectiveness for early childhood educators," in Spodek, Saracho, and Peters, *Professionalism and the early childhood practitioner* (pp. 137–160). New York: Teacher's College Press.

Wach, T.D. and G. Gruen (1982) *Early experiences and human development.* New York: Plenum.

Walsh, P. (1988). *Early childhood playground: Planning an outside learning environment.* Melbourne, Australia: Martin Educational, in association with Robert Andersen and Associates.

Whitebrook, M., C. Howes, R. Darrah, and J. Friedman (1982). "Caring for the caregivers: staff burnout in child care," in *Current topics in early childhood education,* Vol. 4. Norward, NJ: Ablex Publishers.

Whitebrook, M., C. Howes, and D. Phillips (1990). *Who cares? Child care teachers and the quality of child care in America. Final report of the National Child Care Staffing Study.* Oakland, CA: Child Care Employee Project.

Willer, B. (1987). *The growing crisis in childcare: Quality, compensation and affordability in early childhood programs.* Washington, DC: NAEYC.

Winter, S. (1994/95, Winter). "Diversity: a program for all children." *Childhood Education,* 91–95.

Index